DATE DUE			
OCT 1 2 2001			
3·14·03			

201-9500 — PRINTED IN U.S.A.

RAISING A CHILD WITH A
NEUROMUSCULAR DISORDER

RAISING A CHILD WITH A NEUROMUSCULAR DISORDER

◆ ◆ ◆

A Guide for Parents, Grandparents, Friends, and Professionals

Charlotte E. Thompson, M.D.

New York Oxford
OXFORD UNIVERSITY PRESS
1999

Oxford University Press

Oxford   New York
Athens Auckland Bangkok Bogotá Buenos Aires Calcutta
Cape Town Chennai Dar es Salaam Delhi Florence Hong Kong Istanbul
Karachi Kuala Lumpur Madrid Melbourne Mexico City Mumbai
Nairobi Paris São Paulo Singapore Taipei Tokyo Toronto Warsaw

and associated companies in
Berlin Ibadan

Copyright © 1999 by Charlotte E. Thompson, M.D.

Published by Oxford University Press, Inc.
198 Madison Avenue, New York, New York 10016

Oxford is a registered trademark of Oxford University Press

Library of Congress Cataloging-in-Publication Data
Thompson, Charlotte E.
Raising a child with a neuromuscular disorder :
a guide for parents, grandparents, friends, and professionals/Charlotte E. Thompson
p. cm.
ISBN: 0-19-512843-5
1. Neuromuscular diseases in children.
2. Musculoskeletal system—Abnormalities.
3. Children—Diseases.
I. Title.
RJ496.N49T47 1999 618.92'744—dc21
99-30834

1 3 5 7 9 8 6 4 2

Printed in the United States of America
on acid-free paper

Dedication

To all the special infants, children, and teenagers I have cared for, whose lives were tragically shortened by neuromuscular diseases, but who taught me so much about living fully each day: Ron, Brian, Kenny, Joshua, Dianne, Curtis, Jeffrey, Sasha, Korie, Douglas, Dianna, Craig, Tim, Stephen, Daniel, Austin, Job, Joseph, Deon, Mark, David, Danny, Jim, Steven, Charlie, Anthony, George, Janice, Alex, Leroy, Don, and others too numerous to name.

Contents

Foreword

In this important book, Dr. Charlotte E. Thompson has provided a tremendous service to parents of children with neuromuscular disorders and their families. She has given a bird's-eye view of all the common muscle disorders in childhood and also some of the less common ones—and has interwoven the basic medical information with practical advice on how to cope with the problems of a disabled child, and how to ensure that the child achieves his or her full potential.

Dr. Thompson is one of the few people with the capacity to write such an informative and practical book, combining her interest, knowledge, and expertise in the medical aspects of the muscle disorders—including their diagnosis and management—with a compassion for her young patients and their families, and a genuine commitment to help and guide them. She has, in fact, spread the net even wider and devoted a chapter to coping with a child with a neuromuscular disorder as a parent, a sibling, a family member, and a friend.

This book is written in plain, down-to-earth English and has successfully avoided much of the usual medical jargon. We all have much to learn from Dr. Thompson's book, and I am sure it will prove a useful resource not only for families but for professionals and other caretakers as well.

Victor Dubowitz, M.D., Ph.D., F.R.C.P., D.C.H.
Professor of Paediatrics
Royal Postgraduate Medical School
University of London
Consultant Paediatrician
Hammersmith Hospital
Medical Director, Neuromuscular Unit
Hammersmith Hospital, London

Preface

I t has been a privilege to be a part of the neuromuscular world for the last thirty-eight years, and I owe a tremendous debt to many who have been both guides and friends. Dr. John Walton (now Lord Walton) in his days at the University of Newcastle first offered wise teaching and insights, followed by Dr. Ted Munsat, formerly at the University of Southern California School of Medicine, and Dr. James Peter at the University of California in Los Angeles. Dr. Paul Vignos, Dr. Stirling Carpenter, Dr. Byron Kakulas, Dr. Margaret Thompson, Dr. Lewis Rowland, Dr. Andrew Engel, and Dr. Michael Brooke have also contributed greatly to my knowledge.

My greatest debt of thanks goes to Professor Victor Dubowitz of Hammersmith Hospital, University of London, and his associate, Dr. Caroline Sewry. Their leadership in the world of pediatric neuromuscular diseases, muscle pathology, and research has been a source of knowledge, as well as friendship for many years. My frequent trips to London to spend time in their neuromuscular center at Hammersmith Hospital have kept me abreast of the latest in both clinical pediatric neuromuscular disorders and research. The ongoing willingness of both Professor Dubowitz and Dr. Sewry to answer questions, discuss cases, and review muscle biopsies has made all the difference in my ability to continue seeing complex patients in the six neuromuscular programs that I have directed.

Professor Victor Dubowitz, despite his exhausting schedule, has also been extremely gracious in reviewing parts of this text. His international stature in the pediatric neuromuscular world has always left me in awe, and his friendship and support over many years have truly made a difference in my life.

Dr. Margaret Thompson, a longtime special friend, and professor emeritus at the University of Toronto, author, and pediatric geneticist, has spent many hours reading and rereading the manuscript. Her suggestions and corrections have been invaluable, and I owe her an enormous debt of thanks.

My agent, Laurie Harper, has made such a difference over the years with her strong support and friendship, as well as her expert knowledge of the book world.

Joy Tassi, a friend for many years, as well as one of my special parents, has also spent a great deal of time reviewing the book, both from the viewpoint of a parent and in her present role as a hospital social worker. Her contribution has been invaluable.

Others I would like to thank for their professional contributions are Dr. Mary Phyllis Cederberg, pediatrician and former chief, California Children's Bureau, Santa Barbara; Dr. Anthony Cosentino, pulmonologist; Sarah Clarke, special education attorney; Donna Winters, physical therapist; and my anesthesiologist son, Dr. Geoffrey Thompson. Also, a very special thanks to Lee Botsford and to Joan Bossert, my editor at Oxford University Press, for her wonderful help and enthusiastic support of the book.

Lastly, a special tribute and thanks to all the parents who have generously contributed wise advice scattered throughout the chapters in the special boxes, and reviewed chapters. The book would not be the same without their willingness to help.

It has been awe-inspiring, in many ways, to watch the development of interest in the neuromuscular field from a small group of concerned individuals at the first few international neuromuscular congresses, to now see the involvement of geneticists, biochemists, immunologists, and others from all over the world. All of this will surely pay big dividends, in the future, for children with neuromuscular disorders and their parents.

I know all those I have mentioned join me in hoping that our joint efforts will make a real difference in the lives of both parents and children with neuromuscular disorders.

RAISING A CHILD WITH A NEUROMUSCULAR DISORDER

Introduction

This book is about the most common disorders that cause muscle weakness in infants, children, and young people. Because it may be the first book you have turned to, as parents or family members, I have tried to make it as comprehensive and all-inclusive as possible. My hope is that not only will parents find it of value, but also family members or friends who have specific questions about how they can help a child with muscle weakness. Also, special education teachers, nurses, physical therapists, occupational therapists, adaptive P.T. teachers, and hopefully even physicians will find information of value in each of the chapters. Answers to your questions about children of any age, from infancy to adulthood, will be addressed, but I would like to offer the following advice: *Please don't try to read this book from cover to cover right away, because that could be overwhelming.* Instead, I would suggest that you refer to it, a chapter at a time, when you want to find answers to some specific questions or need words of support.

The first chapter is to help you survive the shock of the initial diagnosis and to start making some plans and thinking about what lies ahead. Of course, the most crucial question, once some of your initial numbness and shock have worn off, is to be sure that the diagnosis of a neuromuscular disease is correct. Once this is established, then if you are parents, I would urge you not to look too far into the future. None of us can really guess what it will hold, and this is particularly true with neuromuscular diseases, because exciting research discoveries are being made daily.

The hardest job you will have as a parent is to keep on with your usual daily activities and not center everything around your child's diagnosis. Life does go on, and there are probably others in your family who need some attention. Remember that their needs are important, as well as your own. You will probably find it difficult to get everything done during the days and develop some balance. But hopefully some of my suggestions will help you accomplish this.

Finding some real quality time in each day will be difficult if there are additional tasks that you need to accomplish for your child with a neuromuscular disorder. As one parent said, "Twenty-four hours in one day are just not enough when you're parenting a special-needs child." Just the physical care of your child alone may be wearing, and then the added emotional drain can take a real toll. One mother said she felt as though she were running a marathon every day. Things got better once she began to take care of herself and planned time for some daily exercise, as well as time for herself. Getting through a day at a time was the best way to cope, she discovered. So, for now, I would suggest that each of you just try to get through one day at a time and read this book only a chapter at a time, as the need arises.

ONE

◆ ◆ ◆

Coping With the Diagnosis

The greatest fear that we all share as parents and grandparents is that something will happen to one of our children. If problems arise and medical advice is sought, there is always the terrible anxiety that the answer will be devastating.

If you have been given the diagnosis of a neuromuscular disease or disorder in one of your children, *the initial reaction was probably shock.* This, then, was most likely followed by numbness, or will be at some time, and then denial. For some parents these feelings may even last for years, but I want to reassure you that these reactions are perfectly normal. Shock and numbness are nature's way of giving you time to adjust and develop your coping mechanisms. One parent said to me, "I don't think that you ever accept your child's terrible diagnosis, but gradually, over time, you do learn to adjust to it."

> Don't try every new treatment that comes along, and don't believe everything you read in the newspapers.

If your numbness persists for a long time, however, so that all feelings of grief and anger are buried, then you could be just doing things mechanically or at such a frantic pace that you don't allow the reality of the diagnosis to surface. Though we can try to bury pain by walling off our feelings, I can guarantee you that it will come out in some other way now or in the future—as accidents, headaches, back pain, sleeplessness, or anxiety.

Anger

Once the numbness begins to lessen, you may find it is replaced by tremendous anger. Some parents feel they want to strike out at God, the physician who gave them the bad news, their mate, or their co-workers. These feelings, too, are perfectly normal, but hopefully your anger will gradually begin to lessen and life slowly become less of a blur so that your coping mechanisms can develop.

> It may seem really rough at first, but you'll get to a point where you can't imagine life without your child.

Both mothers and fathers have told me that after receiving the diagnosis of a neuromuscular disorder in a child, they felt such intense anger and pain that they wanted to walk away and not even try to cope with all the problems that lay ahead. Sometimes parents even wish a child had not been born or were dead because their anger, grief, and resentment are so intense. I can assure you that these feelings are perfectly normal, too; but if they take over your life, I would urge you to talk to a close friend, minister, rabbi, priest, or counselor. Support groups for fathers, mothers, or couples can also provide a safe setting for feelings to come out and let you realize that they are okay and others have reacted in exactly the same way.

As coping mechanisms develop, destructive feelings can be channeled into productive activity, allowing life to go on. The questions "Why me?", "Why us?", "What did we do wrong?", will always be there, but, as one parent said, "For me, not receiving an answer to 'Why me?' was an answer itself." She added that she felt there were no answers to some questions, and hated it when someone said, "Oh, you're special. You were chosen to have a child with a problem." "Then," she went on, "I yell inwardly," saying, "I don't want to be special, I don't want to be chosen, I want my life back again just as it was before we got the awful diagnosis."

Grief

When your dream of having a normal family life and perfect children is destroyed, grieving is a natural reaction. All of us have times in our lives when things work out far differently from what we had planned.

But if we can allow ourselves to grieve, as Dr. Elisabeth Kübler-Ross and other physicians have taught us, some healing will occur.

Grieving does have almost a life of its own, and we must work through its different stages to finally reach a place where we feel at least some inner peace. If we wall off our grief and don't allow our inner pain to surface, then unanticipated problems will most likely develop that could have a strong impact on our lives.

Many parents are afraid that they will become so overwhelmed by their grief that they will lose contact with reality. One father said to me, "I felt as if time had stopped, and I could no longer function. I couldn't think straight and do my work or even stand being around people. I slowly withdrew from most of my activities and functioned just at a mechanical level. Then, once I allowed myself to do some grieving, I began to heal. I had to allow the pain to come up, but only in short bursts. Otherwise I couldn't have made it; I would just have been overwhelmed."

> Try to channel your energies into coping with the problems of the muscle disease rather than grieving.

We do have to honor our pain and allow it to come up for even just a few minutes at first, and then for longer and longer periods. Crying can help healing to occur. A counselor or support group is another source of aid, but it is important to find a therapist who has felt real pain; otherwise he or she cannot really understand what you're feeling and help you to heal. On-line support groups are developing now, and since an individual does not have to physically be with others to participate, these groups may be of help to those uncomfortable about sharing feelings with a therapist or group. It would be particularly important to get some counseling if you begin to distance yourself from your mate or your children, have marked sleeplessness, or show other signs of tension.

Even when you think your grieving is over, from time to time a terrible feeling of pain and grief may suddenly surface and is something of which to be aware. Parents tell me this happens especially when their child can't do something that another child is doing, such as skateboarding, playing Little League, or even climbing on a jungle gym. Learning to handle this pain and grief, which may surface at totally unexpected times, is part of parenting a child with a special problem. My advice to parents or to anyone who has to learn how to handle grief is to allow yourself a few minutes of grieving and then get on with what you were doing. Sometimes you may even need to excuse yourself and go for a short five-minute walk, sit in a quiet place, or listen to some music. I have a favorite place to go when I need to do a little grieving. It's on a cliff above a beautiful expanse of ocean, and somehow, as I look out at the waves breaking against the rocks, the pain that I'm feeling ebbs away, and I can go on with what I need to do. Any of us who have had real pain in our lives need to find a place of solace, where we will be undisturbed so that our pain can surface; the more we allow pain to come up and work through it, the more quickly we can get back in balance and feel at peace. It's easy to handle grief and pain by running helter-skelter like the White Rabbit in *Alice in Wonderland*, but eventually the grief and pain will catch up with us and may do real damage.

> Enjoy the moment and stay in the present; the future may be too frightening.

Many parents look so far into the future that they anticipate all the terrible things that might occur. Their child's possible death is always on their minds. One mother even said: "I wish it was all over now." Her fourteen-year-old son with Duchenne dystrophy was beginning to develop more and more muscle weakness, and because she was a single-parent mother, the responsibility was weighing heavily on her shoulders.

> Don't give up. When you hit a wall, look for a way around it.

"I just know I can't do it," she said. "I'm having a hard enough time coping now. What will it be like later on?"

Any parent caring for a child with a disorder that becomes worse over time probably has had similar thoughts, even though they may have neither expressed nor acknowledged them. It is perfectly natural to fear what lies ahead for your child, so early on I would urge every parent to fill his or her survival kit with the following:

1. Have faith in your ability to get through a day at a time.
2. Know that your courage will increase as you get through still another day.
3. Think positively and see the good things that happen each day, not the bad.
4. Be aware of the joys your child brings, and not the sorrows.

5. Learn to rely on your ability to handle new situations.
6. Don't allow fear to paralyze you.

By letting fear become a motivating force rather than a paralyzing one, it can give you the energy to accomplish what you need to do. Professional actors and singers who are honest about their feelings say that before a performance fear gets them moving and keeps them focused on their performance. I promise you that fear can do the same thing for you if you use it as a positive force and let it push you rather than make you immobile.

The sleeplessness that fear often causes can also be used in a positive way. It can be used as a time for thinking, grieving, or making plans about how to get through still another day.

Stress

One of the greatest problems you have to fight as the parent of a child with neuromuscular disease is stress. Fear, worry, and fatigue all can increase stress, so you constantly have to fight these dark forces. Finding a balance in life is one of the hardest things that we all have to learn as parents, but some individuals never do. Instead, they go helter-skelter through life, never achieving any balance. We all take on too much, but if we can learn to eliminate all but the essential tasks in a day, balance is much easier to achieve.

> You'll need to scrape your knees before you learn to take care of yourself.

Spending time with family, friends, or co-workers can be enjoyable, but eliminating unnecessary gatherings or meetings gives you extra time to do something *you* want to do. Cutting down on telephone conversations can save lots of time and energy, and fax machines help a great deal, too. Many parents find that having an inexpensive home fax machine gets information quickly to doctors, agencies, and schools. An answering machine can be lifesaving also, particularly if occasionally you allow it to receive your calls and don't always feel that you have to answer the telephone.

It's important for both mothers and fathers to find as many short-cuts as possible to lessen fatigue, and parents who get up frequently at night with their children are particularly at risk. Even one good night of uninterrupted sleep now and then can make a real difference in how dark or bright the days look.

Handling the Stress of a Hospitalization

When illness occurs or hospitalizations are necessary for children, family life is completely thrown out of balance. One parent often takes on most of the extra burden of a child's hospitalization but, by doing this, he or she may end up feeling resentful and angry.

> It takes a lot of courage to parent a child with a neuro-muscular disease.

Some parents seldom leave the side of their child's hospital bed, which I understand, but would urge some kind of a trade-off be worked out with family members or friends. Someone else should be able to take over at least part of the hospital watch because getting away from the hospital for even ten minutes, morning or afternoon, can make a great deal of difference. By meeting a friend for a cup of coffee at a neighborhood café or taking a short walk or jog, the day will be much better. As parents, you put yourself at risk for accidents and all kinds of medical problems if you don't take the time to care for yourself. Our bodies can handle only so much stress, and long periods of worry beside a child's hospital bed are pretty hard on even the toughest parents.

You can use the hospital time to find something new and creative to do. Some parents develop new hobbies that they can do by the side of the bed such as sketching, whittling, knitting, needlepoint, or crossword puzzles. Just as you pack your suitcase with essentials for a long trip, do plan for your hospital stays. This can also be a time to make new friends among the staff or parents of other children, and often these friendships survive the test of time, since they are forged during periods of intense emotion. There will be days when you may need to open up to those around you just to survive the turbulence of your emotions.

Rather than continually showering your child with flowers, balloons, and gifts, try putting aside a little of the money for yourself. A good dinner out now and then, or even the wonderful treat of a massage, can make a real difference in your ability to get through this time of heightened stress. A new CD or some other treat, or splurging for some steaks for a special dinner at home, can make the days shorter and less gray. Stormy, dark days will still be ahead, but by digging way down and using all your inner resources and creativity, you can stay afloat and in balance.

Creative Outlets

If your child has a progressive neuromuscular disorder, such as Friedreich's ataxia or Duchenne muscular dystrophy, having one or more creative outlets can be lifesaving for you, as a parent. This can be something as easy as sketching, building models, painting, or writing poetry. Planning a few minutes a day to do something you enjoy allows you to put your cares and worries aside for that little while, so you can enter a different world. Art and music are particularly good for this purpose.

Exercise, too, helps fight fear and work off the nervous energy that can accumulate. Even a brisk ten minutes spent walking or jumping rope can make a difference, but each of us has to find a form of exercise that we can work into our days. Please do something! People who are completely sedentary generally fight fear far less effectively than those who get up, get out, and get moving.

Fun

A few minutes of fun each day will also help ease the stress and burdens that you carry as parents. As with exercise, each of us has to find our own ways to have fun when we are going through a stressful period. A short time spent throwing a football with a friend, walking through an art gallery, or having some good coffee in a pleasant setting, can make the day easier.

> If you can get beyond the pain, life can have some fun in it again.

Children, too, need some fun each day, particularly if they have a neuromuscular disorder. It's easy for them to get on a treadmill of school, doctors' appointments, and special lessons or therapy sessions. Remember, their fears and worries are no less real than yours, and this is particularly true if they have a progressive neuromuscular disorder.

Once in a while it's a good idea to declare a family "mental health day." When you can take a day off from work, surprise your children with a special trip to a nearby park, zoo, or a lunchtime picnic. Lots of money doesn't have to be spent, but the goal should be to have some family fun together.

Joy

The ninety-year-old woman who is frequently quoted as saying something like, "If I had my life to live over again, I would smell more flowers, run barefoot in the sand, and hug more babies" was certainly wise. Perhaps by taking a few minutes to think about the things that bring you happiness or joy, you can pare your life down to the bare essentials. Is it your job, your family, friends, or sports? Many parents run so fast each day that they never take time to smell the roses or enjoy a beautiful view. Nor do they take time to really enjoy their children's funny sayings and hugs. One hug from a child can make a whole day much better if you let yourself feel how precious it is.

What many adults wouldn't give for a daily hug from a child. Think of lonely seniors living in a single, cold room, or couples who desperately want children but are unable to have them. Most children give hugs and love without restraint if this is what they've known, and even those with real health problems often show a concern and love for the people around them that is very special. I am often amazed at the beautiful spark or spirit that some children with chronic illness exhibit. Kids can do more for us than we can possibly imagine unless they have become spoiled. So enjoy each day or the moments you have with your children and try to make these times as special as possible.

> A spoiled child is an unhappy child, and a spoiled child with a disability can become very depressed.

TWO

◆ ◆ ◆

When to Ask for a Second Opinion

U nfortunately, errors do occur more often than they should in the diagnosis of childhood neuromuscular disorders. This is because there are few pediatric neuromuscular training centers in the world, and muscle diseases are given little emphasis in the training of neurologists, orthopedists, and pediatricians. Often, too, the physician who makes the diagnosis of a neuromuscular disease in a child may be an adult neurologist, so a child's growth and development don't play an important part in the work-up.

Find a doctor who is a children's neuromuscular specialist as soon as possible. Otherwise, you'll waste precious time and energy.

◆

If your child doesn't see someone really knowledgeable the first time, many unnecessary laboratory tests and even one or more muscle biopsies will be done.

One of the major problems in the diagnosis of neuromuscular diseases is the following scenario: one physician does the history and physical, a second performs the muscle biopsy, a third reviews the biopsy slides and makes a diagnosis, and a fourth may do an electromyogram or electrical test of the muscles. Also, now that many physicians are depending just on genetic studies to make the diagnosis of a neuromuscular disease and not on doing a muscle biopsy, further errors can result. *A diagnosis must never be made based on on a single examination or procedure.* Instead, all the pieces of the puzzle—that is, history, physical examination, muscle biopsy, and genetic studies—must be considered together by the same physician for the most accurate diagnosis to be made.

Often, parents are not given the final answer by the first physician they consult, but are sent to several other physicians before a diagnosis is made. This can result in laboratory tests and even a muscle biopsy being repeated one or more times. I have examined children who have had as many as five muscle biopsies because the specimens were either taken from inappropriate muscles, inadequately processed in the laboratory, or interpreted incorrectly. Even muscle biopsies performed in major university medical centers are subject to error, since general pathologists usually don't have extensive training in the interpretation of muscle biopsy slides. Most childhood muscle diseases are not difficult to diagnose if the physician has had specialized pediatric neuromuscular training, as well as considerable experience. To find such a physician, I would suggest that you first ask your primary doctor to make inquiries about a children's muscle specialist and not just accept a referral to a big clinic.

> Be sure that your child is not just a file for the doctor you see. We had a doctor who put our child's file away in a drawer and forgot about her between visits.

The usual neurology training program concentrates on seizures and problems or diseases of the brain and spinal cord, so that neuromuscular diseases are either studied as an elective or are skimmed over lightly. At the present time, there are no specific requirements or examinations for physicians who see only children with neuromuscular diseases and not neurological disorders in general.

> If your doctor doesn't seem to have the knowledge or special training your child needs, then find someone who does.

Establishing a Diagnosis

When muscle weakness is found in a child, a costly and time-consuming medical workup is seldom needed unless other symptoms are present, such as vomiting, heart, or lung difficulties. However, to establish an accurate diagnosis, there are some basic things that should be done.

> You may need to do some research yourself about your child's disorder. If we hadn't done our homework and then changed doctors, the right diagnosis would not have been made.

The first is a *history and physical examination,* which should include a child's birth history; age at which he or she sat, walked, and talked; a detailed family history; and a good general review of problems such as headaches, ear and chest infections, feeding, bladder difficulties, and muscle cramps.

For a physical examination to be adequate, a child *must* be undressed down to his or her underpants or shorts, and girls should be provided with a gown. A child must be observed walking and, ideally, going up and down stairs.

> Don't ever let a doctor intimidate you.

A complete physical examination means examining a child from head to toe to look for medical problems, clues to a genetic disorder, and evidence of muscle weakness or nervous system problems.

Laboratory Tests

After a complete history and physical examination, the next step is for the physician to order some basic laboratory blood tests. The principal one needed is creatine phosphokinase, or CPK (CK in Europe and Canada). Sometimes other tests will be ordered, such as an SGOT (serum glutamic-oxalocetic transaminase) or SGPT (serum glutamic-pyruvic transaminase), and an LDH (lactic dehydrogenase). Tests to measure electrolytes, which are substances in the blood such as sodium, potassium, and chloride, may occasionally be ordered. The most important of all these tests is the one for creatine phosphokinase.

This is an enzyme or substance that performs a specific function in different body tissues. A particularly high concentration is present in muscles, so with muscle loss or destruction, some of the CPK enzyme may leak into the bloodstream. Extremely high CPKs are found in disorders such as Duchenne and Becker muscular dystrophy. A CPK, however, may be normal in the congenital myopathies and spinal atrophies, though occasionally an elevated level is found even in these disorders. *All children with muscle weakness should have a CPK test done at least once to check if it is abnormal. When it is, it can be of major diagnostic importance.* Also, if you, as a parent, have some muscle weakness, curvature of the spine, or an increase in the size of your calves, a CPK test is indicated. You could have the same disorder as your child but in a milder form, or be a carrier of the gene causing the muscle weakness.

> Be careful that you don't feel handicapped by thinking your child inherited the muscle disorder from you and that people are pointing their fingers.

If a markedly elevated CPK level is found, I would suggest that the test should be repeated, because errors do occur. For example, if a child struggles during the drawing of the blood, a CPK can be quite elevated. In most laboratories, the normal value of CPK is 0–270 millimeters per milliliter, but this is not true in all laboratories.

It's important to note that the SGOT, SGPT, and LDH enzymes can be elevated when problems exist in other parts of the body—for example, with a liver disorder. I have seen children who were scheduled for liver biopsies because of a markedly elevated CPK level when, in truth, they had a muscle disease and did not need the biopsy. Normal values for SGOT, SGPT, LDH, and CPK may vary in different laboratories, and the interpretation of these tests should be left up to your physician.

> Be aware of the medical care your child receives. It may range from barely adequate, to well-intentioned, to inaccurate and inappropriate, to plain wrong and physically and emotionally damaging.

Electrolytes do not need to be measured unless there is an indication of a more widespread problem or involvement of other systems in the body. For example, a blood sample for potassium may be necessary if there is a question of periodic paralysis, which will be discussed later. In this disorder, the potassium in the blood may be either too high or too low, depending on which form of periodic paralysis it is.

EMG and Nerve Conduction Studies

Your physician may also order a study called an electromyogram, or EMG. This test measures the electrical activity of muscles. Also, nerve conduction studies may be ordered. These measure the speed at which nerves conduct the messages from the brain and spinal cord. Usually, these tests are not necessary in most childhood neuromuscular diseases, but some physicians like to have them done for completeness' sake. Unfortunately, the accuracy of both tests is very much dependent on how well a physician interacts with a child and also on how cooperative the young person is on that particular day.

Some centers put a great deal of emphasis on EMGs and don't do muscle biopsies. When this occurs, the level of diagnostic errors can be quite high, because a child's muscle tissue does need to be viewed under the microscope except in rare instances. ENG's and nerve conduction studies are a little uncomfortable, but if a physician enjoys working with children, there should not be a problem.

The principal indication for ordering nerve conduction studies is the possibility of nerve involvement, such as that seen in *Guillain Barré syndrome* and other disorders. There is a group called hypertrophic motor and sensory neuropathies, or Charcot-Marie-Tooth, in which nerve conduction times are important. These will all be discussed later on.

An electromyogram is more uncomfortable than a nerve conduction test, so sometimes mild sedation is needed. This procedure consists of having a tiny needle inserted into specific muscles. The results of the tests are seen on a screen, and a paper tracing can also be produced. It is fun for kids to take home a strip of the tracing to share with family, friends, or classmates.

If your child has a possible diagnosis of myotonic dystrophy and is under age five, an EMG will not be helpful, whereas it may be in older children. With a suspected myotonic disorder, parents should also have an EMG, because often myotonia, or increased muscle tone, can be shown to be present in parents, particularly mothers.

Other tests may be ordered by your physician, depending on what disorders are suspected. In general, procedures such as a CAT scan and MRI, which show detailed pictures of a specific portion of the body, and blood tests other than the ones mentioned above are not needed. If there is a question of an inflammatory disease of the muscle, such as polymyositis or dermatomyositis, a sedimentation rate, HLA antigen testing, or antinuclear antibody testing may be needed. If so, these specific tests and the reasons for having them done should be discussed with your physician. Now that genetic testing is available for many of the neuromuscular disorders, it plays an important part in a diagnostic workup. *However, a genetic test should not be the entire basis for a diagnosis in a child; it is just one piece of the puzzle.*

A muscle biopsy is indicated in every child suspected of having a neuromuscular disease unless there is a strong family history of a disorder. A muscle biopsy consists of having a small piece of muscle removed and then examined under a microscope. The muscle biopsy *MUST* be done under a local anesthetic, on a come-and-go basis, unless another surgical procedure is being performed, in which case a general anesthetic is needed.

When a muscle biopsy is performed, a small piece of tissue about the size of a fingertip is removed from an easily accessible, moderately involved muscle. In the past, when a muscle disorder was suspected, the calf muscle was used as the biopsy site. However, now this muscle is seldom appropriate for a biopsy, since it is often one of the strongest muscles in children with muscle weakness. When a muscle biopsy is performed, a local anesthetic is injected around the incision site. The incision does not need to be very large, and if the thigh muscle is used, the biopsy can be done somewhat to the side so that the resulting scar is not very visible.

In some centers around the world a punch biopsy is used to remove the muscle rather than obtaining it by an open procedure. The instrument used is a small, leatherlike punch that allows a tiny core of muscle tissue to be removed. This leaves a smaller scar than does an open procedure, but, unfortunately, few centers in the world are equipped to do punch biopsies.

The physician performing a muscle biopsy is usually a general or orthopedic surgeon, but in a few pediatric neuromuscular centers the same physician who examines the child also does the muscle biopsy and interprets it. This is ideal but, unfortunately, is usually not the case.

Specific studies need to be done on the muscle that is removed, and a piece of tissue should also be sent to a laboratory for genetic interpretation. A muscle biopsy should never simply be performed and the tissue then put in the old-time preservative formalin: this practice is extremely out of date. Nowadays, several different stains should be done on *frozen* muscle tissue. Then, if the diagnosis of congenital muscular dystrophy is being considered, a substance called merosin should also be looked for. This can be of both diagnostic importance, as well as an aid in predicting a child's future outcome.

If, as parents, you feel that your child has not had a complete pediatric neuromuscular workup and you want to obtain a second opinion, it is an easy thing to have records transferred from one physician or center to another. Either a note or a call to the doctor's office or the clinic's secretary will let them know that you wish your child's records to be reviewed by someone else. Most likely you will be sent a records-release form, which you will need to fill out with the second consultant's name and address. Be sure to sign it also before returning. It sometimes takes a little time to get records transferred, so you may have to make a few phone calls and even be a bit pushy to have this done. Muscle biopsy slides, EMG and nerve conduction results, blood and genetic findings, and history and physical examination results can all be transferred from one doctor or center to the other. A cost is not usually involved in doing this, and, if it is, it should be minimal.

> If your child doesn't follow the textbook description of a particular neuromuscular disorder, please get a second opinion.

> If your doctors and the other professionals you see don't seem to have a clue about what is wrong with your child, find those that do.

So, if you have any doubt at all that your child has not had a thorough, complete, neuromuscular consultation, then I would urge you to seek a second opinion, even if you have to go some miles to find a qualified pediatric neuromuscular specialist.

◆ ◆ ◆

THREE

Neuromuscular Disorders: History, Incidence, and Genetics

O nce you have found a pediatric neuromuscular consultant with whom you feel comfortable and are sure that the correct diagnosis has been made, you'll want to start learning a little more about your child's specific disorder. In general, neuromuscular diseases are divided into three groups: myopathies, or muscle diseases; neuropathies, or disorders involving the nervous system; and conditions in which changes in the metabolism of the internal tissues of the body result in muscle weakness.

History of Neuromuscular Disease

The earliest picture of a child with a muscle disease, which appears to be Duchenne dystrophy, comes from Egypt in about 2500 B.C.

The first recognized description of a muscle disease in the medical literature was by Dr. Edward Meryon, who lived in England in the mid-1800s. He described a child with apparent early-onset muscular dystrophy, but the credit for the description of rapidly progressive, early-onset, childhood muscular dystrophy is given to Dr. Guillaume Duchenne (1806–1875). Dr. Duchenne was also the first physician to do a muscle biopsy by use of a metal punch, similar to the one that is used in some centers today. Accurate diagnosis of most neuromuscular disorders was not possible until specific stains were developed, so that frozen muscle tissue could be examined under the microscope.

New types of neuromuscular disorders are still being identified, particularly in the group known as mitochondrial myopathies. Also, the treatment of neuromuscular diseases has changed a great deal over the years as physicians have learned more about lung care and life-support systems.

Incidence of Childhood Neuromuscular Diseases

When parents are initially given the diagnosis of a neuromuscular disease in their child, the first thing many of them say is, "But no one in our family has ever had such a problem. How can it be? I've never even known anybody with a muscle disease. How often do these conditions occur?"

If a neuromuscular disorder appears for the first time in the family, a history may be obtained that several infant deaths or miscarriages have occurred in some family members for which the cause was not known. A neuromuscular disorder can occur for the first time in a child, and we speak of this as a mutation or change in the child's own genes.

Muscle diseases are found worldwide in all ethnic groups, and, in the Middle East, because of the practice of interfamily marriages, some children with muscle diseases develop weakness much more rapidly than is usually the case. When relatives marry, it is possible for a child to inherit half of the recessive gene pair from each parent.

In answer to the question: Can both boys and girls have neuromuscular diseases? The answer is "Yes, depending on the specific type." Some of the disorders, such as Duchenne and Becker muscular dystrophy, hardly ever occur in girls unless there is another genetic abnormality. But most disorders affect the two sexes about equally.

"Did We, as Parents, Do Something Wrong to Account for our Child's Neuromuscular Disorder?"

When the diagnosis of a neuromuscular disease has been made, most parents continually ask themselves, "Why did this happen? Was it because we did or did not do something?"

Let me reassure you that because most neuromuscular diseases have a genetic basis, you had no control over the development of the disorder unless a genetic disorder was known to be present in your family, or you had genetic testing and chose to ignore a positive result.

If we are aware of genetic problems, then, as parents, we can make informed decisions about whether or not to have one or more children. Unfortunately, the diagnosis of a neuromuscular disease is often not made until a second or even a third child is conceived. Thus, it is possible to have three or more children with the same disorder in a family.

Genetic Questions

Because most parents have no interest in learning minute details about genetics, I want to give you just a general outline. However, in Appendix A you will find a more complete description, which Dr. Margaret Thompson, one of the leading neuromuscular geneticists in the world, has been kind enough to edit. I know that you have much more to do than be weighed down with a great many facts about genetics, but if you're interested, please do turn to Appendix A. Here, I will give you just some basic information about different ways genes can be inherited. Then you can either go into more detail with your physician or genetic counselor, or turn to the back of the book.

Not all neuromuscular diseases are due to changes in genes, as far as we now know. Also, in spite of the pace of current research, the cause of many of the disorders is still unknown or just beginning to become clear. We do know that the disorders dermatomyositis and polymyositis appear to be due to abnormalities in the body's reaction to foreign substances, a so-called autoimmune response. Changes in the body metabolism, or the internal chemical workings of the body, also cause some of the neuromuscular diseases, as I've noted previously. The neuromuscular conditions for which we have no real understanding at this point are the large group of mitochondrial encephalopathies, some of the limb girdle syndromes, and Dejerine-Sottas disease, if this indeed exists as a separate entity. (Professor Dubowitz and others have raised the question of whether this disorder should be classified by itself.) Extensive worldwide research is going on daily to find the causes of all the as yet unidentified neuromuscular diseases.

Important Genetics Terms

If a child receives an altered gene from a parent who has a neuromuscular disorder, he or she can develop the same problem. This is called *autosomal dominant inheritance.* Examples would be facioscapulohumeral and myotonic dystrophy. For example, if a father has facioscapulohumeral muscular dystrophy, he can pass the gene on to one of his children, so that either his sons or his daughters can have the same condition. However, if a mother has a gene on her X chromosome that causes a condition such as Duchenne or Becker dystrophy, then 50 percent of her sons can have the disorder, and this is called an *X-linked* or *sex-linked recessive disorder.* In turn, each of her daughters has a 1-in-2 chance of being a carrier, which means that a carrier daughter can pass the disorder on to 50 percent of her own male children. *Carriers* sometimes show signs or symptoms of disorders themselves, but this is not the usual situation. For example, in Duchenne dystrophy, a mother who is a carrier can have heart problems, curvature of the spine, or even enlarged calf muscles in her legs.

In addition to autosomal dominant inheritance and sex-linked (or X-linked) inheritance, there is also *autosomal recessive inheritance.* This is where one altered or mutant gene comes from each parent. An example of this type of inheritance is spinal atrophy, where a child receives an altered gene from both his mother and his father.

When both parents are carriers of the same recessive gene, each of their children has a 1-in-4 (or 25 percent) chance of having the disorder, since they would receive an altered gene from each parent. This does not mean that if one child has the disorder, the next three will not, and *the incidence of problems occurring in a family is always greater if one genetic disorder has developed.*

This is important to note because, in my experience, many parents have been told by physicians and genetic counselors that there is no chance of a problem reoccurring, and then it does one or more times.

Other Questions

Another question I'm often asked is why one child with a neuromuscular disorder may have a much more rapid progression of muscle weakness, while another one doesn't seem to have such a severe problem. There is a term in genetics, *expression,* which answers this question. If a gene is completely expressed, then the full-blown picture of a genetic condition occurs. Myotonic dystrophy is a good example of this because, in the same family, one child may have a mild disorder while a sibling may be severely involved. We still do not have many of the answers as to why one child may have an incomplete expression of a disorder while another has a full-blown picture. Probably other background genes are involved, but it will be some time before we know all the answers.

A physician with wide experience in neuromuscular diseases can often give you a fairly good idea about what is ahead after seeing the results of your child's tests and physical findings because of similar cases he or she has seen. However, one of the most important indicators of what lies ahead is whether your child's muscle weakness improves, stays the same, or gets worse over a period of several months' time.

Do All Parents Need to See a Genetic Counselor?

I am hesitant about suggesting that parents talk to a genetic counselor unless he or she has specific training in neuromuscular diseases. If the counselor knows just the results of the DNA testing and not the muscle biopsy interpretation and other tests, the information given may not be accurate or up to date. Without all the pieces of the diagnostic puzzle— that is, the history, physical examination, CPK, and muscle biopsy interpretation—an accurate diagnosis *cannot be made.* However, a well-trained genetic counselor who is knowledgeable about childhood neuromuscular diseases can be a real asset. Also, if your physician cannot answer your specific questions about whether any unborn children will develop the disorder or the possible involvement of siblings, then I would seek a genetic counselor who has had special training in neuromuscular diseases.

First, I would discuss the need to see a genetic counselor with your physician. *Don't hesitate to ask about a genetic counselor's background and training in childhood neuromuscular diseases, since, unfortunately, there are no good sources to check on his or her background.*

Thus, I would urge you to use great caution in choosing your experts. If you don't have a good feeling about one, or your questions are not answered, please do look elsewhere. There are many excellent, caring professionals in the neuromuscular field, though it may take some searching to find those who will help guide you through the rocky shoals ahead.

I would also caution all parents about rushing off to a public or a medical school library. Unless you have a medical background, it is often difficult to interpret the vast amount of material that can be found about neuromuscular diseases. Also, many textbooks are out of date almost as soon as they are published, and articles and chapters in books may not be written by experts in children's neuromuscular disorders. Long-term follow-up reports from physicians who have seen children from the time of diagnosis to adult years are rare. (Frequently, children are seen by many different doctors over the years, or in clinics where physicians change frequently.)

I would caution you, too, to be careful about accepting at face value what you read in newspapers, lay presses, or even agency newsletters. Frequently, it takes considerable training and experience to spot these inaccuracies, so please do be careful about trying to read everything available. My best recommendation is that you find a children's neuromuscular expert whom you trust and with whom you feel comfortable. Then I would urge you to keep an ongoing list of questions to discuss with him or her. Hopefully, the information given in the following chapters will provide a good foundation on which you can build a storehouse of facts about your child's specific disorder.

When it comes to questions about practical day-to-day matters, on the other hand, other parents or lay individuals are often far better sources of information and referrals than are physicians.

FOUR

◆ ◆ ◆

Neuromuscular Disorders: Descriptions and Treatment

I f your child has been diagnosed as having a neuromuscular disorder, you'll probably want to learn as much as possible about the specific condition. Now that a great deal of information is available on the Internet and in lay publications, it may be difficult to know what is fact, fiction, or somewhere in between.

Recently, I came across a list of medications of which to be beware in a lay neuromuscular newsletter published on the Internet. When I faxed it to Professor Dubowitz in London, his immediate reply was, "Beware of what you read on the Internet." I think this is wise advice about all medical information put out by lay groups. However, practical information given by these groups is usually excellent, because it is written by parents who have "been there."

Because you will want to have as much accurate information as is available, specific details are given in this chapter about the primary conditions in which muscle weakness is found in children and young people. There is almost an explosion of new information now about many of the specific disorders, but I will try to be as complete as possible about what is known to date.

Disease in the muscles themselves can be the cause of weakness, or the problem may be with the nerves that send impulses to different muscles. Also, abnormalities in the internal workings, or metabolism, of the body can cause muscle weakness in specific cases. We do know now that most, but not all, of the various muscle disorders are caused by changes in genes. Disorders can either be inherited from a parent or grandparent or occur for the first time in the child due to a change or mutation in a gene. Because most parents have no interest in a great deal of technical genetic information, only basic facts will be given. Those who want more detailed information can find it in Appendix A.

Myopathies

MUSCULAR DYSTROPHIES

Because of the Labor Day Telethon, the one muscle disease of which most parents are aware is Duchenne muscular dystrophy. In this disorder, a progressive loss of muscle strength occurs in boys. Girls can develop this condition only if they have another genetic abnormality, such as a condition called Turner's syndrome.

Duchenne Muscular Dystrophy

History: First described by Dr. Edward Meryon in 1851, although the credit is given to Dr. Guillaume Duchenne, who published a detailed description in 1861.

Incidence: Approximately 1 in 3500.

Ethnic Groups: All.

Sex Involved: Boys, and some girls with an additional genetic disorder.

Inheritance: X-linked (sex-linked) recessive, transmitted through a carrier mother to 50% of her sons. Many cases are due to a new mutation in the gene; this then is the first case in a family.

Site of Gene Mutation: Xp21, causing a failure of production of the protein dystrophin.

Laboratory Findings: Markedly increased creatine phosphokinase (CPK), serum glutamic-oxaloacetic transaminase (SGOT), serum glutamic-pyruvic transaminase (SGPT), and lactic dehydrogenase (LDH) may also be increased.

DNA: Genetic studies usually show abnormalities in the gene, but this test must not be the only one used for diagnosis.

Onset: Age 2+ years (the condition is present at birth but not detectable early on unless a CPK, muscle biopsy, or DNA tests are done).

Initial Signs: Often the boys are late walkers, fall and trip, have difficulty with steps, and problems keeping up with children of the same age.

Later: A progressive loss of muscle strength occurs, with wheelchair use usually necessary by 12+ years.

Complications: Curvature of the spine (scoliosis), contractures (tightness of specific muscles), heart and lung involvement. Less than 15% have heart problems before age 14, but about 57% have difficulties after age 18.

Problems to Be Aware Of: A learning disability can be detected in a large number of the boys, and delayed intellectual development may also be present.

Necessary Diagnostic Tests: CPK, muscle biopsy, dystrophin staining, DNA studies.

Treatment: Daily exercise, physical therapy with good stretching, and swimming in a warm pool. Special exercises can be done in the water by a physical therapist that help keep the muscles functioning as well as possible and also provide a much greater feeling of well-being. Muscle contractures are much easier to stretch in warm water than on a therapist's table. (Lifts are available if there is difficulty in transferring a patient from a wheelchair to the pool.) Night splints can make a real difference when heel cord contractures develop, and short-leg braces, or AFOs, may also be needed. If the heel cord contractures do not improve and are making walking difficult, then surgical lengthening of them by what is called a percutaneous procedure may be necessary. (This entails just a tiny slit through the tendon, and the procedure does not necessitate having a large incision made which can be much more painful and heal more slowly.) Any surgery should be followed by good physical therapy and walking as soon as possible in a short-leg cast.

Genetics: Prenatal testing can now be done either by chorionic villus sampling (CVS) of the placenta or after birth. Amniocentesis, a procedure in which fluid is removed by a needle through the mother's abdomen, can also be used. Testing siblings and other family members can be important in looking for carriers or detecting early cases in young boys. Also, it is important for mothers to remember that one-third of carriers after age 30 may develop signs of heart problems.

Treatments That Have Been Tried:

Myoblast transfer—despite widespread studies, this has proved unsuccessful.

Prednisone (a cortisone-like drug) is now being prescribed in varying doses in some centers but has long-term side effects.

Drug trials—different drugs are tried periodically, but none has been successful to date.

General Notes: There is much cause for optimism about finding a treatment for Duchenne dystrophy now that worldwide research is occurring. Thus, the most important thing that you can do as parents is to keep your son as active as possible and involved in normal daily activities. It is extremely easy to spoil a child who has Duchenne dystrophy, but in the long run he will suffer, as will family members, friends, and classmates. A boy with this disorder should be treated just like his brothers and sisters and be expected to carry his own load in the family. This means he should have his daily chores and do as much as he can for himself. If he is given special treatment, then both he and any brothers or sisters may pay a high price in the future.

> CASE: An 18-month-old child was seen in a child development center at a large teaching hospital because of slow development. He could pull up on furniture but had not started walking and spoke only a few words. During the workup, a CPK of 19,000 was found on examining his blood, so he was referred for a neuromuscular workup. On examination, muscle weakness was found, particularly around the hips. His muscle biopsy showed a typical picture for Duchenne dystrophy. Walking began at two years of age, but then he developed hyperactivity, as well as some learning problems. Social interactions have been difficult for him, but, with his supportive family, he has gradually adjusted to his disability and found a great release in art. (The family history is interesting in that the mother is one of eleven children, and there are no other cases of Duchenne dystrophy or muscle disease in the family.)

Becker Dystrophy

History: Described by a physician, Dr. Peter Becker, and by Dr. Franz Kiener, a psychologist in 1955.

Incidence: 1 in 20,000.

Ethnic Groups: All.

Sex Involved: Male.

Inheritance: X-linked (sex-linked) recessive—i.e., transmitted through a mother to 50% of her sons.

Site of Gene Mutation: Located at Xp21, which is the same location as the Duchenne dystrophy gene.

Laboratory Findings: Markedly elevated CPK (SGOT, SGPT, and LDH may also be increased). Abnormalities in size and amount of dystrophin generally, *but this is not one hundred percent true.*

Onset: Age 2+, but generally somewhat later than Duchenne dystrophy. Mild cases may not be detected until the teenage years or even adulthood, and then there may be just cramps on exercise, with perhaps some mild weakness.

Initial Signs: Difficulty in walking and running and keeping up with friends.

Later: Slowly progressive loss of muscle strength, with ability to walk generally into the thirties or forties.

Problems to Be Aware Of: Heart (cardiac) problems may be difficult to detect and yet can occur when there is not a great deal of muscle weakness. Less than one-third of individuals have signs and symptoms before age 35, but greater than two-thirds have signs and symptoms after age 35. Also, a third of the carriers of the gene may have some signs of heart problems after age 30. Contractures do develop but are less severe than those seen in Duchenne dystrophy.

Medical Tests: CPK, muscle biopsy, dystrophin staining, and DNA studies.

Treatment: Daily exercise is important, and swimming is particularly beneficial. Physical therapy is needed if muscle tightness develops, and night splints or short-leg braces (AFOs) may also be needed if heel cord contractures develop.

Genetics: Prenatal tests are available, and because the risk of Becker muscular dystrophy occurring in the next generation is quite high, prenatal testing for mothers who have had one child with this disorder is advised. If men with Becker dystrophy have children, the sons will be unaffected, but all the daughters will be carriers and therefore at risk for having sons with Becker dystrophy.

> CASE: A 3-year-old boy was found to have a CPK of 19,000 during lab work taken when he was ill with diarrhea and vomiting. The pediatrician also noted mild muscle weakness and referred the child for a neuromuscular workup. The mother's brother was in a wheelchair because of muscle weakness, but no diagnosis had been established for his disorder.
>
> On examination, the little boy was found to have mild muscle weakness but was able to hop on one foot or the other. He also had large calves, as did his mother, and tightness of the heel cords. A muscle biopsy showed a typical picture of muscular dystrophy, and a diagnosis of Becker dystrophy was made. He is now 17 and about to graduate from high school. In general, he has done well, but now is showing some increasing difficulty going up and down stairs and getting out of chairs. He is a good student and, in general, has had few problems relating to his Becker muscular dystrophy.

Emery-Dreifuss Muscular Dystrophy

Incidence: No accurate figures are available, since this disorder is often incorrectly diagnosed.

Ethnic Groups: All.

Sex Involved: Male.

Inheritance: X-linked (or sex-linked) recessive, so mothers can transmit the disorder to 50% of their sons. Carriers can easily be detected by skin biopsy. An autosomal form has been described also for which the gene has not yet been found.

Site of Gene Mutation: The gene is located at Xq28 on the long arm of the X chromosome, and the missing defective protein is called emerin. The gene product is known as EMD.

Laboratory Findings: Markedly increased CPK. Also, the presence or absence of emerin can be looked for in skin or muscle biopsy with special techniques.

Muscle Biopsy: The picture is quite unusual, because small or atrophic fibers may be present that are not usually seen in biopsies associated with muscle weakness due to disease in the muscle itself.

Onset: Usually childhood, but it can present as early as age 2.

Initial Signs: Tightness of the heel cords and a specific pattern of muscle weakness of the lower extremities.

Later: Slowly progressive loss of muscle strength, particularly in the lower extremities. (The distribution of muscle weakness is quite unlike that of Duchenne or Becker muscular dystrophies, because gradual loss of strength occurs in both the legs and the shoulder muscles. Tightness of the back muscles develops, which limits forward bending.) Increasing tightness of the arms results in right-angle, or 90-degree, contractures at the elbows. *This is the most important diagnostic clue, but the reason for this is unknown.*

Problems to Be Aware Of: Attention to the heart is of extreme importance, because, as the boys reach their teens, conduction problems of the electrical system of the heart can cause cardiac arrest or heart stoppage. Thus, after puberty, boys should see a heart doctor, or cardiologist, at least yearly. Their hearts should be checked with a Holter monitor at this time.

Treatment: Daily exercise and ongoing physical therapy to treat developing contractures.

Later: In the late teens or early twenties, it is usually necessary to surgically implant a small device called a pacemaker in the chest muscles in order to regulate the heartbeat. I have had male patients in their late teens or early twenties who did not want to see a cardiologist, saying that if they were going to get weaker and weaker, they saw no reason to have a pacemaker. *Note: Dr. Linton Hopkins, an authority on this disorder, says that he has Emery-Dreifuss patients in their fifties and older who with pacemakers, have a good quality of life.*

Genetics: Testing siblings and mothers, to see if they are either carriers or have the disorder, is important.

Note: If you are the mother of a youth with Emery-Dreifuss muscular dystrophy, your heart should be checked at least once a year by a heart doctor, or cardiologist. If you are a carrier of the disorder, you, too, are at risk for conduction problems in the heart that can cause sudden cardiac arrest, or heart stoppage.

> CASE: The mother of one of my Emery-Dreifuss boys complained to a cardiologist of fatigue, breathlessness, and some light-headedness. The physician did not connect this with her son's Emery-Dreifuss muscular dystrophy until I called him. A pacemaker was put in place almost immediately then, and the woman quickly improved and was able to return to work.

Limb Girdle Dystrophies

Patients with so-called limb girdle muscular dystrophies have muscle weakness close to the body, or proximal involvement. The clinical picture may resemble Duchenne and Becker muscular dystrophy to a certain extent, but the inheritance is autosomal recessive rather than sex-linked. In other words, an individual with muscle weakness receives one gene from each parent rather than inheriting the disorder through the mother, a so-called sex-linked inheritance. At this time, the group is divided into:

Calpain3 (limb girdle muscular dystrophy 2A, or LGMD2A)

Age of Onset: 8–15 years.

Gene Location: 15q.15.1–q21.1.

Inheritance: Autosomal recessive.

Progression: Variable.

Sarcoglycanopathies—Severe Childhood Autosomal Recessive Muscular Dystrophy(SCARMD)

History: These forms were described in 1983 and are a subgroup of the limb girdle dystrophies. It is important to distinguish these because a rapid progression of muscle weakness can occur.

Gamma Sarcoglycanopathy

Incidence: Unknown.

Ethnic Groups: Particularly prevalent in North Africa.

Sex: Either.

Inheritance: Autosomal recessive, with a gene coming from each parent.

Age of Onset: 2–10 years.

Gene Location: 13q.12. The affected protein is gamma sarcoglycan, 35DAG.

Abnormality: Absence of or decreased gamma sarcoglycan.

Progression: Extremely variable.

Initial Signs: Enlargement of the calves (hypertrophy) and weakness in muscles close to the body (proximal).

Later: Rapid progression of muscle weakness can occur.

Problems to Be Aware Of: Respiratory difficulties are not as prominent as in Duchenne dystrophy, and heart problems may not occur or may just be mild, but should be watched for.

Alpha Sarcoglycanopathy

Incidence: Unknown.

Ethnic Groups: Particularly prevalent in North Africa.

Sex: Either.

Inheritance: Autosomal recessive, with a gene coming from each parent.

Site of Gene Mutation: 17q.12–q21.33.

Abnormality: Absence of or decreased alpha sarcoglycan protein called 50kDAG (dystrophin-associated glycoprotein).

Age of Onset: Can be in early childhood.

Laboratory Findings: CPK can be quite high.

Muscle Biopsy: Large (hypertrophic) fibers may be seen, and splitting of fibers can also occur.

Initial Signs: Enlargement of the calves (hypertrophy) can be present, plus weakness in muscles close to the body, or the proximal muscles.

Later: Loss of ambulation can occur at about age 12 as rapid progression of muscle weakness occurs.

Comments: Respiratory difficulties are not as prominent as in Duchenne dystrophy, and heart involvement may not occur or just be mild. The back should be checked for signs of scoliosis, or curvature of the spine. Also, muscle contractures may develop.

Life Expectancy: Death can occur even in the thirties if there is rapid progression of muscle weakness.

Treatment: Daily exercise, particularly swimming, and ongoing physical therapy. *Note: If a patient becomes overweight and sedentary, the use of a wheelchair may be required in the twenties or earlier.*

Genetics: Prenatal testing is important if there is a known case in the family.

Note: Exercise, along with any needed pulmonary and cardiac care, can make a real difference in life expectancy, as well as the quality of life.

> CASE: This teenager had a fracture of her leg at age 8 and subsequently seemed to have more and more difficulty in walking. She developed a waddling gait and fell two to three times a day. Thus, it became difficult for her to walk even short distances. On examination at age 13, she had considerable loss of muscle strength, very large calves, and showed a positive Gowers' sign. (This is the need to push up on the legs in order to get up from a sitting position on the floor.)
>
> The family history revealed that all members of her father's side of the family had large calves, and a cousin had died at age 32 with muscle weakness. Both the muscle biopsy and the laboratory work confirmed the diagnosis of severe childhood autosomal recessive muscular dystrophy. A deficiency of adhalin, or 50kDag protein, was found, and her dystrophin was normal.

Facioscapulohumeral (FSH) Muscular Dystrophy

Incidence: 1 in 20,000.

Ethnic Groups: All.

Sex: Either.

Inheritance: Autosomal dominant, with the gene going from parent to child.

Site of Gene Mutation: The long arm of the chromosome at 4q35.

Onset: May be in infancy, but usually much later on.

Initial Signs: Weakness of face, shoulder, and arm muscles, with loss of ability to smile, wrinkle the forehead, or close the eyes. Speech difficulties may also occur.

Later: Increasing weakness in arm muscles and also in the legs.

Problems to Be Aware Of: Curvature of the spine, or scoliosis. Also, hearing loss and visual problems can occur.

Treatment: Ongoing physical therapy. Surgery may be necessary if curvature of the spine or severe upriding of the shoulders occurs.

Genetics: Prenatal tests are available, but there is some question about whether the disorder, which is usually mild, justifies these. Siblings and other family members should be examined and tested for the disorder.

Note: In general, children and teenagers with this disorder develop muscle weakness rather slowly, but this is quite variable. Usually, those with the disorder live as long as their unaffected siblings.

> CASE: A 2-year-old boy was noted to have some facial weakness and mild weakness around his shoulders. The child's father and grandfather both had evidence of facioscapulohumeral muscular dystrophy, and a neuromuscular workup confirmed the diagnosis. The boy has developed more muscle weakness than the father and also began to develop curvature of the spine as a teenager.

Congenital Muscular Dystrophy

The name unfortunately causes a great deal of confusion because parents, and sometimes even physicians, link the disorder (or group of disorders) with Duchenne dystrophy and other severe types. *There is no connection.* Congenital simply means that the problem is present at birth or soon after, and the children can improve in strength.

Incidence: No good statistics are available.

Ethnic Groups: All races, but the Fukuyama type occurs more frequently in Japanese patients.

Sex: Either.

Inheritance: There are X-linked, autosomal dominant, and autosomal recessive types. Four specific types have now been identified:

> Pure type
> > Merosin-positive
> > Merosin-negative
>
> Fukuyama
> Santavuori
> Walker-Warburg

Laboratory Findings: CPK may be markedly elevated.

Muscle Biopsy: The amount of muscle involved on the muscle slides does not relate to the degree of the child's involvement. Severe changes may be seen on the biopsy, yet a child may show just mild weakness.

Site of Gene Mutation:

> Pure type:
> > Merosin-positive: ?
> > Merosin-negative: chromosome 6q2
>
> Fukuyama: chromosome 9q31-q33
> Santavuori: ?
> Walker-Warburg: ?

Age of Onset: Birth or soon afterward.

Initial Signs:

Widespread muscle weakness.

Pure type:

Merosin-positive: usually normal intelligence.

Merosin-negative: higher CPKs and changes on the brain picture, or MRI (may not be seen until after six months); usually intelligence is normal.

Fukuyama: usually severe developmental delay with an abnormal MRI of the head, seizures, and elevated CPKs. Most children can never walk, but there are exceptions. The severe changes in the brain seem to correlate with the amount of muscle weakness.

Santavuori: muscle weakness, plus eye abnormalities, causing visual problems, and in the brain, resulting in retardation and seizures.

Walker-Warburg: brain abnormalities, causing retardation.

Later Signs:

Pure type:

Merosin-positive: may improve and walk independently.

Merosin-negative: the outcome is dependent on the amount of muscle weakness and whether or not respiratory muscles are involved.

Problems to Be Aware Of: If a child with congenital muscular dystrophy has recurrent lung infections, such as pneumonia, then he or she is at high risk for a much shortened life expectancy. Colds and coughs should be treated aggressively with antibiotics, and sometimes daily small doses (maintenance antibiotics) are necessary during the winter months. Also, children with the Fukuyama congenital muscular dystrophy generally develop hydrocephalus, or enlargement of the ventricles of the brain, and require shunts. Most of the Walker-Warburg children require shunts because they develop progressive hydrocephalus.

Life Expectancy: No specific number of years can be given, because this is dependent on the severity of the respiratory infections and the kind of pulmonary care that is received.

Treatment: Physical therapy with aggressive stretching of contractures and rapid treatment of colds and coughs.

Genetics: Prenatal testing is available.

Note: It is extremely important to know whether or not merosin is present or absent, because this can help in predicting, to some extent, the severity of problems that may occur. As parents, you may need to request that this test be done, since it is not routine in all centers. (Muscle-biopsy tissue can be sent to prominent researchers, such as Dr. Eric Hoffmann at the University of Pittsburgh, if the test for merosin is not available where your child's muscle biopsy is performed.)

> CASE: A 19-month-old boy was seen because he was not walking by himself. A CPK of 340 had been found by the pediatrician, and he was referred for a workup and muscle biopsy. On examination, he had some mild muscle weakness both close to the body, or proximally, and of the arms and legs, or distally. A muscle biopsy revealed the typical picture of congenital muscular dystrophy. The biopsy showed marked pathology, which was not consistent with the mild disorder that the little boy showed. (This is a common finding.) He did walk alone at 22 months.
>
> The child has done very well except for the development of contractures. However, he has had an intensive swim therapy program three times a week from the time he was a little boy and now, as a teenager, is going to school, is holding an after-school job, and also has a radio program.

Congenital Myopathies

The following are the most common types:

Central Core Disease
Minicore Disease
Congenital Fibre type Disproportion
Myotubular Myopathy
Nemaline Myopathy
Miscellaneous types with subcellular structural changes
Minimal Change Myopathy (nonspecific)

New ones are described from time to time but may constitute just a single case report.

History: Described by Dr. G. Milton Shy and Dr. Kenneth McGee in 1956.

Incidence: Unknown because of frequent misdiagnosis.

Ethnic Groups: All.

Sex: Either.

Inheritance: Either dominant or recessive, depending on the particular disorder.

Age of Onset: Usually at birth or within the first few months.

Initial Problems: Muscle weakness and often respiratory infections.

Later: There is generally an improvement in muscle strength, particularly with good physical therapy and exercise.

Problems to Be Aware Of: Development of contractures, or areas of muscle tightness. Also, respiratory infections, particularly pneumonia, can be a real problem if there is weakness of the chest muscles. Sudden death can occur because of respiratory or breathing failure.

Treatment: Good stretching and physical therapy with orthopedic surgery as needed.

Genetics: Siblings should be watched for evidence of the disorder.

Central Core Disease

Age of Onset: Birth.

Initial Problems: One or both hips may be dislocated because of diffuse muscle weakness. Most patients have some weakness of the facial muscles, which can be seen in the inability to completely bury the eyelashes when the eyes are tightly closed.

Later Signs: May improve considerably and then the muscle strength may reach a plateau.

Inheritance: Dominant.

Laboratory Findings: CPK, EMG, nerve conduction times are usually within normal limits. Genetic studies can now be performed, but a good biopsy should also be obtained for the highest diagnostic accuracy.

Muscle Biopsy: *It is extremely important that the muscle biopsy be done under a local anesthetic, because the anesthetic risk in central core disease is high due to the frequently associated condition called malignant hyperthermia.*

Gene Location: 19q, which is the same site as that of malignant hyperthermia. However, several patients with central core disease have been found not to have the malignant hyperthermia defect.

What Lies Ahead: Most of these children do well, although there are a few case reports of adults who develop progressive muscle weakness later on in life. Also, this disorder has been seen with heart, cardiac, enlargement due to an abnormality of the heart muscle called a cardiomyopathy.

Precautions: A muscle biopsy should *always* be performed under a local anesthetic because of the risk of malignant hyperthermia. If a general anesthetic is needed for some other reason, then Halothane and succinylcholine anesthetics should be avoided, and malignant hyperthermia precautions should be taken by the pediatric anesthesiologist with a cooling blanket and the drug Dantrium, available in the operating room. *Also, the anesthetic machine should be flushed prior to use to be sure no traces of previous anesthetics are present.*

> CASE: A 6-year-old boy was seen because his teacher had noticed a funny gait on the playground plus inability to keep up with the other children in the class. He was seen by an orthopedist, who said that the child would outgrow the problem. The boy continued to complain of difficulty keeping up with his friends and also muscle cramps, so his pediatrician ordered a CPK, which was found to be 522 (0–235 is normal). The pediatrician referred him for a neuromuscular workup and, on examination, the child was found to have slightly decreased muscle strength both in his arms and legs. Also, he walked with his feet wide apart, a so-called wide-based gait. Because of questionable big calves in the mother and father, EMGs were done on all three individuals but were found to be within normal limits. A muscle biopsy revealed a classic picture of central core disease. The youth has gradually improved in strength and now is able to take part in most activities with his friends.

Minicore Disease (Multicore Disease)

History: Described by Dr. Andrew Engel in 1971.

Incidence: Rare.

Ethnic Groups: All.

Sex: Either.

Inheritance: Unclear, but may be autosomal recessive.

Site of Gene Mutation: Not known.

Laboratory Findings: CPK is usually normal.

DNA: No studies are available at this time.

Age of Onset: Birth or somewhat later.

Initial Problems: Marked muscle weakness at birth or mild muscle weakness in early childhood.

Later Signs: Generally improvement in strength.

Problems to Be Aware Of: Scoliosis, or curvature of the spine, may develop. Also, sudden death can occur due to weakness of the diaphragm and lung failure.

Precautions: Anesthetic risk similar to that in central core disease. Infants are more likely to have respiratory or breathing problems. Sleep studies should be done to see if there is a decrease in oxygen at night.

Treatment: Ongoing physical therapy with good daily exercise. Prompt medical care for coughs or colds so that pneumonia does not develop. Mask ventilation can be used if there is an oxygen lack during the night.

Genetics: No prenatal testing available.

> CASE: A 9-year-old boy was seen because of difficulty going up and down stairs and frequent falling. There was no family history of any muscle problems, and the child walked at 15 months.
>
> CPK was within normal limits. On physical examination, he was found to have some weakness in his legs, as well as in the muscles around the hips. No calf enlargement was seen, but the boy walked with his feet wide apart. The muscle biopsy showed a typical minicore disease. The youth has done well with a good exercise program and some weight loss. He prefers to watch many hours of television a day and snack between meals, so it takes hard work on his mother's part to keep him out of the refrigerator and off the couch.

Congenital Fibre type Disproportion

History: Described by Dr. Michael Brooke in 1973. Many physicians feel this is not a clear-cut entity, since there seems to be some overlap with some of the other congenital myopathies.

Incidence: Unknown.

Ethnic Groups: All.

Sex: Either.

Inheritance: May be either dominant or recessive.

Laboratory Findings: CPK usually within normal limits.

Muscle Biopsy: Shows a difference in the size of one of the types of fibers. Normally two types of fibers are present in muscle, called types I and II. In fibre type disproportion, the type I fibers are smaller than type II fibers, and they should be of equal size in children.

DNA: None present.

Age of Onset: Birth or somewhat later.

Initial Problems: A dislocation of one or both hips may be present, as well as clubfeet.

Later Signs: Curvature of the spine, or scoliosis, may develop, as well as muscle contractures.

Treatment: Ongoing physical therapy and orthopedic surgery as needed for foot and hip problems, as well as contractures.

CASE: This child was active at birth, but then, soon after, seemed to have somewhat decreased ability to move. He did sit at 6 months and walked at 15 months, but he did not have normal strength. At age 6 he was seen in a teaching center, and his CPK was found to be 39 (normal is 0–130), and his nerve conduction times and EMG were reported as normal. Despite these findings, the child was sent home with the diagnosis of Duchenne muscular dystrophy.

When the diagnostic workup was repeated, the muscle biopsy showed a fibre type disproportion. The patient has had no progression of muscle weakness but has developed some contractures, which have necessitated stretching, short-leg braces, and an aggressive exercise program.

Myotubular Myopathy

History: Described by Dr. Spiro in 1966.

Incidence: Unknown.

Ethnic Groups: All.

Sex: Either, except in the X-linked (or sex-linked) form, which affects just males.

Inheritance: X-linked recessive, autosomal recessive, or autosomal dominant forms are known.

Site of Gene Mutation: Xq28.

Laboratory Findings: CPK is usually within normal limits. The defective protein is myotubularin (MTMX).

Muscle Biopsy: Shows a specific picture. *One problem in diagnosing this disorder is that not all the muscle biopsy sections may show the changes, so it may be necessary to review several slides.*

Age of Onset: Birth or late childhood with the autosomal recessive type. The infantile X-linked form can be quite severe and may even lead to an early death.

Initial Signs: Diffuse muscle weakness; unusual facial features, with long, thin faces and weakness of the eye muscles.

Later Signs: Curvature of the spine, or scoliosis, may develop, and also frequent pneumonia because of respiratory and diaphragmatic muscle weakness.

Treatment: Physical therapy and good exercise, as well as treatment of orthopedic problems; ongoing attention to respiratory problems is important.

Problems to Be Aware Of: The amount of muscle weakness and the difficulties that a child has will vary with the specific type of myotubular myopathy. Although the X-linked form can be quite severe, most patients with the other types do quite well. Even in the X-linked form, infants are now surviving because of the pulmonary care that is available. Curvature of the spine and respiratory, or lung, problems may develop later on in the other two types and must be watched for carefully. Also, sleep studies should be done to see if there is decreased oxygen during the night. If this is present, mask ventilation can be used.

CASE: At birth, this child was noted to be very floppy and had deformities of his feet (pes cavus). At 2 weeks of age he developed considerable respiratory distress and had to be hospitalized. This occurred again at 7 weeks of age, at which time he seemed to have even less muscle strength and tone than he did previously. At this time it was also noted that he had some weakness of the facial muscles. A neuromuscular workup revealed a normal CPK and nerve conduction times. *A muscle biopsy done in the nursery revealed myotubular myopathy.* A biopsy was done somewhat later on the mother to see if this was the sex-linked form of myotubular myopathy. Her biopsy showed minimal changes, so it was difficult to establish that clearly. The child ultimately was able to be discharged from the hospital and seemed to improve in strength to some extent.

Nemaline Myopathy ("Rod Body Myopathy")

History: Described by Dr. G. Milton Shy in 1963. The name comes from tiny clumps of threadlike bodies seen in the muscle biopsies (*nemaline* = "thread" in Greek).

Incidence: Unknown.

Ethnic Groups: All.

Sex: Either.

Inheritance: Usually autosomal recessive, but there is a rare autosomal dominant type.

Site of Gene Mutation: The 1q21–q23 is autosomal dominant; the 2q21.2–q2 is the autosomal recessive type.

Laboratory Findings: CPK may be within normal limits. The gene product is the protein tropomyosin.

Age of Onset: Birth or somewhat later.

Initial Signs: Diffuse muscle weakness; respiratory failure because of weakness of the diaphragm. Children have long, narrow faces in addition to high-arched palates that create dental problems. It is important to note that swallowing difficulty may be the presenting sign of this disorder. Long, narrow feet with high arches and curvature of the spine may occur. Joint fixation or arthrogryposis has been present in several cases.

Later Signs: In general, the infants improve in muscle strength and then plateau, or stay about the same. However, normal muscle power does not develop, and the children usually have thin, narrow bodies.

Complications: Curvature of the spine (scoliosis) and problems with respiratory infections. Diaphragmatic weakness may be present, and heart failure has occurred in one teenage patient.

Problems to Be Aware Of: There is a question whether or not this is a distinct entity, because these rods have been found in some of the other congenital myopathies. Sleep studies should be done to determine if there is a decrease of oxygen during the night. Mask ventilation can be used during sleep if this occurs.

Treatment: Immediate attention to colds, coughs, and respiratory infections, physical therapy, and treatment of scoliosis or orthopedic problems.

> CASE: A 12-year-old girl was seen with a complaint of muscle weakness and curvature of the spine. She was quite thin and, on examination, had weakness both in her upper and lower extremities. The curvature of the spine was quite severe, and there had been a history of several episodes of pneumonia. Her neuromuscular workup revealed a normal CPK, but the muscle biopsy showed many nemaline rods. She continued developing recurrent pneumonias, which necessitated frequent hospitalization.

Inflammatory Myopathies

Myositis

History: Polymyositis was first described by Dr. Wagner in 1863, and dermatomyositis by Dr. Unverricht in 1891. Dr. John Walton (Lord Walton) wrote the basic text on myositis in 1956 and has written many subsequent reviews on the subject. Two primary forms of myositis occur in children: dermatomyositis, with muscle weakness and skin changes; and polymyositis, with just muscle weakness.

Incidence: Unknown.

Sex: Either.

Site of Gene Mutation: No specific gene is known to be involved.

Laboratory Findings: CPK may be markedly increased, as may the sedimentation rate and other studies that show the body's reaction to a foreign substance. Several blood tests should be done, including a complete blood count (CBC), sedimentation rate, ESR, antinuclear antibodies (ANA), and HLA Class I and Class II antigen testing. These should be done before steroid (or prednisone) treatment has been started.

Muscle Biopsy: If the biopsy does not show inflammation or the type of cells that appear in infection, it is important that the frozen muscle tissue be processed with special stains. The so-called NADH stain can show fibers that look like coiled-up snakes and are called "whorled" fibers. Some variation of the fiber size is also present, and both these changes indicate that an abnormal process, or myopathy, is present. Doctors Stirling Carpenter and George Karpati in Canada have shown that changes may be seen on highly magnified pictures of the muscle fibers, by a technique called electron microscopy.

Onset: Any age.

Initial Signs: There may be either a sudden or a gradual onset of muscle weakness in a child who has been healthy. The involved muscles are usually those close to the body, but weakness can be widespread. Muscles can become quite painful, but this is not always so. If the skin is involved (i.e., dermatomyositis), it becomes red and shiny over the cheeks and bridge of the nose (this is called a malar flush). The knuckles of the hands, or metacarpophalangeal joints, can also become red or scaly; and this is called a Groton's sign.

Complications: Children may be extremely ill with fever and widespread muscle weakness, which can become worse quite rapidly. When it develops slowly, the diagnosis may be difficult to make. Calcium deposits under the skin, or calcinosis, occur in some children and may be quite painful. Small deposits can work to the outside and poke through the skin. Also, with widespread disease, respiratory problems can develop, and weakness of the respiratory muscles and diaphragm have been reported.

Problems to Be Aware Of: It should be noted that in 25 percent of cases of myositis the CPK can be within normal limits, and 25 percent of muscle biopsies may show few or no changes. This prevents physicians who are not familiar with the disease from considering myositis as a diagnostic possibility.

Treatment: Prednisone in high doses (the recommended dose is between 1 and 2 mg per kg per day given in divided doses by mouth over a 24-hour period for the first four weeks) should be started as soon as the diagnosis is made. It should not be given on an every-other-day basis, but given daily, and after the first month tapered down to what is called a maintenance level. If children are extremely ill, other drugs may be needed, such as cyclophosphamides, methotrexate, and cyclosporin. Also, intravenous immunoglobulins have been given in some centers, with good success. *Note: The prognosis is very much dependent on how quickly prednisone is started, the dose used, and the type of exercise and ongoing physical therapy that a child receives. A child can return to normal or almost normal strength, but the earlier the treatment, the better the chances are that a child will have the best possible outcome.*

> CASE: A 12-year-old girl was seen because of the rather sudden onset of muscle weakness both in her shoulders and in the muscles around the hips. She also had developed a skin rash over her face, elbows, and hands and was in considerable distress. The diagnosis was felt to be dermatomyositis, and subsequent laboratory work showed this to be the case. Her CPK was 25,000 (normal 0–270), the sedimentation rate was 40 (normal 0–10), and her muscle biopsy showed diffuse inflammation. With high daily doses of prednisone, which were tapered after a month to a lower so-called maintenance level, she did well. The improvement was due not only to the medication, it was believed, but also to the physical therapy that she received.

Infantile Myositis

History: The first case described in the medical literature was a beautiful baby I first saw at 6 months of age. She had widespread muscle weakness, and her CPK was in the thousands instead of below 200. Her muscle biopsy showed many clumps of inflammatory cells, and, although myositis had not been reported in infants, the diagnosis of infantile myositis seemed to be the most appropriate one. I started her on a good dose of prednisone, and within 1 to 2 weeks she was holding up her head and showed much-improved muscle strength. Subsequent to the time that I submitted this first case for publication, there have been several others reported in centers all over the world. Thus, infantile myositis is something that should be considered if a baby is floppy at birth and shows inflammatory changes in the muscle biopsy. The CPK may or may not be elevated.

A child's outcome is dependent on the extent of muscle weakness, how quickly prednisone is started, and good general care. Some infants have been reported to return to almost normal strength.

Prader-Willi Syndrome

History: This disorder was first described by Doctors Prader, Labhardt, and Willi in 1956.

Incidence: 1 in 25,000.

Sex: Either.

Inheritance: Usually from the father. (This syndrome has a very complicated inheritance, and often the deleted gene inherited from the father is the one responsible.)

Site of Gene Mutation: A deletion or defect on the father's chromosome 15 is the usual cause. Some children with the disorder can be shown to have inherited both chromosome 15s from their mother and to lack a copy of their father's chromosome 15. This, however, is an unusual occurrence.

Laboratory Findings: CPK may be within normal limits. Growth hormone and thyroid tests can be important to be sure they are within normal limits.

Muscle Biopsy: Generally normal.

Onset: Birth.

Initial Signs: Widespread muscle weakness with difficulty swallowing and sucking, but no breathing problems. Children have specific facial characteristics, including small eyes, high foreheads, and somewhat triangular mouths. Also, their hands and feet may be small. In males, the genitalia may be undersized, with the testes not down in the scrotum.

Later Signs: May show some developmental delay, but a few children have IQs in the normal range. Muscle strength can improve, though the children may be late walkers with considerable delay in growth.

Complications: Marked obesity and difficulty in controlling food intake.

Problems to Be Aware Of: If children constantly want food, refrigerators and cupboards need to be locked.

Treatment: Weight control, physical therapy, and exercise on an ongoing basis.

> CASE: One of my little patients with Prader-Willi syndrome showed not only a lack of growth hormone but also an abnormally low amount of thyroid hormone. He responded well to thyroid medication and also had a good increase in height with growth hormone treatment. Thus, I would recommend that both growth hormone and thyroid function be measured in all children with Prader-Willi syndrome.

Disorders of Muscle Contractures

Arthrogryposis

Cause: This is a very complex group of disorders for which we have few answers. Thus, no exact classification is possible.

Incidence: Unknown.

Ethnic Groups: All.

Sex: Either.

Inheritance: Usually autosomal recessive, but can be dominant if a parent has the disorder.

Laboratory Findings: CPK may be within normal limits or elevated.

Muscle Biopsy: May show the typical picture of congenital muscular dystrophy, or just widespread changes in the muscle. The muscle biopsy may reflect nervous-system problems. Also, nemaline rods have been found in a few cases, which is puzzling.

Site of Gene Mutation: No specific gene has been identified.

Age of Onset: Birth, with the findings of fixed contractures of two or more joints and sometimes other malformations.

Initial Problems: Muscle weakness and joint contractures.

Later Signs: With good physical therapy and orthopedic surgery, contractures can often be improved, but this is variable. Lung hemorrhage, or bleeding, has been reported, leading to a fatal outcome.

Problems to Be Aware Of: A child's length of life will depend on whether severe respiratory infections accompany the muscle weakness and joint contractures. Because of the need for frequent surgery, there is always the risk of anesthetic problems, as is true with most of the other neuromuscular disorders. Also, some children have malformations of their facial structure, which makes anesthetics particularly difficult to give. *An experienced pediatric anesthesiologist should always give the anesthetic if surgery is needed for a child with arthrogryposis. In addition, great care needs to be used when the breathing tube is removed, particularly if mechanical ventilation has been needed. Otherwise, a fatality can occur, as happened with one of my little patients.*

> CASE: One little girl with arthrogryposis walked amazingly well after several surgeries, even though her orthopedist felt she would never walk. However, her mother refused to give up, and the little girl was also very determined. Together they proved an unbeatable combination.

Neuropathies

The muscle weakness found in the group of disorders called *neuropathies* is caused by changes either in the spinal cord or in the nerves themselves. Many of these are due to genetic changes, which will be discussed later. One of the major groups is the spinal muscular atrophies, of which there are three types:

SPINAL MUSCULAR ATROPHIES

Werdnig-Hoffmann (Type I)
Intermediate (Type II) (previously called
    Arrested Werdnig-Hoffmann disease)
Kugelberg-Welander (Type III)

Because the long-term prognosis, or outcome, for each of the disorders is quite different, it is important that any infant or child suspected of having one of these disorders be accurately diagnosed as early as possible.

Werdnig-Hoffmann (Type I)

History: Described by Dr. Guido Werdnig in 1891 and by Dr. Johann Hoffmann in 1893.

Incidence: Approximately 1 in 10,000 in the United States.

Ethnic Groups: All groups.

Sex: Either.

Inheritance: Autosomal recessive, with one gene coming from each parent.

Site of Gene Mutation: Defect is on 5q11–q13; abnormalities in the SMN (survival motor neuron) gene and the NAIP (neuronal apoptosis inhibitor) gene have been described.

Laboratory Findings: CPK usually within normal limits.

Onset: Birth, with decreased fetal movements usually during the last few months of a mother's pregnancy.

Initial Signs: Respiratory or breathing problems, as well as feeding problems. The diaphragm itself is always spared—that is, it is not weak.

Later Signs: Rapid progression of the muscle weakness, with death usually by one year.

Problems to Be Aware Of: If a baby is admitted to the hospital because of respiratory problems or pneumonia, physicians may insist on mechanical lung support. Parents do have a right to say that this is not what they want for their infant, since it essentially prolongs life for just a short period and a fatal outcome will still occur.

Precautions: Careful attention to colds, coughs, and lung infections.

Genetics: Because each parent carries the gene for this disorder, some parents elect to use artificial insemination or make a choice to adopt rather than having further children. Even though the risk is that one in four infants of carrier parents should have the disorder, I have cared for families in which two and even more infants have succumbed from the disease. Prenatal testing is available and is important if further pregnancies are planned.

Treatment: None is available at this time, although from time to time drug trials are carried out.

> CASE: One mother who lost two infants with Werdnig-Hoffmann disease told me of the terrible time she and her husband went through with their first baby in a prestigious medical school hospital. When the doctors insisted that a ventilator be used because the baby had developed pneumonia, the mother said that she and her husband essentially lived in the hospital to be near their child. Then, finally, even the respirator did not keep the baby alive, and the infant was in no more distress. When the second baby was found to have Werdnig-Hoffmann disease, the parents asked me if they could keep their baby at home. They had an excellent, caring pediatrician, so together he and I offered the support they needed. The mother and father told me afterward how much better it was to have their baby with them during those difficult days rather than in a cold, gray, impersonal hospital. So parents do have a choice about where they want their baby to be, although it may take a very aggressive approach to convince the physician in charge that the baby should be at home or in some place other than a hospital.

Intermediate Spinal Atrophy (Type II)

History: Described by Professor Victor Dubowitz in 1964 and by Doctors Ted Munsat and Roger Woods in 1968.

Onset: Usually after 6 months of age.

Incidence: No good statistics, because this form is often not separated from other kinds of spinal muscular atrophies or some of the other neuromuscular disorders.

Ethnic Groups: All groups.

Sex: Either.

Inheritance: Autosomal recessive, with a gene coming from each parent.

Site of Gene Mutation: At 5q11–q13.

Laboratory Findings: Normal CPK (usually).

Muscle Biopsy: A specific picture is seen that should not be difficult to diagnose.

Initial Signs: Babies appear to be healthy at birth and then, after the first few months, gradually develop muscle weakness. A child may sit independently but almost never has the strength to crawl, pull up, or walk. Some little ones take one or two steps but then gradually develop muscle weakness and even lose the ability to crawl.

Later Signs: Children may gradually improve somewhat in their muscle strength as they grow and develop, but then seem to reach a plateau. There have been ongoing discussions about whether or not intermediate spinal atrophy is progressive, but most experts feel that it is not.

Problems to Be Aware Of: With an increase in weight, which is seen particularly in teenage girls, as well as a decrease in exercise, many teenagers lose the ability to walk.

Treatment: A good exercise or swim program and ongoing physical therapy is extremely important. KAFOs, or long-leg braces, may help patients maintain the ability to walk.

Complications: Curvature of the spine, or scoliosis, with usually the need for spinal fusion in the teens.

Genetics: Prenatal testing is advised. *Note: The life expectancy for a young person with this disorder can be within normal limits if he or she has stayed active, has had few lung infections, and has not had a severe curvature of the spine.*

CASE: A child was first seen at age 2 who had been given the diagnosis of Werdnig-Hoffmann disease in a large medical center. The mother had been told that the child would not live beyond two years of life, and yet she seemed to be doing quite well. After a diagnostic workup, the child appeared to fit into the type II spinal muscular atrophy group and was fitted with lightweight braces and put on a good exercise and physical therapy program. This young lady has now graduated from college and continues to ambulate with crutches, using a wheelchair for long distances. Her mother never allowed her to feel sorry for herself, but expected her to keep up with other children as much as she could. Her advice to other parents is "Don't be afraid to urge, coax, push, prod, or shove if necessary." She said that her daughter was more than willing to try to manipulate, cajole, persuade, or con other people into doing things for her. "It was a continual battle to circumvent her attempts to find the easy way out and be lazy. But I never sold short her capabilities, and I encouraged her every step of the way to believe in herself and know that she could have a good life."

Kugelberg-Welander (Type III Spinal Atrophy)

History: Doctors Wohlfart, Kugelberg, and Welander described this disorder in 1955 and 1956.

Incidence: No true figures because of errors in diagnosis.

Ethnic Groups: All groups.

Sex: Either.

Inheritance: Autosomal recessive, with a gene coming from each parent.

Site of Gene Mutation: At 5q11–q13.

Laboratory Findings: Normal CPK.

Muscle Biopsy: Similar to other forms but may see small groups of abnormal round fibers (group atrophy).

Initial Signs: Within the first two or three years of life, with the development of mild muscle weakness. The children may be late walkers and may also have difficulty in going up and down stairs and keeping up with others their own age.

Later: Slowly progressive muscle weakness may develop, so children may be mildly affected and thus have a fairly normal life expectancy.

Problems to Be Aware Of: Decreased activity, lack of exercise, and a large weight gain may cause loss of muscle strength or the ability to walk.

Treatment: Active ongoing physical therapy and daily exercise are important, with careful attention to weight gain.

Genetics: Prenatal testing is important if parents are willing to terminate the pregnancy if the disorder is diagnosed.

> CASE: A 3-year-old boy was seen because of difficulty keeping up with his friends. He walked at 12 months but then, around 18 months, seemed to be having some difficulty walking and going up and down stairs. When a neuromuscular workup was done, the CPK was found to be within normal limits, but he did show muscle weakness around the shoulders and hips as well as twitching, or fasciculations, of the chest muscles. Steps were difficult for him to navigate, and he did have a positive Gowers' sign. A muscle biopsy showed the picture of spinal atrophy and, with the progressive course, it was felt that the proper diagnosis was Kugelberg-Welander spinal muscular atrophy. He has continued walking well into his late teens and early twenties.

Note: Frequently these children are diagnosed as having Duchenne muscular dystrophy because the weakness is close in around the body, or proximal. However, they do not have the developmental delay that is frequently seen in Duchenne dystrophy, nor do they have the same pattern of muscle weakness. It is important to make a correct diagnosis because of the difference in life expectancy as well as cardiac and pulmonary involvement.

Note: All three forms of spinal muscular atrophy are autosomal recessive, with the gene coming from each parent. Prenatal diagnosis is not always possible in each case, but if there has been one case in the family, it generally is. The field is changing, but a knowledgeable neuromuscular genetic counselor should be able to discuss the possibilities of future children having spinal atrophy if this diagnosis has already been made in one of your children.

I must caution you that if you choose artificial insemination, it is not entirely safe, since one individual in about 50 is a carrier. If, as parents of a spinal atrophy child, you do decide to have a second pregnancy, it is possible that an uninvolved child may be born. Each child has a 25% risk of having this disor-

der, but the statistics do not always play out in real life. I have seen two out of three babies and three out of four in a family with spinal atrophy. Thus, if you already have one child with spinal atrophy, a great deal of discussion and soul-searching should take place before another pregnancy is planned.

HEREDITARY MOTOR AND SENSORY NEUROPATHIES (HMSN) or CHARCOT-MARIE-TOOTH SYNDROME (CMT)

History: Described by Dr. J. M. Charcot in France in 1886, and by his student, Pierre Marie, and Dr. Harold Tooth from England.

Incidence: 125,000 to 150,000 cases in the United States and about 1 in 2,000 worldwide.

Ethnic Groups: All groups.

Sex: Either.

Inheritance: Variable, depending on the type. Unfortunately, the classification is still very much in flux, as many new molecular studies are being carried out. The inheritance is autosomal dominant or recessive, depending on the type, but there is a rare, rapidly progressive, X-linked recessive type.

Hypertrophic Neuropathy or Peroneal Muscular Atrophy (demyelinating type) (HMSN Type I)

Initial Signs: Usually in childhood. Children develop muscle weakness in the lower legs, so may seem clumsy because of tripping and falling.

Later Signs: Muscle weakness then begins to be found in the hands. Also, the feet often develop high arches, which makes buying shoes a problem.

Site of Gene Mutation: Chromosome 17p11.2 in most children, but in other families chromosome 1q21–23 is involved.

Laboratory Findings: CPK is usually within normal limits, as is the muscle biopsy, but changes resembling those found in nerve dysfunction—i.e., neuropathic changes—have been reported. EMGs may be abnormal, and motor-nerve conduction times can be quite markedly decreased.

Problems to Be Aware Of: Several members of the family may have the disorder and not be aware of it. Often they will complain just of difficulty in buying shoes. Thus, it is very important that nerve-conduction times be done on as many family members as possible, and molecular genetic studies as suggested by a knowledgeable clinician or geneticist.

Treatment: A good exercise program and ongoing physical therapy can make a real difference. A surgical procedure called a triple arthrodesis, performed on the ankles, can help individuals walk with less difficulty and for more years. Short-leg braces may be needed, as well as special shoes.

Genetics: This disorder can cause either minimal or quite severe weakness, with rather rapid progression. No general statements can be made.

> CASE #1: One little boy had rather severe Charcot-Marie-Tooth disease, which had originally been diagnosed as Duchenne dystrophy. The parents were first cousins from the Middle East. Despite excellent physical therapy, braces, and a good exercise program, the boy lost his ability to walk around age ten. This unusual case suggests a "double dose" of a dominant gene because the parents were related.

> CASE #2: One Charcot-Marie-Tooth patient who is now in college has always loved sports. Fortunately, because she has a mild disorder, she still can take place in many activities. She has had recurrent injuries, probably because of increased stress to her bones, with her muscle weakness. However, this has not seemed to stop her. She did have stabilizing surgery on both ankles when she was a teenager, which made a real difference in her ability to continue being an active participant in sports.

Neuronal Type (HMSN Type II)

Incidence: Not clearly defined.

Ethnic Groups: All groups.

Sex: Either.

Inheritance: Autosomal dominant.

Site of Gene Mutation: 1p35–p36 and 3q13–q22.

Laboratory Findings: CPK usually within normal limits, and the nerve-conduction times may be normal or just mildly abnormal.

Muscle Biopsy: May be normal or show changes in the muscle—i.e., myopathic changes.

Initial Signs: Generally occurs in later years, but can develop in children and young people. Initial weakness of the legs occurs, accompanied by tight heel cords and high arches of the foot.

Later Signs: Long-term outcome is dependent on whether the weakness is progressive and, if so, at what rate.

Problems to Be Aware Of: Other family members may carry the gene and have mild manifestations that will not be picked up without nerve conduction or genetic studies.

Treatment: Good exercise program, physical therapy, surgery, and braces as needed.

Dejerine-Sottas (HMSN III)

History: Described by Dr. Joseph Dejerine and Dr. Jules Sottas in 1893.

Incidence: No good figures.

Ethnic Groups: All groups.

Sex: Either.

Inheritance: Autosomal recessive, with a gene coming from each parent.

Site of Gene Mutation: 17p11.2 and 1q21–q23.

Laboratory Findings: CPK is most often normal, but nerve-conduction times are usually slow.

Initial Signs: In the first three years of life. Some of the children are late walkers.

Later Signs: Weakness gradually develops in the muscles of the hands and feet, and a tremor or fine movement of the fingers can be noted when the hands are extended. Curvature of the spine (scoliosis) can develop. The progression of the muscle weakness may be variable. Later, several things determine whether or not an individual will have real difficulty with this disorder. These depend on the rate at which progression of the muscle weakness occurs. Some individuals have very mild disease, while others have much more severe weakness and have to use a wheelchair later on in life.

Problems to Be Aware Of: Other family members may be affected, so it is important to do nerve conduction times on as many as possible and genetic studies when indicated.

Treatment: Good physical therapy and an active exercise program. Orthopedic surgery may be necessary to help stabilize the ankles.

Note: In the last one to two years there have been such major advances in pinpointing the specific genetic changes in this disorder that the classification I have just given may not stand up in the future. For now it offers a broad outline, and your physician or genetic counselor can note any differences as they develop.

Friedreich's Ataxia

History: Described by Dr. Nikolaus Friedreich in 1863.

Incidence: 1 in 50,000.

Ethnic Groups: All groups.

Sex: Either.

Inheritance: Autosomal recessive, with a gene coming from each parent.

Site of Gene Mutation: The abnormal gene is present on the long arm of chromosome 9, 9cen–q21. There is also a type that occurs with vitamin E deficiency—the so-called FAVED type. The location of this gene is 8q.

Laboratory Findings: Normal CPK but abnormal heart tracings (EKGs). The protein frataxin is decreased. Nerve conduction times are generally decreased also, but more so in the type without the vitamin E deficiency.

Initial Signs: The presenting problem can be difficulty in maintaining balance when walking, or ataxia. Within five years of the onset of this, other problems may develop including scoliosis, rapid eye movements (nystagmus), deafness, diabetes, and high arches (pes cavus). Also, an unusual, angulated toe that looks like the head of a hammer can develop. This is called a hammer toe.

Later Signs: Slurring of speech, as well as difficulty in reading and writing, may also occur. The latter is due to movements or tremors in the hands and arms. Heart involvement can also be present, as well as mental deterioration.

Problems to Be Aware Of: As the disorder progresses, children may have to use walkers and, later on, wheelchairs. However, this is very dependent on how quickly muscle weakness develops. Other individuals, and even brothers and sisters, may have a mild disorder with no progression. Thus, the outcome is extremely variable. The age of onset is an important predictor of the amount of disability, as well as the length of life.

Treatment: Ongoing physical therapy and a good exercise program, as well as attention to heart and feet problems and curvature of the spine.

Genetics: Prenatal diagnosis is possible. Sometimes this disorder is difficult to diagnose because of either very mild involvement or slow progression. A muscle biopsy and good neurological exam are both extremely important, as are molecular diagnostic studies. Vitamin E is now being given for both types. The dose recommended is between 300 and 800 mg by different experts, so you will need to check with your own physician.

> CASE: A 7-year-old boy was seen because of tremors of his arms that resulted in inability to throw a ball. Also, he had trouble running, with falling and stumbling. He was able to ride a bike and swim. Balance was also a problem.
>
> When he was first examined by physicians at age 5 for these problems, he was given the diagnosis of cerebral palsy. When a neuromuscular workup was done, it was found that he had weakness of his hands and legs as well as beginning curvature of his spine. He also had some rounding of his back, called kyphosis, and some loss of the mus-

cle bulk, or atrophy. His CPK was 48 (normal: 0–270), and the muscle biopsy showed no abnormalities. However, his nerve conduction times were quite decreased, and his EMG showed a neurogenic pattern, or one reflecting nerve damage.

It was interesting that in the family history two of the mother's brother's children had died, at ages 5 and 6 of some kind of muscle weakness, and a cousin had also died in the first few years of life. A paternal grandfather was said to have died of muscular dystrophy, as had the mother's one brother.

Based on the progressive muscle weakness, the abnormal nerve-conduction times and EMG, a normal CPK, and the physical findings, a diagnosis of Friedreich's ataxia was made. The patient's subsequent course has proven this diagnosis correct, and he has been followed carefully for the scoliosis and heart problems that developed.

Metabolic Myopathies

Muscle weakness occurs in this group of disorders because of difficulties in the chemical functioning of the body. If, for example, there are errors in the way an individual's body handles the production of a specific protein, one group of symptoms may result, whereas if there is an abnormality in the way sugar is used, another group of problems may result. For simplicity's sake, the metabolic myopathies can be divided into three catagories:

Glycogenoses
Lipid Disorders/Mitochondrial Disorders
Ion Channel Disorders

GLYCOGENOSES

In these disorders, the body is unable to process glycogen properly, which is a substance composed of units of the sugar glucose. Glycogen is produced in the liver and muscles and, when the body needs energy, the muscles convert the glycogen to glucose, or sugar. There are specific chemical substances, called enzymes, that are needed to help all these processes take place.

Nine conditions have been described in which muscle weakness occurs because of enzymatic defects, but not all affect children. Types I,

IV, and VI do not involve muscles, so just types II, III, VII, VIII, IX, X, and XI will be discussed.

History: There have been many individuals who have been prominent in the identification of these disorders, some for whom a specific disorder has been named.

Incidence: Good figures are unknown.

Ethnic Groups: All groups.

Sex: Either.

Inheritance: Dependent on the type.

Laboratory Findings: Dependent on the type.

Initial Signs: Dependent on the type.

Type II—Pompe's Disease, or Acid Maltase Deficiency

History: Described by Dr. J. C. Pompe in 1933.

Incidence: Unknown.

Ethnic Groups: All groups.

Sex: Either.

Inheritance: Autosomal recessive.

Laboratory Findings: Deficiency of acid maltase. CPK is usually within normal limits, but the EMG (muscle tracing) and EKG (heart tracing) can be abnormal.

Muscle Biopsy: Specific changes are seen, with increased glycogen being present.

Site of Gene Mutation: The genetic changes are on chromosome 17q23.

Initial Signs: Marked muscle weakness occurs at birth or soon after. Enlargement of the heart and liver are generally present.

Later Signs: The infantile type is unfortunately usually fatal within a few months after birth. This does depend, however, on the severity of involvement of the different organs, especially the heart.

Problems to Be Aware Of: If the breathing muscles are affected, the help of a good pulmonary doctor is needed. Sudden death can occur.

Treatment: Cardiac and nutritional help.

Note: There is a much less severe form in which children can do well and have just mild muscle weakness. One of the things to note about this type is that it is often not correctly identified, since some of the children have a pattern of muscle weakness similar to type III spinal muscular atrophy or Duchenne dystrophy.

Type III—Cori/Forbes Disease, or Debranching Enzyme Deficiency

History: Described by Doctors Cori, Cori, and Illingsworth in 1952, and by Dr. Forbes in 1953.

Incidence: Unknown.

Ethnic Groups: All groups.

Sex: Either.

Inheritance: Autosomal recessive.

Site of Gene Mutation: Chromosome 1.

Laboratory Findings: CPK and EMG can be within normal limits. The enzyme deficiency can be found in the white blood cells or in tissue taken during muscle or liver biopsies.

Note: Electron microscopy pictures of the muscles may make the diagnosis much clearer, but biochemical studies are the key to diagnosis.

Initial Signs: Infants and children may have just mild muscle weakness, but their livers can be enlarged, and problems can occur with sugar metabolism.

Genetics: Prenatal diagnosis is possible.

Type VII—Tarui Disease, or Phosphofructokinase Deficiency

Incidence: Unknown.

Ethnic Groups: All groups.

Sex: Either.

Inheritance: Autosomal recessive.

Initial Onset: This can occur at any time. The initial symptoms may just be exercise intolerance or increased tiredness, but a number of atypical, severe cases have been described that have a fatal outcome. One was an infant who also had arthrogryposis.

Later Signs: The problems that present are dependent on the degree of involvement, as there can be just mild weakness with exercise intolerance and increased muscle fatigue.

Site of Gene Mutation: Chromosome 1cenq32.

Laboratory Findings: Diagnosis is established by measuring the enzyme in muscle and blood cells.

Treatment: A high-protein diet seems to make a difference, and a ketogenic diet was helpful in the infant with arthrogryposis.

Note: The prognosis generally is good with good medical care, and careful watching of the diet, and exercise.

Type VIII—Phosphorylase B Kinase Deficiency

Inheritance: Either X-linked or autosomal recessive.

Initial Signs: Children can have muscle cramps with exercise, and stiffness and weakness can also occur. There may be enlargement of the liver.

Later Signs: Muscle problems are generally quite mild, but heart disease that can lead to a fatal episode has been described. The general outcome is very much dependent on the extent of involvement of muscle, heart, and liver.

Laboratory Findings: Diagnosis is made by muscle and liver biopsies.

Type IX—Phosphoglycerate Kinase (PGK) Deficiency

Inheritance: X-linked recessive.

Sex: Only males are involved.

Site of Gene Mutation: Xq13.

Laboratory Findings: The diagnosis is made by measuring PGK in the muscle and blood cells.

Initial Onset: This can be at any age after extremely strenuous exercise. Initial symptoms are muscle pain, weakness, and loss of protein in the urine, which is called myoglobinuria. The presenting complaint of myoglobinuria is usually dark, reddish-brown urine.

Later Signs: Patients can just have mild problems with muscle cramps and myoglobinuria, but slowly progressive muscle weakness has been reported.

Problems to Be Aware Of: If myoglobinuria develops, it needs to be treated very quickly in a hospital setting.

Type X—Phosphoglycerate Mutase Deficiency

Sex: Either.

Inheritance: Autosomal recessive.

Gene Location: 7p12–p13.

Laboratory Findings: Special biochemical studies are needed.

Muscle Biopsy: This is important, and specific changes should be seen.

Initial Signs: Problems may not develop until after excessive exercise; then muscle pain, fatigue, cramps, or myoglobinuria can develop.

Problems to Be Aware Of: Dependent upon the amount of muscle involvement, but with recurrent myoglobinuria, severe restriction of exercise is necessary. Hospitalization may be needed if strenuous exercise occurs and myoglobinuria develops.

Type XI—Lactate Dehydrogenase (LDH) Deficiency

Sex: Either.

Inheritance: Autosomal recessive.

Gene Location: Chromosome 11p15.4.

Laboratory Findings: Marked increase in CPK after exercise; abnormalities in lactate and pyruvate levels in the blood.

Muscle Biopsy: This shows an increased amount of glycogen. Specific studies can be done to determine the presence or absence of the LDH enzyme.

Onset: This can be at any age, dependent on the amount of exercise that occurs.

Later Signs: Problems are dependent on the degree of involvement and whether or not hospitalization is necessary for myoglobinuria.

Problems to Be Aware Of: With rapid treatment, patients should do well and have a normal life expectancy.

LIPID DISORDERS

Carnitine Deficiency

A lack of carnitine can be caused by increased output, inadequate intake, or decreased production by the liver. Other internal changes in the body can also result in too little available carnitine.

Sex: Either.

Inheritance: Autosomal recessive.

Laboratory Findings: There can be abnormal levels of carnitine in the blood; in some cases, the CPK is elevated.

Muscle Biopsy: This is diagnostic and shows a markedly increased amount of fat, as does a liver biopsy if one is done.

Initial Onset: This can be in infancy or may not be detectable until adulthood if mild symptoms, such as muscle weakness, pain, or myoglobinuria occur.

Later Signs: The ongoing problems depend on the degree of involvement. Muscle weakness can be mild, or there can be slowly progressive weakness. Cardiac involvement has been reported, with death in a 2-year-old child.

Treatment: Carnitine by mouth has been given to some patients who have done quite well, though others do not seem to have been helped.

Note: A second kind of carnitine deficiency occurs that involves not only the muscles but also the liver. The symptoms of this type are nausea, vomiting, and changes in the body metabolism that cause a coma-like picture.

Carnitine Palmitoyl Transferase (CPT) Deficiency

Sex: Either, but for some reason males seem to have more difficulty.

Inheritance: Autosomal recessive.

Site of Gene Mutation: 1p32.

Laboratory Findings: Diagnosis is dependent on biochemical studies to document the CPT enzyme deficiency.

Muscle Biopsy: The biopsy can appear essentially normal if an individual is not having problems.

Initial Onset: This is usually in childhood, although diagnosis may not be made for many years. Primarily muscle pain and myoglobinuria, or loss of protein in the urine, with strenuous exercise. Also, attacks can be precipitated by cold exposure or fasting. The outcome is very much dependent on the severity of involvement, the diet, and how quickly myoglobinuria is treated, if it occurs.

Treatment: A change in diet is necessary, which should be high in carbohydrates and low in fat. Regulation of exercise is also important. In some cases, mechanical ventilation is needed.

Note: Muscle cramps are not usually present, but in the intervals between severe episodes pain, tenderness, and weakness of the muscles may occur. Also, difficulty with breathing can develop and mechanical ventilation may be needed.

MITOCHONDRIAL DISORDERS

This is a very complex group of disorders that has only recently stimulated much interest, and many of the entities are just now being described.

This is an important group, since mitochondria play a vital part in the use of our muscles, acting like furnaces in the cells to fuel muscle energy. If they do not work effectively, muscle weakness can occur.

Incidence: No good statistics exist, because many new types have just recently been defined.

Sex: Either.

Inheritance: Variable, depending on the specific disorder. It is important to note that children inherit mitochondrial disorders from their mother because the mitochondrial DNA is not in the chromosomes but is passed from a mother to a child with the egg or ovum. The mitochondria are not in the nucleus or primary part of the ovum but in the surrounding tissue, which is called cytoplasm. It is interesting to note that mitochondrial DNA is not always the same in a family or even in a specific person, because it does undergo frequent mutation or change. It appears that the mitochondria are transmitted more or less haphazardly, not precisely like chromosomal DNA. A great deal still needs to be worked out in these disorders, but discoveries are being made almost daily. The principal syndromes now recognized are the Kearns-Sayre (KSS), MELAS, and MERRF.

Kearns-Sayre Syndrome

Laboratory Findings: The CPK is usually within normal limits but may be slightly elevated.

Muscle Biopsy: This shows specific changes, as do the electron microscopy pictures.

Initial Onset: Usually within the first few years of life, but it may not be present until later on. Initially muscle weakness is present. There can be weakness and paralysis of the eye muscles, as well as some weakness of the muscles of the face.

Later Signs: Heart block and mental deterioration can occur. Sudden death can result from heart stoppage.

Treatment: None at this time, although many different things have been tried.

Problems to Be Aware Of: Surgical implanting of a pacemaker may be lifesaving.

Note: Most patients survive into their thirties or forties, depending on the degree of heart problems and whether or not good cardiac care is received.

MELAS

This abbreviation stands for mitochondrial encephalopathy, lactic acidosis, and strokelike episodes. The word *encephalopathy* means there is involvement of the brain. *Lactic acidosis* reflects the increase in the blood of the specific substance lactic acid.

Initial Onset: Generally, this occurs before age 40, and the presenting complaint may be just fatigue, although recurrent vomiting and developmental delay can also occur.

Later: There is a loss of intellectual ability, or encephalopathy, and an increase in the lactic acid of the blood, as well as muscle weakness.

Genetics: In approximately 25% of cases, other family members have been found to also have the disorder.

Treatment: There is none known at this time, but the future looks bright, with tremendous interest now in mitochondrial disorders.

Problems to Be Aware Of: It is important to note that in children the presenting symptoms may be just poor appetite, failure to grow and gain weight, as well as difficulty in keeping up in school. Behavior problems have also been recognized along with this syndrome.

Note: There is usually a progressive loss of muscle strength and intellectual ability. The age at which this occurs depends on the severity of the symptoms.

MERRF

This abbreviation is derived from the two features of the disorder, which are myoclonic epilepsy, a type of convulsion in which there is uncontrollable jerking, and ragged red fibers, seen in the muscle biopsy.

Initial Signs: Muscle weakness and mental deterioration.

Later: Weakness and mental deterioration are progressive.

Treatment: None is known at the present time except medication for seizures and the maintenance of proper fluid and nutritional balance.

Problems to Be Aware Of: There have been cases reported where the ragged red fibers are seen in the muscle biopsies and yet there is only mild weakness. Unfortunately, in some of these cases brothers and sisters can be severely affected.

Cytochrome Oxidase (COX) Deficiency

Cytochrome oxidase is an important part of the process that transforms different substances into oxygen in the body. Thus, when there is a deficiency of this enzyme, patients show muscle weakness and mental deterioration. There is a fatal form and also a mild infantile type, which manifests as weakness of the muscles.

Fatal Type

Initial Findings: Onset is in infancy, with muscle weakness and kidney problems.

Later Signs: Death usually occurs by one year of age because of respiratory breathing problems.

Benign Infantile Type

Inheritance: The inheritance of the defect is still being researched. Some cases seem to be dominantly inherited by the DNA of the nucleus, whereas others seem to be inherited by mitochondria from the mother.

Initial Findings: Severe weakness occurs, so babies may need to be put on a ventilator or be tube-fed.

Treatment: The substance coenzyme Q, called ubiquinone, has been tried, and there are some reports of improvement. Other patients show no change. A nondairy diet is used in some centers, but the general consensus of opinion by experts is that it is not effective.

Problems to Be Aware Of: It is important to note that within the first few years of life infants can recover completely.

Note: The disorder can be fatal, depending on the respiratory problems and whether or not mechanical intervention with a ventilator is needed and successful.

ION CHANNEL DISORDERS

Periodic Paralysis

Sex: Either but, for some reason, boys tend to have more serious attacks than girls.

Inheritance: Dominant, from one parent.

Initial Findings: Can be in infancy or childhood. Cold, hunger, or exercise can bring on an initial attack of muscle weakness, with involvement of the muscles that control swallowing, the eyes, the legs, and the arms. The weakness lasts from 30 minutes to as long as 3 hours, with the blood potassium rising during these periods of weakness.

Problems to Be Aware Of: In making the diagnosis, the increase of blood potassium during periods of weakness as well as the muscle biopsy picture are essential.

Treatment: None may be required, but with severe attacks intravenous calcium or glucose may be helpful. Also, diuretics, which are drugs used to promote fluid loss, have been used to help prevent episodes.

Note: A fatal outcome has not been reported from one of the attacks of muscle weakness, and an individual can have a normal life expectancy. Also, it is important to note that the weakness usually starts at somewhere between 10 and 20 years of age, and then, as young people reach 20 to 35, fewer and fewer attacks tend to occur.

Hypokalemic Periodic Paralysis

Sex: Either.

Inheritance: As a dominant trait from one parent.

Initial Onset: Usually between ages 10 and 20. Muscle weakness may develop quite suddenly and last for a few days.

Laboratory Findings: Diagnosis is made by looking for low levels of potassium in the blood during attacks and also by obtaining a muscle biopsy.

Problems to Be Aware Of: Exercise, cold, anxiety, and an excessive amount of carbohydrate or sugar containing foods will trigger attacks.

Treatment: Potassium given orally or by vein.

Note: The cause of the disorder is unclear at this time. The outcome is good, as the attacks may stop completely, although some permanent weakness can result.

Myotonic Syndromes

Myotonia Congenita (Thomsen's disease)

History: Described by Dr. Asmus J. Thomsen in 1876 in members of his own family.

Incidence: 1 in 8,000.

Sex: Either.

Inheritance: Autosomal dominant, but there is an autosomal recessive variety described by Dr. Becker.

Initial Findings: Onset can be at birth, in the first few years of life, or in the teens. Initial symptoms may be very mild and consist simply of mild muscle weakness or myotonia, which means an increased tension or tone of the muscles. Firm, rather large muscles can be found in the arms and legs. Thus, it may be appear that children are quite strong when in fact they usually have mild muscle weakness.

Site of Gene Mutation: In both the dominant and recessive forms the involved gene is at 7q35.

Laboratory Findings: CPK can be within normal limits. EMG can also be normal in small children, but later on may show the specific electrical pattern of myotonia.

Muscle Biopsy: May be either normal or show minimal changes.

Treatment: Dilantin, procainamide, quinine, mexiletine, and steroids have all been used to help prevent increased muscle tone, or myotonia. I have had the most success with Dilantin and found it to be very helpful in many patients. Some of the other drugs have quite severe side effects, so they should be prescribed only by a physician who is experienced in treating myotonia.

Problems to Be Aware Of: Myotonia can be much more severe in the morning after a night's rest, and can also be present with cold or fatigue.

The diagnosis is primarily a clinical one, with a good history and physical examination of prime importance.

Note: One of the difficulties with this disorder for parents is that because it is sometimes hard to diagnose, physicians, as well as mothers and fathers, may think that children are simply not trying and are lazy. Thus, if a child has big muscles and tends to develop some stiffness with cold, or if the stiffness is present first thing in the morning, this disorder should be considered.

> CASE: One of my teenage patients with this disorder complained that, though she loved to dance, once she was up on her toes she could not get her feet back flat on the floor. Her older sister complained of having difficulty releasing objects when she was trying to cook, and both sisters were delighted when their symptoms were relieved by daily doses of the drug Dilantin.

Paramyotonia Congenita (Eulenburg's disease)

History: First described in 1886 by Dr. Albert Eulenburg in a large East German family.

Sex: Both children and adults can develop the disorder.

Inheritance: Autosomal dominant.

Site of Gene Mutation: Chromosome 17.

Initial Findings: Stiffness of the hands and feet with cold weather, and the eyelids may seem to get "stuck" because of the increased tension, or myotonia, of the muscles.

Later: Muscle weakness, in general, is not a problem but can occur for short periods, such as for a few hours.

Laboratory Findings: No specific findings, with the diagnosis based primarily on clinical symptoms and family history.

Treatment: May be helped with one of the drugs used for myotonia congenita.

Genetics: If a parent has the trait, each child has a 50-50 chance of having the disorder.

Note: Most often the disorder is quite mild, with a normal life expectancy and no permanent weakness.

Chondrodystrophic Myotonia (Schwartz-Jampel syndrome)

Sex: Either.

Inheritance: Usually autosomal recessive, but some cases that may be dominant have been described.

Laboratory Findings: No specific findings.

Muscle Biopsy: Not helpful in making the diagnosis.

Gene Location: 1p34–p36.

Initial Findings: At birth, children are noted to have unusual faces, with narrow openings of the eyes, small jaws, and quite a harsh cry. Short necks, rounded chests, humping of the back (kyphosis) with some muscle weakness, myotonia, and quite large muscles can all be present. Mental retardation or developmental delay occurs in about 20% of the cases.

Problems to Be Aware Of: The muscle biopsy is not helpful in making the diagnosis; instead, the diagnosis is based on clinical findings.

Myotonic Dystrophy (Steinert's disease)

Incidence: 1 in 80,000, or even higher in some areas.

Sex: Either.

Inheritance: Autosomal dominant.

Site of Gene Mutation: 19q13. In the congenital (infantile) form, the disorder is nearly always inherited from an involved mother. With the later onset, the gene can come from either parent.

Initial Findings: In the infantile form, babies have marked muscle weakness and difficulty in feeding. Paralysis of the face muscles and a somewhat triangular mouth, as well as difficulty in completely closing the eyes, are seen.

Later Signs: Developmental delay with late onset of sitting and walking can occur, as can mental retardation of variable degrees. Improvement in muscle strength often occurs, but when late childhood or early teens are reached, some patients develop progressive muscle weakness, as well as clouding of the lens of the eyes, or cataracts. Other problems that occur later are difficulty with bowel movements because of intestinal slowing, heart block, or heart irregularities. In adults, miscarriages can occur in females and sterility in males.

Laboratory Findings: CPK is usually within normal limits, as is the EMG under age 3. Later, some children and adults show myotonia on the EMG.

Muscle Biopsy: This is usually normal.

Treatment: If myotonia becomes a problem later on, Dilantin or one of the drugs used for myotonia congenita can also be used.

Genetics: This disorder can become increasingly severe with each generation.

Problems to Be Aware Of: Eye drops may be needed if there is difficulty closing the eyes completely during sleep. Other family members may have such mild involvement that they are not aware of having the disorder. Often they will sleep with their eyes partly open, which is a real clue to the facial weakness that accompanies the disorder. Mothers should always be checked for this disease if it is found to be present in a child.

Note: Because it is important to make the diagnosis early, a muscle biopsy can be performed in the newborn nursery if needed. The babies generally get stronger, and some, as they get older, can lead fairly normal lives for quite a few years. It is important that this diagnosis be considered, so that mechanical ventilation can be provided for the newborn to get over the first few rocky weeks. Otherwise, physicians may decide not to use mechanical ventilation.

Myasthenia Gravis

Incidence: Between 5–10 per 100,000.

Sex: Either, but in the childhood form, girls are affected about four times as often as boys.

Types: Transient neonatal myasthenia
Congenital myasthenic syndromes
Acquired autoimmune myasthenia gravis of childhood

Transient neonatal myasthenia: This occurs in about 20% of infants born to mothers with active myasthenia gravis. (The disorder has also occured in some babies born to mothers in remission). About 30% of infants born with weakness and respiratory difficulties require ventilation, but generally there is complete remission.

Congenital myasthenic syndromes: These disorders are inherited. The onset can be within the first year of life or later on. Symptoms may be so mild that diagnosis can be somewhat difficult. Facial weakness, difficulty swallowing, and weakness of the eye muscles, as well as generalized weakness can occur.

Acquired autoimmune myasthenia gravis of childhood: In this disorder, the weakness can develop fairly quickly or somewhat more slowly. Cases have been reported after an illness; symptoms can include weakness of the eye muscles, the face, and generalized weakness. Swallowing and speech can also be affected.

Treatment: Because the outcome and treatment are different in each of the types, the care of a child with myasthenia gravis should be undertaken only by a physician with wide experience in treating children with this disorder. It is important to note that myasthenia can be associated with other disorders such as arthrogryposis, so it is important that physicians and parents keep this in mind.

FIVE

◆ ◆ ◆

Your Medical Team

T he mother of a child with a neuromuscular disease said to me one day, "I have to deal with a whole group of professionals now. Many think they have all the answers, and they just don't listen to anything I say; others are great. I have found a real advocate in my son's physical therapist, and she often goes with us to doctors' appointments."

The specialists that your child will probably see in addition to your primary care physician and your pediatric neuromuscular consultant are an orthopedist, physical and occupational therapists, and lung and heart doctors. It's very important that you find professionals with whom you feel comfortable and whom you trust. If any of them belittle you or don't listen, then I would quickly find someone else. *Mothers and fathers are the experts with their children, and if a physician does not listen, problems often arise that could have been avoided.*

Soon after the diagnosis of a neuromuscular disease is made in a

> Be aware that you're going to inherit an army of social workers, ministers, teachers, doctors, nurses, psychologists, and counselors who all think they know better than you do what is best for your child.
>
> ◆
>
> Your doctor and other team members all need to talk to each other frequently.

child, I urge the parents to buy a small notebook that they can take with them to medical appointments. It's important to record not only dates of visits but also what was done. One of my parents asked if she could tape-record the visits with me so that she could not only have a record, but also share what I said with her husband. I thought that was an excellent idea and added a quick summary for the daddy.

Test results should also be recorded as much as possible. Keeping a list of test results may even prevent your child from having things repeated simply because records were lost. Some parents keep a special binder for this purpose, or even a briefcase with records, which they take to appointments.

> Be sure that your pediatrician or family doctor gets involved with the problems that are connected to your child's muscle disease. Our pediatrician was in denial and didn't want to get involved.
>
> ♦
>
> If you feel in your heart that your doctor puts you down or doesn't listen to you, change doctors.

With all the fragmentation that is occurring in medical care today, parents need to be more in charge than ever before. Not only are doctors spending less time these days with patients, but also more and more care is being taken over by nonphysician personnel. So you, as parents, need to be more and more knowledgeable about the care your child receives.

What do each of the professionals offer your child, and why do you need them as members of the medical team?

Orthopedic care is particularly important for children with neuromuscular diseases because of the development of areas of muscle tightness, or contractures, joint problems such as those that occur in arthrogryposis, and curvature of the spine, or scoliosis, which can occur not only in Duchenne dystrophy but also in spinal atrophy, the congenital myopathies, and several of the other neuromuscular disorders.

Another person who is an important part of your medical team is the bracemaker, or orthotist. It took me many years to find the special orthotist that we now use for our patients, and some of my parents drive long distances to have him make their children's braces or back supports. An orthotist who not only has had special training with children's neuromuscular diseases but who also has the necessary skill and patience to work with kids is a real find. There is nothing worse than a brace that is constantly rubbing or one that is too small or tight.

Orthopedists

Generally, it's not necessary to see an orthopedist unless there is a specific problem, such as tight heel cords that need releasing, a beginning curvature of the spine, or joint deformities that may need casting or bracing. With the congenital myopathies, an orthopedist may be needed early, because a dislocation of the hip may be present at birth. In central core disease or fibre-type disproportion, this is a fairly common occurrence—one of the diagnostic signs of these disorders. *Hip dislocations also can occur in older children with intermediate type II spinal atrophy.* It is important to note that if a child is not going to walk, trying to put a bone back into the joint may not be necessary. Often the bone will simply re-dislocate, as occurs in type II or intermediate spinal atrophy. It takes a wise, experienced orthopedist to say that if a child is not going to be able to walk, operating on a dislocated hip is not necessary. Often, orthopedists feel that it's important to put the hip back in place because otherwise there will be pain later on in life. However, no real proof of this exists in medical literature or in the long-term follow-up of older individuals with neuromuscular diseases.

Curvature of the spine, or scoliosis, is a very common problem in childhood neuromuscular diseases and should always be watched for whenever a child is completely examined. The child's blouse or shirt must be removed so that the spine can be adequately seen. Curvature of the spine can be one of the most difficult problems with which children and parents have to contend. Eighty percent of boys with Duchenne dystrophy develop scoliosis once they can no longer walk. Also, most patients with intermediate spinal atropy, or type II SMA, develop curvatures that require surgery. Children with congenital myopathies frequently are candidates for scoliosis surgery, as are children with Friedreich's ataxia and most of the other neuromuscular diseases.

The treatment for curvature of the spine is usually a Luque spinal fusion, though other methods are preferred in some centers. If a child's back curve progresses rapidly over just a few months, surgery should be done fairly soon. Thus, it is important to have a child's back looked at during *each* physical examination. Again, this means that your child should be undressed down to the underpants and be given a top or gown that allows the back to be examined.

The orthopedic surgery known as the Luque procedure consists of supports or wires that are inserted up and down the spine. The length of the incision and the number of vertebrae in the back that are stabilized or anchored depends on the amount of curvature and the judgment of the surgeon. In general, once the operation is performed it does not have to be redone, although occasionally wires will break or a curve will reoccur.

When surgery is to be performed, the technical procedure is, of course, of great importance, but the follow-up care is equally important. Thus, I would discuss with your back surgeon what his or her orders will be following surgery. Some orthopedists and neurosurgeons are meticulous about their day-to-day postoperative care, while others simply operate and leave the care to residents or other physicians. Parents whose children have had spinal fusions can tell you which surgeons give the best follow-up care. *Don't be afraid to change surgeons, before the procedure, if you discover that the one you have chosen simply operates and leaves the care to others.*

> Be sure you find a doctor who doesn't just take care of your child's muscle disease but helps you through the bad days.

Before any surgery is performed on a child with neuromuscular disease, it's very important that the child's lung, or pulmonary, function be evaluated. This is done by making an appointment with a pulmonary physician, who will order a test that shows how much oxygen is being exchanged and how effectively your child moves air in and out of the lungs. The chest muscles can become quite weak in many of the neuromuscular disorders, so it's important that a baseline evaluation be done. This will tell the anesthesiologist whether the child's pulmonary function is adequate for surgery. If it is not, back surgery should not be done.

In some centers, back braces are prescribed for curvature of the spine several months prior to surgery, and some orthopedists insist that the braces be worn for some time after surgery as well.

It's important for you, as parents, to know that if a spinal fusion has been performed, your child needs to sit upright as quickly as possible, hopefully within just a few days, in order to start getting the muscles working again. If any of us stay flat in bed for several days, we can develop weakness, but with a neuromuscular disorder there can be a tremendous loss of strength that may be impossible to regain.

When surgeons are extremely hesitant about allowing a patient to sit up after a spinal fusion, it may be weeks or months before a child is permitted to sit upright and get back to normal activity. If you have any reservations at all about how quickly the orthopedist or neurosurgeon is allowing your child to sit in an upright position after a spinal fusion, *please* request a second opinion.

Also, after back surgery or any other surgery, physical therapy should be started as quickly as possible to the extent that the operating surgeon will allow. Hospital physical therapists will hopefully have had training and experience in working with children with neuromuscular diseases and can help a child keep his or her muscles moving after back surgery. A home exercise program should also be outlined to be started right away after discharge from the hospital.

In addition to back problems for which your child may need to see an orthopedist, foot and joint problems can develop as can fractures due to thinness of the bones, and contractures or areas of muscle tightness.

Foot problems are particularly common in Charcot-Marie-Tooth disease and in some of the congenital myopathies. In Charcot-Marie-Tooth disease, high-arched feet—or pes cavus deformities, as they are called—may require either special shoes or arch supports, which an orthopedist can prescribe. A podiatrist, too, can be helpful with foot problems. In Charcot-Marie-Tooth, surgical fusion, or joining, of the anklebones may be necessary for walking to be comfortable. This operation, called a triple arthrodesis, helps stabilize the ankles.

Other foot problems can occur with Friedreich's ataxia. Bending of the toe may develop, and make walking and buying shoes difficult. This is called a hammer toe and is due to muscle weakness produced by the disease process. In the spinal cerebellar group of disorders claw-like toes can also develop due to imbalance of muscle strength.

Joint problems in arthrogryposis can be a real headache for a child, the parents, and the specialist. Professor Dubowitz urges that patients with arthrogryposis not be immobilized as infants. Instead, they should be allowed to move around as much as possible and then have surgery or casting as they begin to walk. It's very difficult to find an orthopedist who will wait to treat the fixed joints of arthrogryposis. Many of them start with early casting in infancy, which then necessitates repeated casting or surgeries.

Fractures occur in children with neuromuscular diseases more than in other children because they are not able to be as active. Anyone who develops muscle weakness and is less active, may begin to lose bone calcium and develop what is called osteoporosis. The result is thinning of the bone, as is seen to varying degrees in the aging process. Thus, children with neuromuscular diseases who are inactive have a greater tendency to sustain fractures because of the thinness of their bones. Even a sudden movement of the leg or twisting can cause a fracture in a child who is not mobile. Thus, it is important that physical therapists show you, as parents, how to move your child if the ability to transfer from a bed to a wheelchair or onto the toilet has been lost.

I would not be afraid of causing a fracture by trying to stretch a contracture or by moving your child. A fracture can occur even with the best methods of transfer or stretching. A child's bones do heal quite rapidly after a fracture and often just a simple brace or support is needed if he or she is inactive. *However, if a fracture is not healing well, positioning a child upright with the help of a stand or tilt table can decrease the amount of time it takes for calcium to deposit around the fracture site and for the bone to become stronger.* Sometimes even orthopedists forget that standing and weight-bearing can accelerate the deposit of calcium. Children with neuromuscular diseases can have fractures just like any other child if they fall from a bike or have an accident. Kids will be kids.

Physical Therapists

Physical therapists are extremely important in the life of a child with a neuromuscular disease. Some schools employ their own physical and occupational therapists for children, while others hire outside therapists or even pay for private therapy if this is written into the child's Individual Educational Plan, or IEP. I will discuss IEP's later on.

When a child first starts developing muscle tightness in Duchenne dystrophy, or some other neuromuscular disease, the services of a physical therapist are not really needed. Instead, simple stretching by a parent or the use of night splints or AFOs is all that is necessary. However, as further contractures develop, particularly in children with Duchenne dystrophy, physical therapy (P.T.) given several times a week at school is extremely important. One of the ongoing problems that parents encounter with school physical therapists is that after a while the therapists get tired of doing the same kinds of exercise and

> You need to experience the work of compatible and involved therapists, so that you know the difference if your child is assigned to detached and noninvolved therapists.

You'll find that it's very difficult to keep bonding and rebonding with new therapists. The high turnover has taught us how greatly individual personalities and styles impact the quality of services that our child receives.

want to stop it. Therapists prefer to see real improvement, and most of those I've encountered are not happy giving what they see as maintenance physical therapy. However, it is often difficult for parents to find either the time or the energy to do stretching exercises at home, so *therapy at school is extremely important on an ongoing basis.*

The other problem with doing therapy at home is that kids are great at manipulating their parents by crying or screaming as if in pain when stretching is being done. They tend to be more adult with school physical therapists and allow them to do stretching that parents are simply unable to accomplish at home. Thus, therapy in school is something that needs to be requested if your child is developing contractures. A physical therapy program does need to be under the guidance of either your pediatric neuromuscular consultant or an orthopedist. A prescription is required to start it, and this prescription should be rewritten periodically as needed to continue the therapy.

Your relationship with a physical therapist or occupational therapist can range from one of total confidence and trust to total horror and alienation.

◆

You'll find that therapists may be given a great deal of power and autonomy. Since opinions vary at times, you must be ready, as a parent, to defend your child's right to have therapy time and specific equipment.

In special children's programs, such as the California Children's Services (or CCS), P.T. and occupational therapy (O.T.) can be provided and paid for by the state or county. Often a real battle goes on between a school and the local children's services provider as to who will pay for the physical or occupational therapy. Unfortunately, many children's therapy programs are underfunded or understaffed, and the excuse is often given that there are not enough physical therapists to go around. This is unacceptable to me, because the reality is that if a child needs therapy, it should be provided. It may take considerable effort on your part to obtain the needed services, and sometimes an advocate or even an attorney is necessary. You do have to decide whether or not you want to use this kind of energy or if you want to go ahead and do the therapy at home or pay for it privately.

Home Exercise Programs

If you do decide to do a *home program* rather than fight to get it paid for by the school or the state or county children's services, then I would make the following suggestions. You need to devise some creative solutions so that your child doesn't complain too much during exercises and add to your already high stress level.

> Teenagers make the world of the disabled seem very easy.

A way that good stretching can be done without an ongoing fuss is that a special video can be watched or a fun story tape played. If somehow the time can be made special and pleasurable for both you and your child, it will be a far easier task to accomplish.

Many parents have shared with me their concern that they will hurt their child while doing stretching exercises. You do have to be careful not to use excessive force, but firm, gentle pressure should not cause any difficulties. Unusually strong pressure on a joint or muscle can cause a fracture or a pulled muscle. On the other hand, minimal force accomplishes little. Also, a cry of real pain should be distinguished from one of just unhappiness. If you do a home exercise program, then I would urge you to communicate frequently with your child's physical therapist to be sure you are doing it correctly.

Occupational Therapists

Occupational therapists play an important role in the care of many young people with muscle diseases. Their primary focus is on upper-extremity activities, particularly strengthening and activities of daily living (ADL). This is the term needed for prescriptions and in a child's school or individual educational plan. Occupational therapists can help children who have problems with hand function by helping them develop adaptations for dressing, feeding, and bathing. There are many different ways these tasks can be performed with or without mechanical aids, and an occupational therapist should be able to demonstrate them.

Another function of occupational therapists is to teach patients breathing exercises, which are particularly important for young people who have weak chest muscles because of neuromuscular disease.

Some occupational therapists are now becoming experts in computer technology and can help adapt computers for children with limited hand function. They hopefully keep up to date on all new kinds of technology, such as touch-talkers, which help communication. If your school has no one with this kind of training and your child needs it, the school district should pay for an outside consultation. Obtaining this help may take some real work on your part, as a parent, but remember that state and federal laws require that it be paid for by the school if it is needed.

An occupational therapist should see a child one to three times a week for as long as the child requires this care. Occupational therapy will be required for varying lengths of time, but you will find that you may have an ongoing fight to have services continued after a period of one or two years. The school or public agency may want to cut down the visits to one a week or one a month, or stop them altogether.

Parents who have the funds to pay for a private pediatric occupational therapist often do so simply because they don't want to fight the school district or the state or local children's services. Also paying for private therapy gives parents more control: they can continue the therapy as long as they can afford it, and don't have to go through a lot of red tape to obtain it.

Private occupational therapists can be used to help teach feeding and dressing, and adapt both equipment and living environments. You should be able to find a good private pediatric occupational therapist by talking to your physician, other parents, or by calling the rehabilitation or therapy department of your local hospital.

Orthotists

A good pediatric orthotist can make a big difference in both your life and your child's. Braces, both for the legs and the back, have to be changed frequently to keep up with growth. This is a real problem, particularly with growth spurts. Often a brace will need some additional padding or just wedging to make it a little bit larger, but it has to be comfortable or a child simply won't wear it. During the hot summer months braces made of plastic can be very uncomfortable. There are perforated materials that can be used, so I would talk to your orthotist about this option if hot weather creates a problem.

One of the important things to remember about working with an orthotist is that arrangements for payment must be made before the equipment can be ordered. Often braces will sit in the orthotist's shop for many weeks while payment is being arranged, which means that a child is not benefiting from their use. Often braces are outgrown before the authorization even comes through. Sometimes a phone call by your physician to an insurance company or agency is needed before approval is given. It is getting harder and harder to get things paid for now that funds are being cut by the insurance companies to such minimum levels.

Other Specialists

Increasing muscle weakness of the arms and legs is often accompanied by chest muscle weakness. This then can lead to respiratory, or breathing difficulties. At this point, a *pulmonary doctor* needs to be seen periodically. Heart problems often accompany the lung difficulties, so that the services of a *cardiologist* may also be needed. This specialist is particularly important for young people with Emery-Dreifuss syndrome, Friedreich's ataxia, and Becker and myotonic dystrophies. All youths with these disorders should have a baseline EKG, or heart tracing, as they develop more muscle weakness. This is done to make sure that there are no undetected cardiac problems. Also, if there is any evidence of heart irregularity, or a feeling of faintness, chest pain, difficulty sleeping, shortness of breath, or morning headaches, a heart doctor should be consulted immediately.

Protect your child from medical people who would use him or her for experiments. Ask lots of questions.

An *anesthesiologist* is of great importance if general surgery is needed. He or she should be sure that the precautions for malignant hyperthermia are taken.

A *rehabilitation doctor (physiatrist)* may be seen if he or she has had more experience than another specialist, such as an orthopedist or neurologist—with the treatment of neuromuscular diseases. Physiatrists are not trained to operate, but they can prescribe equipment and braces. They can also prescribe physical and occupational therapy so that a child's muscles are used as efficiently as possible.

If the eyes are involved—such as, for example, in myotonic dystrophy and some of the mitochondrial myopathies—an *ophthalmologist (eye doctor)* should be seen on a regular basis. There are both pediatric and adult eye specialists. One particular area of concern is when there is weakness of the muscles around the eyes, so that the eyes may not be closed during sleep. Then eyedrops will usually be needed on a daily basis.

Ongoing Care

The medical specialists who care for your child should all be seen at least twice a year. It is very difficult to keep up to date with medical and other problems if a child comes for a visit just every twelve months. Of particular concern are lung problems, curvature of the spine, inadequate nutrition or excessive weight gain, any kind of eating disorders, poorly fitting equipment and braces, contractures, and dislocated joints.

> Be sure that the medical personnel talk to your child as well as to you.

There are also other things that need to be watched for on an ongoing basis because, for each neuromuscular disorder, there are specific areas of concern.

Also, your child's general well-being, emotional adjustment, and any school problems will need to be discussed periodically with your primary neuromuscular specialist.

Establishing a Good Relationship With Your Doctors

The following are some important things to remember in helping your child receive the best possible medical care.

1. Being on time for appointments and providing the secretary with any needed billing information will make you and your child favorites of the staff.

2. If you have to cancel an appointment, try to do it at least twenty-four hours ahead of time unless there is a sudden illness or accident.

3. Pay your bills on time, and if you can't pay the entire amount, then make arrangements for monthly payments.

4. If you leave a message for the physician to call, and then immediately start talking by phone to several other people, it will make a return call difficult.

5. If possible, take just the child with the neuromuscular disease to the appointment, and leave his or her siblings at home or with a friend. That way, you can give the child your individual attention. Also, it's much easier for the physician and staff to handle one child rather than a group of children.

6. An occasional thank-you note or a small gift at holiday times to a special doctor and the staff is always greatly appreciated.

SIX

◆ ◆ ◆

Navigating the Medical Maze

T he days of being able to choose your own physician without the intrusion of health maintenance organizations, insurance companies, and layers of bureaucracy are sadly almost gone. So to get good medical care these days, it is essential to know how to advocate for your child. Because HMOs and insurance companies are for profit, they are interested in providing as little medical care as possible. The salaries and bonuses that the CEOs and administators of the HMOs and insurance companies receive are in the millions in many cases; the less money they have to pay out for medical services, the more they earn. Thus, if a child has a chronic problem that requires more than the usual number of doctor visits or necessitates hospitalization, coverage may be either not offered or quickly canceled.

Health Maintenance Organizations (HMOs)

HMOs and insurance companies don't really care about your child's health. All they care about is money.

Most HMOs now have primary physicians who act as "gatekeepers." Their primary responsibility is to keep the costs as low as possible, which means that anyone with a chronic illness is not too welcome. One medical director of a large

HMO made the statement to me that "HMOs are not responsible for the medical care of children with chronic illness. This is the responsibility of the family, education, or the state!"

Doctors in HMOs are given a set amount of money per patient, so if your child needs a great number of expensive tests or even just one, such as an MRI or an expensive laboratory test, it either may not be ordered or the gatekeeper may deny it. I have had an MRI request take several letters and phone calls over a period of months, before it was finally grudgingly granted. Usually this was only after I suggested that the parents were ready to seek legal advice.

> Remember that most HMO decisions are not made by doctors, so you may need some strong letters from an outside doctor to get what your child needs.
>
> ◆
>
> Don't be afraid to take on your HMO if you need to. We did, and we won, even though it took much time and effort.

If the gatekeeper doesn't grant your physician's request for a specific referral or test, a letter or call from your pediatrician or specialist is the first step. The gatekeeper may not even know anything about the request because it may have never reached his or her desk. In most cases, a nurse assistant handles most of the paperwork and denials. Thus, it is important that calls and letters be as clear as possible. The need for referral to one or more specialists and the reason why specific tests are required should be stated in a pleasant but emphatic way. If you and your physician can avoid any initial hostility against the HMO administrators and their assistants, it is best, even though you may begin to feel more and more angry that your child is being denied access to needed specialists or tests.

> Learn how to work within the HMO if you can't afford to pay for outside care. Otherwise, you'll just end up feeling angry and frustrated.

When you are the parent of a child with special needs, such as a neuromuscular disorder, you have to decide the best places to direct your hostility, because there will be many situations that will fan the flames of your anger. Unfortunately, fighting HMOs and insurance companies is probably one of these.

My advice to parents is to do the best you can, and then, if you are not making any progress, find someone else to be an advocate. Hopefully, your pediatrician or family physician will fill this role; but if not, you may have to seek legal advice.

The one voice that HMOs and insurance companies will always listen to is an attorney's, because there have been several multimillion dollar awards against these large organizations. Also, legislators and others are now beginning to see the perils of managed care and are raising their voices. Unfortunately, some tragedies have already resulted because specific tests and surgeries were denied. Since HMOs and insurance companies want to avoid a lawsuit at all costs, just the suggestion that you are willing to consult an attorney may be what you need to get a positive response to a request. In California, there is now an 800 number you can call to complain about an HMO (1-800-400-0815)—and complain we all must to begin to swing the pendulum away from managed care.

Choosing a Physician in an HMO

If you are assigned (or have been assigned by an insurance company or welfare department) to a particular HMO, you will probably be given a list of physicians you can consult. This list may not include a pediatric neuromuscular specialist or even a physician who has had specialized training with neuromuscular patients. And instead of allowing you to choose a specialist outside the HMO, referral to a free muscular dystrophy clinic is often made. There are now 262 muscular dystrophy clinics in the United States, plus others in different parts of the world. Before registering your child for one of these clinics, I would suggest that you talk to some of the parents whose children are patients there.

> Find a doctor who is a specialist as soon as possible once you realize there is a problem. You can waste much precious time and energy with misdiagnoses, mistreatment, and misinformation from general practitioners or other doctors who are well meaning but do not have the training or knowledge needed to treat your child.

Questions you will want to ask are about the quality of care received and the time specialists spend with each child. Also, I would check to see if any of the doctors have had training in a pediatric neuromuscular program since a clinic may not have a children's neuromuscular doctor, but just adult rehabilitation doctors, neurologists, or internists. Many parents are uncomfortable about taking their child to a large free clinic and prefer individual one-on-one care from a physician they can get to know and trust.

If you feel that you can find care more to your liking outside a clinic, then you do not have to accept this referral. Remember, though, that fighting the system—that is, the HMO or insurance company—takes a great deal of time and energy, so you do have to decide how best to use your energies.

One real plus of the large muscular dystrophy clinics is that you get to meet other parents and children, and good social workers are generally available. They can be worth their weight in gold, because the experienced ones have learned many tricks to help guide you through the maze of agencies, insurance companies, and HMOs. Also, they should be extremely knowledgeable about local resources, such as parent groups, which many of the local muscular dystrophy groups sponsor. Another advantage of the free muscular dystrophy clinics is that often there is a team present consisting of a neurologist, orthopedist, physical therapist, social worker, and sometimes an equipment person, all of whom can see your child and then talk among themselves about any problems your child may have.

Summer camps are also sponsored by local muscular dystrophy groups. However, your child can attend the camp whether or not he or she is a clinic patient.

Insurance Coverage

Frequent changes in HMOs and insurance coverage seem to be the norm these days, as many insurance companies and state welfare programs are trying to push everyone they cover into HMOs. The incentive here is not to provide better care, although this may be the information given. Instead, the incentive is for the financial benefit of stockholders and administrators.

Additional problems arise if you have to change coverage because of a new job, a move, or a cancellation of your insurance. I have been called by many distraught parents of children whose insurance coverage has been canceled, most often because of a large expenditure of money for a child's surgery or extended hospital care. These parents say they are unable to find other sources of insurance and are desperate.

I'm told it is not legal for insurance companies to cancel policies, and the large, reputable companies deny that this occurs. Unfortunately, however, cancellation is quite a common occurrence when there is chronic illness.

You can seek help through the National Underwriters Company and their publication *Who Writes What in Life and Health Insurance?* This is an annual list of all the companies that write high-risk insurance and the disorders that are covered. Remember, though, that with this special coverage you will have a high deductible and large premiums. But at least your child will be covered. The address is 505 Gest Street, Cincinnati, OH 45203, and the phone number is 513-721-2140. Other suggestions I would make are:

1. Call the Health Insurance Association of America hot line at 1-800-277-4486. You will be referred to the publication given above. The people there are very sympathetic, will listen to your difficulties, and may be able to make other suggestions about coverage.
2. Check with your employer regarding specific health insurance coverage.
3. Call your state insurance department. They each have a list of companies that provide health insurance in the state for individuals who have difficulty obtaining coverage. There are also high-risk pools, which are groups of health insurance companies who agree to write insurance for individuals who have difficulty obtaining insurance.
4. Contact an insurance broker for health coverage. He or she should have knowledge about specific health insurance plans.

State Health Services

Each state (see state directories) has services established to care for children with special needs, and these should help cover the costs of some equipment and services, respite care, physical and occupational therapy, and home health aides. However, obtaining aid may necessitate a real fight. Each state, as well as each agency, has different rules and regulations, so it may take a great deal of effort on your part and your physician's to get any help. Sometimes the energy involved is just not worthwhile, unless you are fortunate enough to find an outstanding social worker to help you.

Unfortunately, the really good hospital or agency social workers don't seem to stay too long, though there are exceptions. Developing a good relationship with an assigned social worker is important, but remember that this is a two-way street. If you forget to return calls or keep appointments, you can't expect the social worker to do so either. It's sometimes hard, I know, to keep your phone free when you expect a call, but it's very difficult for anyone to return a call if your phone is busy for a long period of time.

Expressing your appreciation to your social worker, physician, and anyone else who helps you fight the battle of finding good medical care is important. Strong, caring advocates seem to be harder and harder to find these days, but I'm sure we all do work a little harder when we feel that our services are appreciated.

Paperwork

A large number of forms will invade your life if you have to deal with your state children's service, a regional center, an insurance company, or an HMO. These can be overwhelming, so it's a good idea to start right from Day One, if possible, to keep a file or files in chronological order or in specific categories. Some of the files you will need:

1. Medical reports
2. Lab reports
3. X-ray reports
4 Muscle biopsy reports
5. Medical deductions for income-tax reporting
6. Record of physicians visited
7. Immunization dates
8. Dates and times of specific procedures
9. Names, addresses, and telephone numbers of physicians, social workers, advocates, and agencies

I always urge parents to carry a notebook in their purse or jacket pocket to record the date of a doctor's visit, the advice given, and any lab test or X-ray results. A chronological medical account can save both you and others countless time, as well as duplication of tests and procedures. Also, equipment purchases should be recorded.

Now that many parents have computers and are knowledgeable about their use, record keeping should be somewhat easier. Remember, though, to always have a backup disk in a place other than your home or office. Thefts, fires, and storms do occur, so records are lost, but if there is a duplicate record somewhere, then you will be protected. Also, if your hard disk "crashes," you will not lose all your data.

One of the quickest ways to lose the services of a good physician is to inundate him or her with requests for summaries of your child's disorder. Frequently, after I see a patient, I receive numerous requests from parents asking for complete copies of the file to go to the school, other physicians, state and local agencies, and many other places. Preparing these reports is both time-consuming and expensive, with rarely any payment. This is one of the reasons that few physicians will care for patients with chronic medical conditions. Lawyers bill by the minute or every fifteen minutes for paperwork and telephone calls, but there are few instances when physicians can do this. So please, do be aware, when you fill out medical release forms, of the amount of work you are asking of your physician. Parents often feel that they have no choice about filling out these forms if their child is to receive services. However, an appreciative note or phone call to your physician after asking for voluminous paperwork would be much appreciated, I know. Hospitals and clinics have medical records staffs to process forms and other information, but most physicians in private practice have to prepare reports themselves and are becoming more and more burdened with paperwork. This takes time away from patient care and is slowly driving many doctors out of medicine.

When you take your child to a physician or hospital, do carry your medical coverage information with you. Many private physicians and clinics refuse to see a patient unless this information is available prior to the visit. Numerous times patients have promised to mail insurance information to my office and yet, even after being given stamped, self-addressed envelopes, have neglected to do so.

So good medical care is a two-way street, and, as parents, you do need to do your part to ensure the best possible care for your child and really learn how to navigate the maze of HMOs and insurance companies.

SEVEN

General Medical Care

O ne of the things that often falls by the wayside when parents have a child with a special problem is general medical care. I've seen children who had never received any immunizations or were lacking several important ones. Thus, continuing your child's regular checkups with your family doctor or pediatrician is an important part of maintaining good medical care. A blood count, urinalysis, and tuberculin skin test should be done yearly, and these, too, are often forgotten.

> Be careful that your doctors don't get so overwhelmed by the neuromuscular disease that they forget to take good care of ordinary things like immunizations, and blood counts.

Your child's yearly physical examination, should be a time to talk over your concerns and to keep the doctor up to date on how things are going. Don't ever be afraid to insist that he or she be thorough and that your child gets a complete examination. Just a quick five to ten minute visit once a year just will not do it. Ongoing good medical care, by a concerned physician, is still available if you look for it. So don't let anyone tell you that it's impossible to find a doctor who will spend time with you and really listen. It may take a lot of networking and many phone calls, but somewhere out there is a doctor who can give your child the general pediatric care that is needed.

Unusual Findings or Symptoms

Whenever a medical problem occurs, except for colds or stomach upsets, it's common for both physicians and parents to suppose that it is somehow related to the neuromuscular disorder.

Recently, I saw a teenager with limb girdle dystrophy who was going to the bathroom almost hourly. When I discussed this with her physician, he said, "Oh, well, that's just because she has muscular dystrophy." My reply was that her urinary problems had no connection with the muscle disease and that she needed a good workup by a urologist. Subsequently, she was found to have an infection in the urinary tract, and some problems that she had apparently had since birth. After these were taken care of, she went to the bathroom just three or four times a day, like a normal teenager.

It's true that with some of the neuromuscular diseases problems can develop in other parts of the body. For example, in myotonic dystrophy slowing of the bowel can occur, leading to constipation. Constipation can also be a real problem in children with neuromuscular diseases because weakness of the stomach, or abdominal, muscles can cause difficulty in pushing out, or expelling, stool. Also, kids with considerable muscle weakness often try to avoid going to the bathroom so as not to cause embarrassment or be a problem to their parents or caretakers. Or, they may drink just small amounts of fluid to prevent frequent urination, which can increase the hardness of stool.

Preventing Constipation

Drinking more water and juices helps make bowel movements softer. Six to eight glasses of some kind of fluid—water, juice, or milk—should be the daily goal for all of us, though it is often hard to achieve, particularly with kids. The little boxes of children's juices that can be purchased are good to keep in the refrigerator or on the shelf so that one or more can easily be carried to school or activities. Inexpensive sports bottles can also be carried in a backpack or wheelchair. You do have to be careful, however, that your kids don't fill up on juices and not good food, because a whole day's calories can be obtained that way.

Parents have told me some amazing stories about their children's bowel problems. One mother said, quite hesitantly that she hadn't realized her daughter's constipation was so bad until we added more laxative foods to her diet. Prior to this, the plumber had had to come monthly to their house because the child's large stools had plugged up the toilet! Not only can constipation cause plumbing problems, but large bowel movements can cause fissures, or breaks in the skin, around the rectum and can be quite painful. There is a real relationship, too, between bladder infections and constipation. So if your child has repeated infections of the bladder or kidney and is also constipated, please think about this association.

If there is a real problem, I would keep a three-day record of everything your child eats to see if more fiber-containing foods, fruits, or vegetables need to be added. If three days is not enough to identify difficulties, then a week's record may be necessary. Once you have this, it can be mailed to your physician or gone over with him, or her, or one of the office assistants. It is usually quite easy to spot problem areas once the child's diet record is in front of you.

Some of the diet records that I have seen have been quite amazing, including only fast foods and snacks with little protein, fruits, or vegetables. Bowels do need these to function properly, and muscles and brains need a good diet with protein, carbohydrates, and fat. If we live on foods that have little substance, or fiber in them, it is much like putting a poor quality of gas or oil in an expensive car; before long the car would begin to have problems with its motor and become plugged, as we can if we don't eat foods of good quality with lots of fiber. Foods that can be constipating are milk and milk products—particularly cheese—also apples, bananas, rice, and potatoes.

If dietary changes do not prevent constipation, then your physician may want to prescribe a stool softener, some of which are combined with a mild laxative.

Obesity

Obesity, which is weight gain to a greater degree than is normal for the person's age, is something any of us can develop if we don't have the opportunity to get much exercise. So, if a child cannot run and play like others, he or she may be at risk for gaining a large amount of weight. When parents or caretakers have to lift a heavy child, painful backs or muscle spasms can result. If your child is diagnosed with a muscle disorder, it's important early on to start a high-protein, low-calorie diet if excessive weight gain begins to occur. By keeping a three- or four-day diet history, you can add up the number of calories eaten each day and, with the help of your child's doctor, decide what the correct number should be. Each of us has a different caloric need, depending on the way our bodies burn food, our age, and how much exercise we get.

Some children with muscle diseases, particularly the congenital myopathies, have just the opposite problem since they can be quite thin. These kids need diets high in protein and calories. Here again your physician should be able to help you work out a good food plan. A child in the first few years of life needs about forty calories per pound of body weight daily, but then, from four to nine years, this decreases to about thirty-five calories per pound. Teenagers, depending on their level of activity, need about twenty calories to a pound unless they are involved in a very active sports program.

Many parents feel so sad and guilty about their child's disability that they cater to every eating whim and feel that deprivation of any food just isn't fair. However, in the long run, a child will be hurt rather than helped if he or she is allowed to eat anything desired.

For some reason that has never been well documented, a large number of boys with Duchenne dystrophy become quite obese, while others get quite thin. So, depending on a child's body needs, adjustments may be needed in the amount of calories consumed. If your physician is too busy, a hospital dietitian should be able to help you determine the number of calories your child needs and work with you to plan a good diet.

Eye Problems

Only a few eye disorders are associated with childhood neuromuscular diseases. One is eye muscle weakness, or ptosis, which ocurs in childhood myotonic dystrophy and several other conditions. This muscle weakness makes it difficult to keep the eyelids up in a normal position.

If children have significant weakness of the eye muscles, they may not be able to completely close their eyes at night, and part of the white portion of the eyeballs will show. If this occurs, an ophthalmologist, or eye doctor, should be seen two or three times a year to watch for problems, and eye drops will most likely be prescribed.

Cataracts, or clouding of the lens of the eye, also develop in myotonic dystrophy, and should be watched for by an eye doctor on a regular basis.

Retinitis pigmentosa, a progressive change in the retina, which is at the back of the eye, occurs in children with Kearns-Sayre syndrome and can lead to visual loss. Children with this condition need an eye examination as soon as the diagnosis is made and then at least yearly.

Hospitalizations

Not only are fewer and fewer procedures being done in hospitals these days, but hospital stays for even major procedures are being drastically reduced by the HMOs and insurance companies to cut costs. This puts a greatly increased burden on your shoulders as parents, so you may have to become extremely assertive to ensure (1) that your child stays in the hospital as long as needed, (2) that either you have adequate help at home, or (3) daily visits or assistance from home health aides, visiting, or public health nurses.

Even parents who are physicians or are medically trained need help in caring for their children after hospitalization for an illness or surgery because this is far different from caring for someone else's child in an office or hospital.

If your child has to be hospitalized, please take along favorite toys or books, and do some preparation ahead of time. Playing "doctor" or "operation" with small children markedly reduces their anxiety level, as does reading books about going to the hospital (see Suggested Readings).

Most children need their mothers and fathers nearby when they are hospitalized, but not if you or your partner get upset or anxious. Fear is rapidly communicated to children who want to feel our strength and love, not our fear and insecurities. So please do your crying or have your hysterics away from the bedside. I've seen even little children assume the parenting role in a hospital, which causes them great anxiety.

Talking About Pain and Procedures

Children are extremely perceptive, and have an unusual ability to know if their parents are telling the truth about a procedure or how much pain there will be. So if you and your child communicate well, I would encourage you, as parents, to answer questions as truthfully as possible. A lot of explanation isn't needed, but do tell your child in age-appropriate sentences, what he or she can expect. Be very matter-of-fact, because otherwise your children will pick up on your anxiety.

For children who have problems comprehending what you are telling them because of developmental delay or retardation, I would just use simple sentences and repeat them two or three times.

Dental Care

In some of the childhood neuromuscular diseases long, narrow faces and small jaw openings, as well as protruding front teeth, can create problems. If this is the case, it may be worthwhile to see an orthodontist earlier than usual. In most large cities, there are special needs dental programs with personnel accustomed to seeing narrow jaw openings, muscle weakness, wheelchairs, and other things associated with children with neuromuscular diseases. These programs are often affiliated with dental schools or children's hospitals, so calling a nearby one may be worthwhile.

Please do remember to alert the dentist about the risk of malignant hyperthermia if a general anesthetic is to be given.

Lung (Pulmonary) Problems

Children and young people with neuromuscular disorders are at increased risk for respiratory problems, colds, and lung infections, which include bronchitis and pneumonia. If it is difficult to cough up secretions and mucus, a child is at increased risk for developing small areas of collapse—called atelectasis—in the lungs.

> A daily dose of penicillin during the winter months makes all the difference in both our child's life and in the family's life because of fewer illnesses.

If severe chest muscle weakness is present, a physician may suggest a tracheotomy and mechanical ventilation or respirator. Pulmonary doctors are the ones to help make this decision and should discuss both choices and the pros and cons. Of concern is that many parents have said that they were not given choices about having a tracheotomy performed or clearly told of the risks and problems. Often, too, other methods, such as mask ventilation, have not been tried prior to a tracheotomy being suggested or put in place.

Tracheotomy

A tracheotomy is an operation performed by a surgeon in the operating room, whereby a small tube is put into the windpipe, or trachea. This tube allows easier air exchange and suctioning of the airway. If there is a sudden, acute problem, such as severe pneumonia, a tracheotomy can sometimes be put in place just temporarily. But then there is the concern whether or not the tube can be removed and the patient restored to some kind of a normal life without the use of a respirator to help air flow in and out of the lungs.

If an infant has the fatal form of Werdnig-Hoffmann disease or a severe sex-linked myotubular myopathy, a tracheotomy is sometimes done when there is great difficulty with air exchange. This can extend a baby's life by a few days or weeks, but the outcome is ultimately the same. Before a tracheotomy is done, a knowledgeable pediatric neuromuscular consultant and pulmonary doctor should discuss both choices, including the pros and cons of each, with parents. Ideally, mothers and fathers should also be able to talk to other parents who have "been there," since they can often offer far more insight than physicians. I am always distressed when mothers and fathers tell me of their anger about not having been involved in the important decision of performing a tracheotomy.

When this procedure is being considered for older children with neuromuscular disease, the young people should get to express their wishes, if physically and mentally they are able to do so. Most of the young people I have cared for are terrified of having any kind of mechanical breathing help or a tracheotomy. Even though these devices are much more functional and efficient now than in the past, the idea of being dependent upon a machine and having a tube in your throat is indeed a scary one for both children, young people, and their parents. So if your child has progressive muscle weakness, some thought needs to go into whether or not a tracheotomy is desired before an emergency hospitalization. Parents, kids, and the physician in charge need to discuss this at an appropriate time before an emergency occurs. This way, everyone is clear about what is desired.

There are some guidelines about when tracheotomies should be performed and when the tube should be removed in patients with neu-romuscular diseases. However, a physician's own ethical values and re-ligious beliefs may also come into play. So, as parents, you may need to be quite assertive to be sure that you and your child, and not the physi-cians, make the final decision about a tracheotomy.

Mask Ventilation

This is a way to help a patient breathe without having a tube put in place surgically. Through either a face or nasal mask, air and oxygen are forcibly pushed into the lungs by positive pressure. One expert advises that a permanent tracheotomy be put in place if mask ventilation is needed more than sixteen hours a day. This method can be used when there is so much muscle weakness that breathing is shallow and there is little air exchange. The principal disadvantage of a mask is that it may be somewhat uncomfortable. Unfortunately, this method of ventilation is not commonly used in the United States but is in England, where Pro-fessor Victor Dubowitz comments: "I think one has to move away from the concept that a tracheotomy is essential, since mask ventilation with positive pressure is preferable and is not invasive like a tracheotomy." This view is supported by many other experts in the field. So, once again, some networking with other parents may be needed here, and perhaps a second opinion from another lung doctor should be sought.

EIGHT

◆ ◆ ◆

Special Needs

Parenting is difficult enough these days without adding doctors' appointments, therapy sessions, and countless other tasks. Then, if there are additional problems, such as the need for special equipment, clothing, or help with bathing or dressing, many days may just seem too hard. As one parent said, "Twenty-four hours are just not long enough to do everything I need to do for my child."

Hopefully, some of the suggestions that follow may make life a little easier for each of you as parents. Remember that any special clothing or equipment you buy should be purchased with the goal in mind of making your child as independent as possible. If children with muscle disease can dress and undress themselves, this not only adds to their sense of confidence but can also be a great time-saver. Clothes that are easy to get on and off are needed for children of all ages; even small children can learn to dress

> You'll have little successes along the way that will help you keep fighting battles. But remember that there will be days when it all just seems hopeless. That is the time to put the problems aside for a while and do something just for YOU!
>
> ◆
>
> Be sure that every piece of equipment that you get for your child makes him or her more independent. You need to shop around and ask a lot of questions.

105

themselves if they have enough time and the garments are simple. Giving your child a few extra minutes to try to dress without help may preserve the maximum amount of dignity and give a feeling of independence.

A child with muscle weakness may need some adaptations, but there are seamstresses or tailors who can do this, or show you, a grandparent, or a friend how to make the necessary changes. Also, other parents of children with muscle weakness can be a good resource, and catalogs are available from which easy-care clothing can be ordered (see Suggested Readings). Clothes can be life-saving that open at the sides with Velcro strips, so a child does not have to raise his or her arms to get them on. Zippers can cause great difficulties, as can buttons, so loose-fitting garments, such as bulky sweaters or warm-up suits, can make life easier for everyone. Kids do want to look like their friends, so making this possible is important.

Occupational or physical therapists should be able to help give your child dressing tips, since there are some tricks that make putting on clothes easier when there is muscle weakness.

Grooming and Hygiene

Skin Care

The skin breakdown that occurs with paraplegics or quadriplegics is almost never seen in children with neuromuscular diseases. Bathing is more difficult for children who are wheelchair users, but daily all-over baths are important to prevent skin problems and body odor. Attention to hygiene is important for all kids since unpleasant smells and an unclean appearance are a real turn-off. If your child has frequent skin infections, a soap such as pHisohex can be helpful, but I would use it just for a few days at a time, since too frequent use can cause dryness.

Dandruff or seborrhea of the scalp can become an ongoing problem for older individuals whose muscle weakness makes it difficult to shampoo their hair. A neck tray similar to the ones used in beauty parlors can make frequent shampoos possible; and these trays can be purchased in either beauty or medical supply stores.

Dryness of the skin can be a problem but should be helped with some of the good skin lotions that are available. Vaseline Intensive Care lotion is one of these, and there are many others. Also, a gentle soap such as Neutrogena or Ivory may be needed.

Bathing

A child who is unable to get in and out of a bathtub or shower can be transferred with the help of a slide board. These can help prevent strain to a parent's back which can occur by lifting a child in and out of a low tub. Also, bath chairs, stools, and handheld shower attachments can be helpful; these can all be purchased through a medical supply house. *Please do remember to always have a rubber mat on the bottom of the tub to prevent your child from slipping.*

Older boys and girls do need privacy when bathing or dressing. A young woman should have a female attendant or helper, and a young man should always have a male attendant. Sometimes mothers get so connected to their sons, if muscle weakness is present, that they forget their boys are becoming young men. But if a mother continues to do daily bathing and dressing for her son as he grows older, it doesn't allow him to have any privacy or be in charge of his own body.

Toileting

A child with considerable muscle weakness may have to be helped onto the toilet, and a raised toilet seat and slide board can make this easier. Many bathrooms are too small for a wheelchair to be rolled next to the toilet, and parents of kids with considerable muscle weakness may have to do a lot of lifting. To prevent this, a commode can be purchased and placed right next to the wheelchair, and if there is a detachable wheelchair arm, the child can be easily moved onto the commode or slide over.

Incontinence is not a problem that is ordinarily associated with neuromuscular diseases. If a child with muscle weakness is having accidents, it could mean that either a bladder or kidney infection is present or that he or she is too shy or embarrassed to ask to be taken to the bathroom. Sometimes, if there are toileting problems, a well-meaning professional may suggest that a boy wear a urine-collection device with a leg bag. I would not recommend this, as they are unpleasant, can leak, and shouldn't be necessary if adequate toilet arrangements have been made.

Constipation can be a major problem for children with muscle weakness, since they may not drink much fluid so as to keep from going to the bathroom. Also, they may be embarrassed about having to ask for help in toileting if they can't go by themselves. Most kids eat few vegetables, salads, or fruits, which may also result in constipation. In this case, bran, in the form of flakes or bran cereal, can be added to the diet, as can apricots, apricot nectar, or, if necessary, a stool softener. Metamucil or a similar product, can also be used to increase fiber in the diet. Remember that apples and bananas tend to be constipating.

Grooming

If muscle weakness is such a problem that a child has difficulty brushing his teeth or combing his hair, long-handled toothbrushes and extralong combs can be purchased through medical supply companies or catalogs. If kids can brush their teeth and comb their hair, it does make them feel more independent.

Equipment

Computers

Every child should know how to use a computer. For kids with a muscle weakness, a computer can be the way to do schoolwork, have fun, and communicate with others; it can also be the lifeline to a future job. Two-thirds of disabled adults are unemployed these days, so every effort should be made to help your child or young person become a computer expert. One caution, though, is that you don't want kids spending so much time with computers that they don't develop good interpersonal skills. As with everything else, there needs to be a balance.

> Sometimes it's a good idea to borrow equipment or have it on loan until you're sure it works. We've had too many different kinds of aids that ended up just getting in the way and being more trouble than they were worth.

Computer technology is getting so complex that few parents have the knowledge or skill to decide what is needed for their child, particularly if there is significant muscle weakness. Thus, enlisting the help of a computer expert can save a great deal of time, money, and frustration. Fortunately, there are now Accessible Technology Centers all across the

United States who employ personnel with training to help youths with special needs. Keyboards can be adapted for weak hands, and devices such as "sticky keys" can help make the time spent at a computer more efficient and more fun.

Computers can also now be adapted to activate things around the house, such as lights, TV, radio, and small appliances. Though these can be expensive adaptations, they can make a great difference in helping your child achieve maximum independence and freedom.

Wheelchairs

Wheelchairs symbolize a loss of independence to most people, and the idea of a child using one is very painful for parents.

One mother of a boy with Duchenne dystrophy said that almost from the day of his diagnosis one of her biggest worries was "How will I deal with a wheelchair? But when my son needed one," she said, "I was very thankful to have it. It was not a barrier or a problem, but a big help and added greatly to the quality of his life. I'm a strong advocate of electric wheelchairs, because they give a person so much more freedom. Rather than being dependent on others, an individual can make his own choices about where he wants to go. I had to search the neighborhood for my son after he got his electric wheelchair, because he was so busy out visiting." The woman made the further point that with progressive muscle weakness, you do have to reassess things almost daily. What works one day may not be appropriate the next day or even the next month.

> Much medical equipment is greatly overpriced, so try to beg, borrow, or trade before you spend your hard-earned dollars.

A wheelchair must be specially adapted for each individual, with attention paid to the length and width of the seat and leg rests, and the height of both the arms and seat-back. A firm back or sturdy insert can make all the difference in a child's ability to sit erect. Also, contractures increase if footrests are too high, because the legs are bent up against the body. Removable armrests are important so that sliding can take place from the wheelchair to a bed or toilet. Slide boards can also be used for transfer.

> You'll find that "custom-made" is really a preconceived design with just a few alterations.

Seat belts are important for any wheelchair user, particularly when there is marked muscle weakness. Shoulder restraints or a harness may be necessary for long trips or bus rides if the wheelchair user has a great deal of neck or trunk weakness.

There are many different models to choose from among manual and electric wheelchairs. Also, there are three-wheel electric scooters called Ponys that are fun for kids and can replace a wheelchair. Many kids prefer the lightweight sport chairs, and there are also expensive chairs that bring individuals to an upright position. A physical therapist or rehabilitation doctor should be able to help you decide on just the right chair when it is needed. Remember that a physician's prescription will be necessary if the chair is to be paid for by insurance, your state children's services program, or the Muscular Dystrophy Association. It may take considerable time and effort to get financial help for equipment, but I would ask other parents and a hospital social worker about ideas for funding sources. It is wise also to check with other parents about which are the best medical supply companies. Parents who have had bad experiences with specific equipment companies are usually more than willing to share this information. Some companies take months to fill orders, and, if repairs are needed, they may not provide loaner chairs and also take considerable time to complete repairs. Unfortunately, in some areas there may just be one big equipment company, but wheelchairs can be ordered through a catalog. However, remember that at some point you will need to have repairs made, so you will want a company that is nearby. Also, as a child grows, the leg rests, arm heights, chair backs, and seats will have to be adjusted periodically.

> A Pony, which is a three-wheeled motorized scooter, has been great for our son at home and at school. It is fun for him to drive, and the other kids envy him.

> There are a lot of expensive, worthless products today for disabled individuals. If you don't shop wisely, you'll have a garage full of equipment that your child can't use.

Wheelchair Cushions

Many kinds of cushions are available for wheelchairs, and it's a good idea to try different kinds to find one that is comfortable. A popular one is the Roho cushion, which has eggcrate-like rows of rubber that can be inflated to a specific shape. There are also two cushions called Jay cushions or Combi cushions—that have molded foam seats.

Wheelchair Trays

Lap trays of plastic or wood are available in different sizes and shapes. A tray should be easy to remove and of a size that doesn't make it difficult to go through a doorway. An occupational or physical therapist should be able to help you decide which one is best. A tray may need to be tried before it is ordered, or it should be returnable.

Lifts

If so much muscle weakness develops that your child can no longer transfer or move out of a wheelchair to the toilet, bathtub, or bed, then a portable piece of equipment called a lift can be helpful. Some of the older models, such as the Hoyer lift, have wide bases and are difficult to operate in small spaces, but there are some new lifts, one of which is the Cindi lift, that have narrow bases. However, the Cindi lift has the disadvantage that the wheelchair seat must be at a specific height. Your local medical supply house should be able to show you pictures of these lifts if there are none in stock. It might be a good idea to rent a lift for a few months to find out if you really find it helpful.

> Your school physical or occupational therapist can be a good resource for deciding on proper equipment.

There are lifts that attach to the roof of a car so an individual can be swung into the car seat. This type of lift should be available through your local equipment company, and at least some funding provided by your state children's services program, the Muscular Dystrophy Association, or your insurance company.

In addition, there are bathtub lifts, which utilize water pressure from the tap, and swimming pool lifts, which can be operated at the side of a pool.

Ramps

If several steps lead into your house and limit wheelchair accessibility, a permanent ramp can be built, or you can order a portable ramp through a medical supply company. The portable ramps are called "roller ramps" and are made in three-, five-, and eight-foot lengths. A physical therapist or contractor should be able to help you decide on the appropriate height and length of a ramp.

Walkers

If your child has considerable muscle weakness, a walker may be needed at some point. Two kinds seem to be most effective for kids; one has the support in the back, the other in front. Your child's physical therapist should help you determine which one is the most appropriate. The height and stability of the walker are important to check, and often this can be done by borrowing one from your child's school or an equipment company.

Stand Tables

Standing for at least three hours a day, when a child is no longer able to walk, was first advised by Dr. Paul Vignos in the 1960s. This has occasioned much discussion over the years, but several studies have shown that standing at least three hours a day results in fewer contractures, a straighter spine, and stronger bones. Standing can be accomplished with the use of long-leg braces (known as knee-ankle-foot orthoses KAFOs) or with the use of standing or tilt tables. These should be obtainable, with a physician's prescription, through your state children's services program, your insurance company or HMO, or the local chapter of the Muscular Dystrophy Association. Stand tables can be used both in the classroom and at home, and with them children can do homework while they are standing or watching a favorite TV program.

Accessibility

Each of us likes to have our favorite things close at hand, and this is important for children as well. Outlet stores, which sell unfinished furniture and closet accessories, make it relatively easy and inexpensive to accomplish this.

Unfortunately, most houses today are not built to accommodate wheelchairs because of their narrow halls, stairs, and small bathrooms, but there are architects who specialize in making buildings accessible for those with disabilities.

Occupational therapists usually have suggestions about possible adaptations for bathrooms and kitchens, and physical therapists can be of help in deciding the necessary height and length of a ramp, if one is needed.

There are some tax breaks for making a house more accessible for people with disabilities, but with the changing laws, I would ask your accountant before claiming any deductions. Financial aid is generally not available for making these changes.

Community Accessibility

A child with considerable muscle weakness, particularly one who needs a wheelchair, may become quite isolated. This is especially true when both parents work outside the home. Since many activities for young people are not wheelchair accessible, this impacts both a child and the whole family. But by doing a little research, it should be possible to find some fun activities. If there is a tourist bureau in your town, or parents' newsletter, these often list what is available for kids with disabilities. Talking to other parents of kids with special needs is usually a good resource. Also, some communities have a hot line you can call to find programs that are both fun and accessible.

Travel

Some of the problems associated with family trips may not be related at all to the special needs of your child with muscle weakness. Instead, the biggest difficulties can be those that all families have in trying to get away for a few days. One mother commented that the worst problem she had was trying to find someone who would take over one son's paper route!

Air travel is much easier now than it used to be, but there still can be some major problems if you don't ask lots of questions ahead of time and anticipate your child's special needs. Do talk to airline representatives, as well as travel agents or someone from American Express. They should be helpful in solving special problems for you. If you wait until the last minute, though, you could have some real headaches. Reading some of the travel books about accessibility can be helpful, too (see Suggested Readings).

One family took a trip to Europe and found that the small shuttle buses couldn't be used to go from terminal to terminal. Also, their child's wheelchair was lost on one occasion, so they advise parents to request that the wheelchair be put in the cabin storage so it is readily available when the plane lands. This family made the further point that if you act confident, you can frequently take a wheelchair many places without too many questions being asked.

Bathrooms in Europe can be a problem for a wheelchair user, because they are often on the second floor, so carrying along a urinal for a male child can prevent some problems. Also, if you go to a restaurant, at home or abroad, check to see if the bathroom is accessible *before* you order. If it isn't, you might want to find another place to eat.

One family said that they took their son to a major U.S. amusement park but found that he couldn't go on any rides because the facility's insurance carrier wouldn't allow anyone in a wheelchair. It started to rain, so one parent ended up standing in the rain with the child, waiting for the rest of the family. So before making any travel plans, it is important to check out the accessibility of bathrooms, dining rooms, and even amusement-park rides.

The Make-A-Wish and Starlight Foundations provide special trips for children with progressive disorders. One parent said: "It's neat for a child to be able to treat the whole family to a special trip, simply because of his or her disability." However, a young person who doesn't have a severe disability may get the feeling that the trip has been given because he or she has a fatal disease. So you do have to weigh the pros and cons.

Safety Precautions

Every individual who uses a wheelchair, and particularly those with marked muscle weakness, should wear a seatbelt, especially when traveling in a school bus or a family van. If the neck and trunk muscles are weak, it may be necessary to attach a harness to the wheelchair and around your child to prevent pitching forward if a sudden stop occurs. Harnesses can be purchased or made at home and will go under a jacket or outer garment.

Handling All Your Child's Special Needs

All these extra problems may make it seem that the days are just too hard. As one parent said, "There just is no training that prepares you to be the parent of a child with a disability." Another added, "Yes, I want my life back." But remember, there are rewards. You will find a whole host of new friends, supporters, and others who care about you, and discover strengths and courage that you never knew you had. Also, each hard-fought battle or problem that you solve will help you to realize how very competent you are or are becoming. Remember that there are a lot of other parents in exactly the same boat, and networking with these and trying to keep some balance in your life will give you the ability to handle all the special problems that come along. I've always been impressed by how well most parents handle their child's neuromuscular disorder and by the almost unlimited energy that they find to do battle whenever necessary.

The Goal of Independence

Every piece of equipment you purchase for your child should help make your son or daughter more independent and your life, as parents, easier. Many parents tell me that they have closets full of unused equipment prescribed by professionals or purchased in hopes that it would make a difference. So do ask lots of questions, borrow equipment before you purchase it to try it out, and be sure that your child is willing to use it before bringing it into your home. Fortunately, wheelchairs and other pieces of equipment are now made with lightweight materials that are much easier to handle and in colors that kids enjoy. Please do involve your child in the purchase of any piece of equipment if he or she is old enough to help make a decision. Since a child or young person will be the one using it, he or she certainly should have some say in the selection.

> Don't let anyone talk you into buying a piece of equipment that doesn't further your goal of helping your child be more independent.

In summary, there are many ways, through special aids, that young people with weakness can achieve independence and keep their muscles in the best possible condition. So it's important to keep abreast of new developments in equipment. But a word of caution is that equipment companies are in business to make money, and their personnel may not be trained to individualize wheelchairs and other equipment for your child or find the ones that are the least expensive and most functional. Thus, the advice of a pediatric rehabilitation physician, an occupational or physical therapist, or another parent is important before any money is spent on equipment. Other parents can be particularly good sources of information about which supply companies are the best and what equipment allows the most independence. Life is so complicated these days that your child's equipment should be as functional as possible to fit in with your family's needs. I would rely on professionals to help guide you, but remember that, as parents, you are the experts for your child and should have the final say about what equipment will or will not work.

NINE

◆ ◆ ◆

Tips for Mothers, Fathers, Grandparents, Brothers, and Sisters

B ecoming a parent doesn't mean that you have to put your own life on hold; that isn't healthy for you, your mate, or your children. But if you have a child with special needs, how do you save any time for yourself when there are so many other commitments?

One mother answered this by saying, "I've had to learn to say no and mean it. It's often hard to do this, but I know I won't be able to make it if I don't."

Another mother said, "I've learned that I have to get enough exercise and have some fun along the way. That's the only way I get through the days."

A father agreed, saying, "Yes, there certainly is no training that prepares you to be the parent of a child with a disability, but if you don't run your own life, someone else will."

> There will be many days when you'll say, "I want my life back," but these will pass. (A mother)
>
> ◆
>
> You'll find that those who do not live with the reality, problems, and issues of special-needs kids have no concept of how precious time is, so you just have to learn to say "No" if you're going to be a strong advocate for your child.

It's easy to get so caught up in the details of life, and particularly in the care of a child with a neuromuscular problem, that not only do you suffer as a mother or father, but so does everyone else in the family.

I often take a prescription blank when I see a harassed mother [or father] and on it write "A few minutes a day just for you, and 1–2 hours a week to do what you want." Many parents, mothers in particular, have said, "But I've forgotten how to do anything by myself or even have some fun." My suggestion to them is that they start by exploring a new neighborhood, having a cup of coffee with a friend, or taking a short walk or bicycle ride. Even fifteen to thirty minutes a day can make all the difference in the world in being able to cope with the multiple problems that you will encounter. By becoming very organized and learning to say "No," you can get your life down to basics and do the things that need to get done, not only for yourself but for everyone else.

> If you don't take any time for yourself, you'll forget what you like to do and who you are. (A mother)

Trying to hold down a full-time job as well as being a parent to a special-needs child can make your life even more complex and stressful. One of the most important things to remember in this situation is to develop a strong support system with family members, friends, and parents of other children with and without disabilities. Learning to say "Yes" in response to offers of help and "No" to taking on more than you can comfortably manage are equally important. Many times you will feel you're taking two steps forward and one step backward, but I suspect along the way you are going to develop new strengths and insights into yourself that would not have been possible if you had not had a child with a neuromuscular disorder. One mother said, "I found a whole new world because of my child's disability. I feel that I'm a better person because of it."

> You'll find a host of new friends, supporters, and individuals who care about you because of your child's disability. (A mother)
>
>
>
> Hopefully, you'll find that the joys your child brings will far outweigh the pain and extra work that his or her care requires. (A mother)

Tips to Find Help

Finding good help is a survival skill that every parent of a child with a disability needs to learn early on. Some good resources for finding help are:

1. Family members.
2. Neighbors.
3. Friends.
4. Child-care facilities.
5. After-school recreation programs.
6. Seniors and retired individuals.
7. College students (live-in or live-out).
8. Live-in sitters.
9. LVNs or RNs (each of these has their pluses and minuses).

> You'll find that child-care workers come and go like a revolving door, and that a good one is hard to find.

Child-care workers do seem to come and go like a revolving door, both in the home and in day-care centers. Unfortunately, you have to be particularly careful about the individuals you hire to help with the care of a child with special needs. One mother said, "We had a respite worker who was a two-hundred-pound chain-smoker and a walking coronary. She let our child fall asleep in a highchair and was too lazy to put him in his bed. When I fired her, she took out her calculator and counted the amount owed her down to the minute: $19.37!"

The following are important points to remember when you are looking for household help:

1. Always check two or more recent references.
2. Ask if the person has had a recent chest X ray or tuberculin skin test.
3. Ask when the individual's last physical examination was, and if there were any problems? (You do have a right to know this as an employer, particularly if someone will be in close contact with your child.)

Home Health Aides

There are visiting-nurse agencies in most towns of any size across the United States. Home health aides who are either licensed vocational nurses or registered nurses can be obtained through these agencies. In large cities, there are home care or home health agencies subsidized by the state or federal government, which should be listed in the yellow pages of your telephone book. Calling a social worker at your local hospital may be another way to find the telephone number for these agencies. Your physicians, too, may have the numbers, since a doctor's prescription is required if these aides are going to be paid for by insurance companies, Medicaid or Medicare.

Family Members

Family members can be a tremendous source of support if they are not critical or controlling. Some, however, simply cannot accept a child who has a disability, and you will quickly find out who your true supporters are. One mother said, "My mother-in-law was determined to make the crooked stick straight." But some grandparents and extended family members are wonderful and can make all the difference in

> Your in-laws may be of tremendous help and support, or they may just not accept your child's problem. (A father)

your life and your child's life. Be sure to let these special individuals know how much you appreciate their help.

Neighbors

There probably aren't too many stay-at-home neighbors who are willing and able to take on the care of your child, but one or two might be willing to do some short-term baby-sitting—if you need an hour or so to do errands or get away by yourself. Don't be shy or hesitant about asking, because all anyone can say is "No," and this shouldn't change your relationship. Often you can do an errand or two for the neighbor while you're out, because the barter system is still alive and well in many places.

Friends

Good friends are important to all of us, but if you have a child with special needs, the support of friends can be irreplaceable. Friends can be there to comfort you in times of need or pain and also act as sounding boards. We all have to be careful, though, about overburdening friends with our problems. Friendship should be a two-way street where both parties have a chance to talk about fears and concerns or share triumphs.

When your child is first diagnosed with a neuromuscular disease, sharing the news with friends may be difficult. They may have noticed that something was wrong with your child and yet been afraid to mention it. The way you share information with friends depends a great deal on the kind of friendship you have. Unfortunately, friends you expect to be there for you often are not. But other people who perhaps you didn't know that well may step in and fill the void. You will develop new friendships as you become more involved in your child's special activities or if you join a parent support group. I would strongly suggest, though, that you not limit your friendships to just parents who have a child with similar problems, because then your viewpoint can become very skewed. It may be hard to interact with parents whose children don't have muscle weakness, or to remember that these parents may be carrying some other kind of burden of which you are not aware. Try to be as open as you can with friends you trust, but do be careful about what you tell them, since many individuals don't want to hear about problems, particularly if they have grown to love your child.

You may have friends who always try to take charge and offer advice. Then I would just smile and say "Thank you" and use either some or none of their advice, as you see fit. There may be other friends who make you uncomfortable because they seem to thrive on pain. It is easier to get through the days if you surround yourself with positive, healthy, well-balanced individuals, rather than those who always see the negative or dark side.

Treasuring your support system—whether it is family, friends, or simply those with whom you have frequent contact in the community—pays big dividends. An occasional thank-you note or simple word of appreciation can pay big dividends. Courtesy seems to be almost a thing of the past, with people always rushing to and fro in a frantic manner. Having even just a few staunch supporters on whom you can depend is critical. Life would be pretty lonely if we had to go it alone, so we are blessed if there are people who will stick by us in times of need or pain.

Child-Care Facilities

There are good child-care programs where children receive excellent care, and others that are pretty awful. So before selecting a child-care facility, you need to play detective and find out about any hidden problems. After an initial visit, I would talk to some of the other parents of children in the program and also drop in unexpectedly once or twice. Questions to ask are:

1. If a child with a fever or illness is brought for care, is he or she sent home, or is the child simply kept away from the other children?
2. What is the ratio of children to adults?
3. How are emergencies handled?
4. What is the training of the staff?
5. Do any of the members have CPR training?
6. Is the facility accredited or registered with the city or state?
7. How close is the nearest hospital or emergency facility?
8. Have the staff had medical examinations or tuberculin tests?

If your child uses a respirator or is medically fragile, then the usual child-care facility will probably not be adequate. In this case, an aide or attendant who cares just for your child may be a better choice. This help may be paid for through community, state, or federal monies. Also, state Regional Centers should help with the expenses of medically fragile children, but it may take a great deal of energy on your part to get any financial aid.

After-School Recreation Programs

Some schools, community centers, and Boys' and Girls' Clubs offer programs that can both be fun and also offer supervision. These programs range from excellent to very inadequate, so do network with other parents to discover the good ones. A hospital or agency social worker might also be able to give you information about the different ones. Many large cities have parent hot lines that can answer your questions about what is available, and in many big cities books can be purchased that list recreation programs and other child-care resources.

College Students

If you have an extra room, it may be possible to find a student who will exchange child-care services for room and board. By calling your local college employment service or placing an ad in their newsletter, you might find just the right person you need. References should be checked, and inquiries made about any medical problems. Also, I would include asking the date of the individual's last chest X ray or tuberculin test. Tuberculosis is on the rise, and every child-care person should be screened yearly; this can usually be done, at no cost, by your local health department. Many children with neuromuscular disorders have weak chest muscles and so are more prone to respiratory infections, so it is important to prevent exposing them to anyone with tuberculosis.

Live-In Sitters

So many people are looking for jobs these days that you might be able to find your own Mary Poppins. One parent found a college student who needed a home for a year until she decided what career to pursue, and this young lady has become invaluable to the two hardworking parents. Again, references and medical problems need to be checked.

Licensed Vocational Nurses (LVNs)
or Registered Nurses (RNs)

If your child is medically fragile and requires constant attendance, then insurance or state coverage for either an LVN or RN should be available. This may take some strong letters from your physician or even some legal help. But if your child needs this type of care, please don't try to do it yourself unless you feel comfortable with a respirator or other medical devices. This can cause a great deal of anxiety for you as parents and also for your child. Even parents who have had medical training need help and support, because caring for your child at home is far different from caring for one in an office or hospital.

Respite Care

Respite care means having a child cared for by someone outside the family, either in the child's home or in another setting. Some Regional Centers and some state or local children's services programs pay for this kind of help, but it is becoming increasingly difficult to obtain this assistance now that less and less money is being allotted to state agencies. When monies are paid directly to parents so that they can hire their own respite workers, some parents elect to keep the money and provide the care themselves. I think this is unwise for several reasons, and would strongly urge that any respite dollars be used to hire outside help.

A Father's Role

A loving father is so very important to all kids. Yet when a child, and particularly a son has a neuromuscular disorder, the extra challenges can be almost overwhelming.

> Take one day at a time and try to make the most of it for yourself and your child.

There are two real difficulties that often arise for the father of a child with a neuromuscular disorder. One is that there may be an increased financial burden which you feel is more your responsibility than your mate's, and the other is that your partner may depend on you for a tremendous amount of emotional support.

One father said, "My wife expects me to always be the strong one, so I've had to find a few special people to help me carry my burden."

Another father said, "I really wished that I could just walk away and never come back. It took me a long time to get over the anger that I felt about knowing my son would never be able to play Little League baseball or varsity football. But now I've learned that the joys he has brought us have far outweighed the pain and the extra work that has been required."

> There will be days when you wish you could throw in the towel and just walk away, particularly if you're having to work extra hard to make ends meet financially. You may find that it's a no-win situation that you keep hoping will get better. (A father)

The financial problems can be lessened somewhat if you learn how to become a strong advocate, network with other parents to fight HMO and insurance company restrictions, and become knowledgeable about support that is available, often at little cost.

One father said he saw his children very little because he had to work two jobs to make ends meet. He said his wife couldn't work because their child needed so much care. In general, he felt it was a no-win situation that he kept hoping would get better. He knew he couldn't walk away, but he certainly often thought about it. Finding other fathers with whom he could talk and also a friend with whom he could play handball made a real difference in his life. Being the parent of a child with a disability does strip the normal gears of parenting, as one father said, and life can become an emotional roller coaster, with some highs and many lows.

> Parenting a child with a disability is heroics followed by release. The ups and downs are very difficult, but you'll develop strengths that you didn't know you had.
> (A father)

It's extremely important to plan weekly time alone with your mate—time when you don't talk about problems but simply try to have fun together. Going one day at a time, or even just a few hours at a time, and not looking down the long road ahead can really help. There will be some moments of joy, I promise you, if you just hold on.

> It's best not to think about the future but just put on blinders and do the best you can. (A father)

Support groups for fathers have their pros and cons. One father felt very uncomfortable with a support group he attended because it had a religious context and that was not within his comfort zone. He went just once or twice. However, another father said he didn't think he could survive without his weekly support group.

You have to find a way that will work for you, and know that taking time for yourself—ideally on a daily basis, but at least weekly—should be your number-one priority. Even the physical care of a child with a neuromuscular disease, if there is tremendous weakness, can be exhausting, so trading time off with your partner is essential. By recognizing and communicating your needs, you can come up with an arrangement that allows you to take over each other's responsibilities a few hours a week so that each of you can have some time to yourself.

Grandparents

If you are a grandparent living close to your grandchildren, they are very fortunate indeed. Only 5 percent of children in the United States have their grandparents close by. When a child is diagnosed with a neuromuscular disease, some grandparents provide tremendous support,

> You may find that your in-laws and other family members make denial the fifth state of the union. They may refuse to believe that your child has a muscle disease.

but others distance themselves and gradually lose contact. One mother told me about not being able to have her child in a wheelchair when her husband's parents were present because everyone had to pretend that there was nothing wrong. This put a terrible strain on all the family members, particularly the child.

If, as grandparents, you feel that you are having trouble handling your feelings about your grandchild's medical problem, then I think it's something that you need to talk over with your mate, if you have one, or a good friend. It is important, too, to discuss your feelings with your son or daughter—and their mate—at an appropriate time. Being honest about how you feel can make all the difference in the world, and you will probably find out that the child's parents feel exactly the same way.

Often, when there is a child with special needs in a family, ongoing communication can bring everyone closer together. One way to start communicating about your pain is to say, at a time and place you can really talk, something like "It's very difficult for me to watch Steve having trouble keeping up with his brothers and sister," then pause and wait to see what comes next. If you're feeling sorry for the child, then this needs to be discussed also. I realize that, in many families, such openness is not easy, particularly if the family is not geographically close by and if it's not something that has happened in the past.

I urge grandparents to avoid either saying or writing anything negative. If you either write or say something, there can be no retraction, so be careful. The time we spend with our grandchildren should be very special, but if their parents are unhappy with our presence because of something we've said, then that time is not going to be made available to us.

Another word of caution is that you may feel so sorry for the child with a special neuromuscular problem that you want to buy expensive gifts and single him or her out for extra attention. This hurts not only the child but also any brothers and sisters. Many parents harbor anger about a child becoming spoiled, yet few feel that they can discuss this with their own parents or their in-laws. The time and attention you give to one grandchild should be no more than that given to another, and any gifts should be given equally to all grandchildren. I speak from experience and know now that I should have spoken up when I was a young parent, but I felt at the time that it would probably cause more problems.

Baby-Sitting a Grandchild with a Neuromuscular Disorder

If you are left in charge of a grandchild with a neuromuscular disorder while both parents work, it is important to ask about the usual schedule and, in general, how the parents want things done. Disciplining grandchildren is particularly hard, and I've heard many grandparents say, "Well, I had to discipline my own children, so now it's my turn to spoil my grandchildren." I think we do both our grandchildren and their parents a real disservice by spoiling children. Both the kids and everyone else suffers. Children are very adept at manipulating grandparents and focusing attention on themselves, so you do have to be careful, especially if the child has a neuromuscular problem.

What children really want is hugs, firm discipline, and lots of structure. So, right from the first, I would try not to step over the line with too many toys, gifts, or too little discipline. If you're not careful, some real problems can result between you and the children's parents, and everyone may suffer. If you are a senior helping with the care of your grandchildren, you have to go back to the basics of parenting and expect your grandchildren to do as much as they can for themselves, obey the rules, and know that when you say "No," you mean it. It's far easier to spoil a child than it is to raise one who has regard for others, a good self-image, and strong feelings of independence.

If you feel embarrassed that one of your grandchildren has a special medical problem, you need to look very deep within yourself and perhaps get some professional help. Every child is a unique, special human being, and if you can find that wonderful specialness, you can look beyond the neuromuscular problem and value that child.

Brothers and Sisters

It's often very hard to be the brother or sister of a child with a medical problem because, to get any attention, you often have to be either very, very good or act out in destructive ways. Even though you, as parents, probably try hard to give each of your children equal attention, it's very difficult. One parent said, "I just don't see how I can keep all the doctor and therapy appointments that Sarah needs and still give my other children the time they should have." My suggestion to her was to find as many support people as she could and, if necessary, pay a baby-sitter or someone outside the family to take Sarah to a few of her appointments.

Another parent said, "Even though we understand that our older daughter is having temper tantrums because her little sister is getting so much attention, no amount of attention seems to be enough. What can we do?"

To this mother I suggested that some play therapy with a trained counselor or a sibling group might be helpful for the older daughter. Art therapy, too, can be beneficial if this is available, because it allows a child to express his or her anger on paper or by doing a creative project. Many art therapists also have degrees in counseling and can help a child talk about things that are bothering him or her.

So if one of your children begins to withdraw from family activities or starts acting out, professional help may be needed. Changes in school performance are also tip-offs that things are amiss and that counseling might be needed.

To find good counselors or a siblings group, I would first ask your pediatrician or family doctor for suggestions. Also, a hospital or agency social worker might be able to help you find resources. As a last resort you could start a group of your own, perhaps asking a professional to help out. If money is short, just getting brothers and sisters of other disabled children together with your kids can be extremely helpful. That way, all the children can share experiences, and mothers and fathers can have time to talk together. Also, there are some good books available for siblings that you might want to investigate (see Selected Readings).

I've held many sibling groups over the years and have heard some amazing stories from brothers and sisters. The most common complaint among siblings is that they don't get the parenting that the child with a disability receives, and are treated in a different way. Also, they feel resentment about being asked to perform tasks or chores that are not expected of their sibling. Some of the tales may be quite exaggerated, but I suspect that there is an element of truth in all of them.

One of the things that siblings often face is embarrassment about having a brother or sister who is not like other children. If you can have some good discussions about these feelings, it should resolve the issue.

Also, when siblings can talk to other brothers and sisters about their embarrassment, it is helpful.

When there is a progressive disorder and the expectancy that a child's life will be shortened, the child's brothers and sisters have a right to understand what is going on. Encouraging them to talk about their fears and giving matter-of-fact answers, rather than going into long explanations, should relieve a great deal of their anxiety.

Older siblings may worry that someday they will pass on the same problem to their own children. A genetic counselor who is knowledgeable and has up-to-date information about neuromuscular diseases should be able to help relieve some of these fears.

One of the great burdens that the brothers and sisters of a child with a disability usually carry is considerable guilt about being "normal." As adults, many of the siblings go into the helping professions in an attempt to make up for their own good health, and probably also to rid themselves of the unconscious guilt that they have carried for many years. So it's important that brothers and sisters be given the opportunity to ask questions in order to gain some understanding of their sibling's disability. They may assume that it was something they did, said, or thought that caused the problem.

Sibling jealousy can easily occur if parents are spending more time with the disabled child than with their other children. So, as parents, it's extremely important to be sensitive to your other children and also to be careful about asking them to serve as caretakers or baby-sitters. Once in a while is okay, but always being the designated baby-sitter just isn't fair and it can cause a great deal of anger and resentment.

One of the best ways to keep problems from arising is for you and your partner to spend as much one-to-one time with each sibling as possible. This helps keep open the lines of communication and lets your kids know that they are valued and loved. But remember, you need to *listen* and not be thinking about something else when you are having a dish of ice cream or a Coke with a brother or sister. Not only do you need to listen with your ears, but also watch the body language, since this will help you understand what your child is feeling. If you can be as honest as possible about answering questions, that will make things better, too.

If the lines of communication are not open with all of your children, and you feel there is anger, resentment or withdrawal, I strongly advise some family therapy, even if only a few sessions. It's natural for both a child with muscle weakness and siblings to feel angry that such a problem had to occur in their family. We all carry a picture of the perfect family in our minds, and a great deal of anger can result if, for some reason, the reality is different.

Remember that the brothers and sisters of a disabled child often pay a high price. Several of them have said to me, "I've never felt that I had parents, and I've just had to parent myself." This loss of a childhood can have many adulthood repercussions: difficulties with interpersonal relationships, constant caretaking of others, and no real feelings of being loved and valued. So do the best you can to spend quality time with all your children. Remember that consistent discipline, listening, and lots of hugs will pay big dividends in the future.

TEN

Tips on Coping With Your Child's Ups and Downs

How can a child or teenager not feel terrible anger about having muscle weakness and receiving the diagnosis of a neuromuscular disorder? Even if parents and doctors haven't told the young person the diagnosis, he or she will certainly know something is wrong if keeping up with friends or siblings is difficult. Also, if there are frequent doctors' appointments or visits to a physical therapist, a great deal of visible or hidden anger may be present. If there is no healthy outlet for this anger, soiled underpants, temper tantrums, forbidden words, or striking out at siblings, parents, or friends can occur. Also, a decline in school performance, a change of personality, or a look of anxiety can all be tip-offs that emotions and feelings are not being expressed. If a healthy means of getting rid of anger is not found, the anger may be internalized and lead to depression.

> Try to give your child as much of a normal life as possible; it's very important.

If your child with muscle weakness refuses to socialize and hides away in his or her room, it could be embarrassment about not being able to keep up with friends or classmates. If braces of any kind have to be used, or a wheelchair, these, too, can add to embarrassment about having others see them. Tip-offs to depression are withdrawal

You'll have to help your child understand that many people often don't want to talk with him or her if they see a wheelchair.

◆

You may often think, What's the point of my child doing well in school or making college plans if she might not make it? If you think that way, you'll get yourself into real trouble.

from normal activities, a change in personality, loss of appetite, or difficulty sleeping.

Some kids with muscle disease just give up, don't try anymore, and have a lack of interest in everything. I've had youths with life-threatening muscle diseases say to me, "Why should I study when I'm going to die in a few years? Why not watch TV all day? It really doesn't matter what I do, does it?"

If you sense a feeling of apathy or depression in your child, manifested by a lack of interest in making friends or going out, counseling or interaction with a peer group could make a big difference. Not having a real interest in living affects not only a child's emotional well-being and physical health, but also that of the entire family.

A child who feels depressed or apathetic may withdraw from everyone and make the problem worse because of loneliness. Unfortunately, the friends of a young person who has a progressive neuromus-

People do a lot of hurting without knowing it, and you have to teach your child to anticipate the hurts so she won't suffer too much from them.

cular disorder do often drop away. If this is occurring with your child, it will help greatly if feelings can be discussed with you, a teacher, or a counselor. Kids should feel comfortable about asking even difficult questions. This is particularly true if they know their life will be shortened with progressive muscle

weakness, heart, or lung problems.

Parents who have read their children's diaries after the children had died have told me of the loneliness and isolation they voiced. How they wished for someone with whom to discuss their fears and feelings. Instead, they wrote that everyone seemed to shy away from talking about what was happening to them, and they were too shy or concerned about others to bring up things they wanted to ask.

One mother said, "I just couldn't let my son say the things that he needed to, particularly toward the end." She spoke warmly of a man in the neighborhood who, toward the end of her son's life, came one or two times a week to see him. He would go to the young man's room, and they would talk and talk. It was the greatest gift anyone could give her son, she said.

In trying to establish good communication with a child who has a neuromuscular disorder, you may have to do some advance planning in order to have the best results. For example, you need a place where you can *really talk and listen*—in a garden, a park, or in a quiet restaurant or ice-cream parlor. Sitting across from your child and being aware not only of what he or she is saying, but also the body language, helps establish real communication. The way a person sits or talks often expresses emotions such as anxiety, fear, or depression.

If you feel there is a communication void because you have been too busy or haven't found a good way to talk to your child about feelings or problems, some help from a counselor might be needed. Even a few sessions can be helpful. To find a good counselor, I would ask other

> The best gift you can give your child is high self-esteem.

parents for names or check with a local mental health agency or family service. Psychologists or therapists with a marriage and family counseling license (MFCC) can be good resources, and sometimes a school counselor can help. Counseling can be written into your child's Individual Educational Program (IEP) if he or she qualifies for special education, but be specific about the number of sessions needed, how often they should occur, and for how many minutes.

Good counseling can make a tremendous difference in how kids handle anger, resentment, depression, fear, and denial, and also in how they deal with sexual fantasies. There are counselors who work just in the area of sex and disability,

> If you respect the freedom of your child's spirit and let it go unencumbered by the physical restraints imposed by the muscle weakness, you'll help him or her develop coping skills.

who are sometimes connected with a medical school or specific agency. If you need to find this kind of help, your physician or other parents might be able to suggest some names.

Outside Help

Art Therapy

A less threatening way for kids to have some help with their feelings, rather than seeing a psychologist or counselor, is to have art therapy. Art therapists have had special training in helping children work through problems with the use of painting or arts and crafts. After a project is completed or while it is under way, an art therapist can talk with a child about what he or she is feeling. Art can be not only lots of fun, but also a healthy way to lessen feelings of anger and depression.

It's always been of interest to me that, for some reason, a large number of the boys I have cared for with Duchenne dystrophy seem to have unusual artistic ability. Their art brought them not only pleasure but also offered a creative outlet for feelings of sadness, anger, and frustration. Over the years I have been given many special drawings and paintings by young people with neuromuscular disorders.

Support Groups

In most large communities there are now not only support groups for kids with special needs, but also many on-line support groups. Not all the young people in these groups have the same disability. Also, it is a good idea for a young person with muscle weakness to realize that there are other kids with perhaps even greater problems.

Realistic Goals and Expectations

One of the hardest things for both kids with muscle weakness and their parents to face is that there are goals that will be impossible to achieve. Thus, realistic expectations are most important as you help your child plan for the future. Remember, though, that most youths will envision several different careers as they are growing up, and their future may not be one that either of you have anticipated.

One father said, "One of the hardest things that I have had to accept is that my son just can't set his sights on something that will not be possible for him. He's always loved sports and wanted to be a professional baseball player. So he and I have become very knowledgeable about all the teams, and hopefully someday this interest will help him get a job as a sportswriter or newscaster. It's really important to channel your child's energy into something that is possible."

It is important that not only kids have realistic expectations, but I think their parents have to have them also. Many fathers who are sports fans find it extremely difficult to accept the fact that their sons with muscle disease will not be able to take part in many sports. Finding something that a young person is particularly good at, then, is important. Hobbies, for example, can widen a child's horizons and be a way to connect with others who have the same interests. With all of the on-line groups available now, kids can make friends around the world who have interests similar to their own.

For example, amateur radio operators can have fun with other ham operators and develop friendships, and occasionally they can even perform important roles by picking up distress messages and relaying them to the proper authorities. This is a way to stay connected to the real world and offer a service besides.

One young person with a muscle disorder loved animals and had a special ability with them. He cared for pets of neighbors and friends, an activity that not only gave him a sense of self-esteem and a special status, but also was a way to earn a little extra money.

Rather than focusing on things your child can't do, please try to focus on the things that he or she can do at each age and stage. If you can live "in the moment" and not constantly agonize about the future, then life will be very much easier for everyone. Every child with a disability has activities in which he or she can participate, though perhaps not at the

> Always stress what your child *can* do, not what he or she *can't* do.

same level as siblings or classmates. However, with adaptations, many things should be possible for your child. By concentrating on the things your child can do, such as using the computer, going to a movie or ballgame, or using the telephone, you will give him or her a feeling of confidence.

One thing that all children do far too well—and particularly children with limited physical ability—is become expert TV watchers, which can be a real escape for both a child and his family. One patient of mine watched six to eight hours of television a day and gradually withdrew from the real world. Unfortunately, this TV watching was accompanied by snacking, and the boy put on weight rapidly. To make matters worse, both parents developed severe back problems as a result because the boy had to be lifted. Thus, the excessive TV watching caused problems not only for the child but also for his parents.

Expectations for children with progressive muscle weakness do have to be changed from time to time, depending on how much weakness develops. However, with the many adaptations for equipment and computers available, these young people should still be expected to get on with their lives and to do the best they can in school, at home, and in

> You need to expect your child to do the best possible. Tell him that you won't always be at his beck and call, so he had better learn to do things for himself.

the community. One parent said, "I treated my son just like his brother and expected him to do whatever he could for himself and for others. If something was particularly hard for him because of his muscle weakness, then we just had to work out a different way that it could be accomplished."

Fear and Anxiety

Two problems that can occur as a young person becomes more aware of his or her muscle weakness are *anxiety* about what lies ahead and *fear* that he or she will become extremely incapacitated or dependent.

As a young person develops more and more muscle weakness, the causes of anxiety may be things such as:

1. Will I make it to the bathroom on time?
2. What if I fall? Who will help me?
3. What if there's a fire? How will I get out of the house?
4. What if I get sick and have to go to the hospital?

Some anxiety is normal for all of us, but when increased muscle weakness develops and children lose the ability to fend for themselves, it's easy to understand how they can become increasingly anxious. Questions for you to think about in this regard are:

1. Does your child seem unduly concerned about where you are going and when you will return?

2. Does he or she have an anxious look?
3. Is your child having headaches or stomachaches?
4. Is it hard for him or her to settle down at night?
5. Are bad dreams or nightmares a problem?

Symptoms such as loose stools, stomachaches, headaches and other physical symptoms can be tip-offs that your child is overly fearful. Some mild medication might even be needed once in a while. For older children who use a wheelchair, a small dose of Valium can make a big difference in the anxiety level. I would discuss this with your physician if you are concerned.

Fear, a powerful emotion for any of us, can be almost paralyzing when it is brought on by thoughts of incapacitation, pain, dependency, or death. Fear can be particularly troublesome for a young person with progressive muscle weakness who senses he or she is becoming more and more dependent. The questions that I am most frequently asked are "Will I be in pain?" and "What will happen if I can't breathe and I have to go to the hospital?" A major fear for many young people with neuro-muscular weakness is the possibility of a tracheotomy and dependency on a respirator. If the tracheotomy and/or life-support system occurs, the decision to go ahead should always be made by the young person, if he or she is mentally competent, and *not* by the family or physician. I be-lieve that each of us has the right to say what we do and don't want to do with our life and be in charge of our own destiny as long as we are intellectually able to do so. It seems tragic to me when a young person's wishes are not respected by the family or physicians.

Privacy

If lung or heart failure caused by extreme muscle weakness is becoming evident in your child, it will be difficult to follow any kind of a normal daily schedule. One of the greatest problems may be how to provide a young person with privacy if he or she is totally dependent on others for care. If you are faced with this situation, you have to be most sensitive to your son's or daughter's desire to be as much in charge of his or her body as possible. This may mean hiring a male aide for a son or some-one other than a mother or sister to help care for a daughter. Parents who assume almost total care for older youths or teenagers put the young people in a position of great dependency, so that they feel just like little kids. This can understandably cause a great deal of anger and resentment, which may come out in countless ways, such as picking on brothers and sisters, inappropriate language, sullenness, or depression. If you see any of these behaviors in your young person with advanced muscle weakness, then I would think carefully about how much privacy you are allowing and how many choices he or she is still able to make about dressing, time alone, and other activities of daily living.

> Let your child decide, as much as possible, what he can and and cannot do. You'll have to learn which of your son's friends you can trust and try to put as many worries aside as possible.

Quality of Life

It is the quality of life that most of us want and not the quantity. Close relationships with family and friends, privacy, freedom, the ability to make choices, and a good sense of one's self are all part of this. When these exist, life can be special, whether it is short or long. I've known many beautiful, healthy young people with every advantage in the world who have had lives filled with pain, loneliness, and a sense of inadequacy because they were missing these things.

The best way to give kids a good quality of life is to expect them to do their share in the family, follow the family rules, and treat everyone with respect. Please don't be afraid to expect your child or young person to do his or her best and to live each day as fully as possible.

One special young man with Duchenne dystrophy, who lived just twenty-two years, exemplified the art of living this way. He was one of the happiest and most secure kids I've ever known, and each day for him seemed to be filled with friends and activities. When he died, more than three hundred people attended his beautiful memorial service. This was a great testimony both to the kind of life he had lived and to the parenting he had received. Several years later, I asked his mother and stepfather, "What was it you did to help make Kenny such a remarkable young man?"

His mother thought for a while and said, "I really don't know. I treated him just like my other children, expecting him to do his share of the family work and also to be sensitive to the needs of others. We didn't look too far into the future, but tried to do the best we could each day."

I think that if all of us, as parents, can follow this example, our young people will be very fortunate. There is an art to living, and having some fun each day, really communicating, lots of hugs, and a feeling of mutual respect are all a part of this art. I hope that you, as parents, will find that your child's neuromuscular disorder acts as a positive force rather than a negative one and that you can survive the many ups and downs you will encounter.

ELEVEN

◆ ◆ ◆

Helping Develop Your Child's Coping Skills

O ne of the most important things that you can do, as parents, is to help your child develop good self-esteem and be as independent as possible. Yes, this may result in some bruised feelings and perhaps even falls, but it's very difficult to develop a good feeling about yourself if you are never allowed to try new things and everything is always done for you. By doing as much as possible for yourself, you develop both coping and problem-solving skills, as well as the ability to handle frustration.

Self-Esteem

Children who feel good about themselves generally reflect their parents' view of them, and do try to rise to the level of their parents' expectations. If you always try to stress your children's positive traits, and not the negative ones, they should feel secure and loved and develop good ego strength. A single derogatory or negative statement may be remembered for years, and I'm sure we all remember one or more from our parents or teachers. It's hard, I know, to be positive and cheerful as a parent in the face of perhaps increasing muscle weakness, but it can be done. For example, looking at things that are working rather than those that are not can make a big difference in your child's overall attitude toward life.

Discipline

One of the hardest things for all of us, as parents, is to learn how to discipline a child. Today, with the advent of HMOs, family doctors and pediatricians are spending less time with parents discussing discipline and other parenting skills. Also, fewer young couples today have parents close by to help teach them about parenting.

It's important for all kids, even those with a muscle disorder, to have consistent fair and firm discipline right from the beginning. Kids with chronic illness learn very early how to manipulate a situation, and particularly their parents, to their advantage.

> It will be hard to discipline your disabled child, but you'll find that he or she wants to be treated just like his brothers and sisters.

It's particularly difficult to discipline a child with muscle weakness, and if the disorder is hereditary, parents may feel considerable guilt as well. Discipline really is love, and by establishing limits, parents teach kids how to survive and hopefully flourish in the real world. Kids will always test the limits; that's just the nature of children. But all of them do want to know what the boundaries are, because only then do they feel secure and loved. Children know that they're not ready to run the family and, if there are no boundaries, they don't know how to act. Kids are particularly clever about playing one parent against the other, so adults in a two-parent family have to stick together and not be separated by a skillfully manipulating child. Tough love pays off in large dividends, both for parents and grandparents. If you spoil kids with neuromuscular diseases, it not only hurts the young people, but everyone who spends any time with them.

> Kids don't want to be treated any differently from their brothers and sisters. They wish that you'd yell at them just like you do the others.
>
> ◆
>
> Kids use behavior modification of their parents and others from the time they are small babies, so you have to be really careful, particularly if they have a disability.

Mealtimes

One of the hardest times to discipline kids is at meals. Because life today is so hectic for most families, meals often consist of fast food or quickly prepared snacks eaten on the run. Unfortunately, today a family that sits around the table and eats together is a rarity. If a family does eat together, the TV or radio may be on, so that no real conversation occurs. In this situation, children don't learn table manners or how to carry on any kind of communication.

My advice is to make dinners, at least, a special time. Talking together and sharing thoughts and feelings helps keep the lines of communication open and also helps develop increased closeness. Topics of special interest to the whole family such as school reports, and even special problems that need to be solved, can be discussed around the table. I know from experience that it's hard to plan a sit-down meal every night, but I urge each of you to think about how to make this part of your daily schedule.

Letting everyone participate in meal planning and even shopping for food together makes mealtime more of a family activity. Also, it helps kids develop tools of independence that they will need in order to live, hopefully on their own later on. Even kids with muscle weakness should be able to put together some kind of meal, or at least do the planning for one, by the time they are teenagers. If they can help with the actual preparation and cooking, that is even better. Some young people with considerable muscle weakness have said to me that they don't see any point in learning to do things for themselves because they know that they will always need help. My reply is that we don't know if that will be true and, if even it is, they still need to know how to do things in order to take charge and tell an aide or helper what needs to be done.

A child with progressive muscle weakness may need to have food cut up or, at some point, may even need help with eating. Adaptive utensils can be ordered from the Preston/Fred Sammons catalog (1-800-631-7277), as well as from other medical-supply houses. Special utensils with hand supports or long handles, and even made-to-order cups can be found in the catalogs of many medical supply houses.

Chewing and swallowing are not usually problems in children with neuromuscular diseases, but occasionally they can be. If they are, soft foods and things that have been cut before being brought to the table make life easier for everyone and may also help a child with considerable muscle weakness feel less conspicuous.

There are children who love to be babied and want to stay dependent, but this isn't good for them or anyone else in the family. It can particularly cause difficulties with siblings if they realize that the young person with the muscle disease could do more if he or she just tried.

> You just have to let your kids scrape their knees sometimes.

Real behavioral issues and discipline problems often develop around food and at mealtimes, so it's very important that your kids know the rules. If a kid has to be sent away from the table because of poor behavior, offering food to the child later simply defeats the purpose. No child is going to starve, so I urge you not to offer food later if a real discipline problem has occurred at mealtime.

Part of making meals as pleasant as possible is setting an attractive table and having the food look appealing. A pretty plant or fresh flowers on the table can also make mealtimes more cheerful. Most kids enjoy setting the table with their own special decorations, or they can use colorful napkins, paper place mats, or ones made of easy-care material. These can be purchased at low cost in many stores.

Children who are small eaters need to be watched so that they don't fill up on juice or milk. Also, kids who snack a lot between meals usually lose their appetite at mealtime. If your child is snacking between meals and not eating at mealtimes, I would cut back on cookies and other treats for a few days and see if more isn't eaten during regular meals. Remember, however, that a child who cannot run and play actively does not need as many calories as he or she would otherwise.

A good breakfast with some protein is important for every child, and particularly for kids with muscle weakness. If you have little time available, I would suggest trying one of the following:

◆ instant oatmeal
◆ instant cream of rice
◆ hard-boiled eggs
◆ instant sausages
◆ bacon
◆ yogurt

Lunches can be prepared the night before, or small lunch packs can be purchased now for kids, although these are quite expensive. Peanut butter is a good food for kids, as are tuna and cheese, and there are individual cans and packets of these foods available now for young people. Remember, though, that peanut butter and cheese can be constipating, so if a child has trouble with hard bowel movements, be aware of what is eaten. Many parents are surprised to find out that apples and bananas can be constipating. If constipation is a problem, as it often is with muscle weakness, things like bran muffins, carrot sticks, fruit rolls, and fresh fruits should be added to the diet. Most kids are not great about eating raw or cooked green vegetables, but often they will eat small carrot sticks, celery, or even broccoli cut up into small pieces.

Chores

With an increasing number of mothers and fathers holding jobs outside the house, most boys and girls have little opportunity to try to do things for themselves. Also, most caretakers don't take the time to teach kids how to problem-solve, since it's easier to do things themselves. But learning new skills usually requires the guidance and aid of an adult. If kids don't learn how to do even small things for themselves, how will they learn to perform adult work and develop the self-esteem that comes from a job well done?

> Tell your child that you won't always be at her beck and call, so she'll have to find a way to do things for herself as much as possible.

Daily chores can teach children the stick-to-itiveness that is needed to finish an uninteresting task, since we all have jobs we don't like to do. If children learn good work habits early on, these will stand them in good stead in the years ahead and also help develop a sense of confidence and good self-esteem.

Chores added to kids' daily routines can seem like an unnecessary burden. But as one outstanding parent said, "The message is that my child is handicapped, yes, but helpless, no! Also, I have repeatedly stressed to her that I have no intention of being her personal servant for the rest of her life."

> Don't adopt a mind-set of handicapped thinking. It's real easy to do this.

Kids can be quite inventive and creative in their play, and they can use these same abilities to devise ways to accomplish things for themselves and to complete household chores. Given the opportunity, children often discover ways to accomplish tasks that wouldn't occur to their parents. First they can learn small things, and then, later on, be given more complex tasks. Some parents feel that planning how to accomplish tasks takes more time and energy than it's worth. On a day-to-day basis, I'm sure that this is true, but not if you look at the long-term results. One excellent parent said, "I demand my daughter's cooperation in figuring out ways to do things she claims are impossible. The benefits are fantastic. This summer, at the age of fifteen, wheelchair and all, she has been hired for her first real job, working in an amusement park. It's the beginning of her road to independence. I would like to believe that making demands on her and rewarding them with an allowance gives her some initiative in this direction."

The chores chart in Appendix C offers some suggestions for chores, which parents can adapt for their child's age and abilities. I suggest, too, that an allowance be tied to the completion of chores, since this helps a child learn that earning money is based on job performance. Some parents argue that chores should be done without a reward or allowance, since that is the kid's contribution to the household. Many mothers and fathers feel, too, that an allowance should simply be given and not earned just because the children are part of the family.

One family who had a child with muscle weakness devised a system of accumulating a certain number of stickers on the chore chart, to be redeemed for prizes. Fifty stickers equaled a trip to the ice-cream store or other treat, which also created a family outing. If a chore was not done, the children were reminded once and then, if the chore was still left undone, five points were deducted. Other parents take away a child's TV viewing or some other fun activity if tasks are not completed.

Choices

As children grow and develop, they need to be given more and more choices about what they want to wear, the friends with whom they wish to spend time, when to do their homework, as well as their chores. Parents of a child who is developing more and more muscle weakness may find it difficult to allow choices simply because of the child's increasing dependency. Even making small choices, though, helps maintain self-esteem and some feeling of independence.

> Appreciate the small things your child can do. Always stress the positive.

Fun

It truly is the quality of life that most of us want and not the quantity. Fun and special times are particularly important to kids who are not able to do all the things their friends can. Daily fun, good communication, and lots of hugs bring a family close together and make life special. But to accomplish this everyone in the family has to work together, and there has to be some good planning.

Parents of children who develop more and more muscle weakness because of a progressive neuromuscular disease often dread the future so much that life becomes bleak. When this happens, depression can start seeping into all aspects of a family's life. If this begins to happen or is happening in your family, some individual counseling, or even family therapy, may be needed. There is no question but that anger and resentment can be strong forces in a family if a child has weakness from a neuromuscular disorder. How can a child or his parents not feel terrible anger, particularly if the disorder is progressive? Kids are amazingly perceptive and may sense things that parents and doctors haven't told them, but they certainly know something is wrong if they can't keep up with their friends, brothers, or sisters. Also, when there are frequent doctors' appointments or visits to a physical therapist, a great deal of either visible or hidden anger can be present. If this anger doesn't have a healthy way of being expressed, it will come out in some other form, such as soiled underpants, temper tantrums, forbidden words, or striking out at siblings, parents, or friends. A decline in school performance or a change in personality may be a tip-off, too, that emotions and feelings are not being expressed or handled well.

> If even a minor triumph occurs, have a celebration. It's important!

Some kids, when they are depressed, refuse to socialize with friends and family and hide away in their rooms. This may be due to anger about the muscle disease, having to wear braces, or being forced to use a wheelchair. Many kids, too, may have a feeling of impending doom or anxiety. Though we all have days when life seems pretty gray, if *every* day seems that way for a child or a parent, some help is needed right away. Tip-offs to depression are withdrawal from normal activities, a change in personality or appetite, weight loss, other medical problems, or difficulty sleeping.

There can be little doubt, then, that finding ways for kids to continue socializing with both nondisabled and disabled friends is important. Children who are gradually forced out of normal activities because of their physical limitations may begin to feel great loneliness. Adaptations could make it possible for a child to continue doing things with his friends. It is amazing how creative both kids and adults can be if they really put their minds to solving problems like this.

Friends

Many parents of children without a disability prefer to have their children play only with other nondisabled children. This certainly creates difficulty when you're trying to find friends for your child with muscle weakness. However, I suspect kids from families like these are not ones with whom you want your children to play anyway.

So you may have to be quite resourceful to find both nondisabled and disabled playmates for your child. I would begin by calling your local YMCA/YWCA or community recreation center. Boy and Girl Scouts, Camp Fire Girls, and Indian Guides are other possible resources. Many cities have parenting hot lines and also newsletters that should give you ideas about numbers to call.

> Children need friends, but if your child has lots of muscle weakness, kids may stay away. So you have to be very resourceful in finding friends and activities for your child.

Any effort you make to keep your child involved with friends and out doing things, rather than just sitting at home watching TV, will bring great rewards.

Living fully each day may become a challenge not only for you as parents, but also for your child. There will be good days and bad days when you think that you just can't go the distance, but all you can do is your best. None of us is or ever will be a perfect parent, but always keep in mind that lots of fun, hugs, and laughter scattered through the days are the principal ingredients to make everyone's spirits rise.

TWELVE

◆ ◆ ◆

Finding the Best School Program

Helping a child become an independent, happy adult depends not only on the family life but also, to a great extent, on the education that is received. Unfortunately, with the increasing bureaucracy and decreasing amount of money available for today's students, it is often an uphill battle for parents to get a good education for their children. And, when special needs are involved, some real barriers may have to be overcome.

Fortunately, the majority of children with early neuromuscular diseases do not need special programs or teachers. If, however, your child has considerable muscle weakness at a young age, or an associated problem, such as a learning problem, he or she may need additional help right from the beginning. This help may include physical therapy, adaptive P.E., special equipment, or accessibility to places in the school. Some of this assistance will or should be provided by the school

School is always a problem for the first few days. Give your child a pat answer to tell the kids what is wrong.

◆

A label such as retardation or progressive muscle disease can be a predictive thing, so be careful about labels.

◆

When your child has special needs, you may find that you are treated like an unwanted salesperson. Don't let anyone do this to you. Just keep on putting your foot in the door.

system; while other help may be available from state children's services. Unfortunately, each state does things a little differently, so I would suggest talking to other parents, a parents' advocacy group, special education personnel at your child's school, and someone at the state children's services if you can't get help at a local level.

> Beware that schools have learned lots of tricks to keep parents in line.

If you feel that your child needs something that is not provided in a regular class or school, it is very important that you know how to navigate the special education maze.

Specific guidelines to help children with many kinds of disabilities were established in 1975 and originally defined by Public Law 94-124. This was amended in 1997 and is now called IDEA. The laws state that if a child's disability is covered, any needed special education should be provided at no cost to parents. It is important to note that kids are covered through their twenty-second birthday if they have not yet graduated from high school.

The law also says that a child's schooling should be in the "least restrictive environment." Thus, if a child needs some special help but can still be in a regular classroom this is required. However, you have to be very careful, because school personnel will often mainstream a child simply because it is less expensive for them. Many times special help is not provided, and the child just sits in a large classroom learning very little. Mainstreaming without special help or aides generally doesn't work for younger children who have special needs, and if a child has progressive muscle weakness or an associated learning disability, mainstreaming may be the very worst possible choice.

> No matter what your child's needs are, be careful that the school doesn't just mainstream him or her because they don't want to be bothered or spend extra money.
>
> ◆
>
> Schools don't usually identify the child's separate needs, but just lump them all together.

I am concerned, as are many educators and other professionals, about the tendency to put even severely disabled children in large regular classes with minimal special help. This may be good for the school budget, but I've seen far too many children left behind when it comes time for junior high, high school, and college. Look at a mainstream program (sometimes referred to as "full inclusion") with somewhat of a jaundiced eye if your child has special needs unless excellent additional tutoring or instructional support services (including consultation with inclusion specialists) can be provided. As one attorney who specializes in special education cases said: "Full inclusion works only if you have the needed support services for the student and support from the regular education teacher. If the regular education teacher does not feel supported by special education staff, inclusion will not work."

The types of disabilities that make a child eligible for special education include problems with bones and joints; muscle weakness; learning disability (which means difficulty with reading, writing, or how information is processed); deafness; blindness; and less than normal intellectual capacity—that is, mental retardation. Also, the category of "other health impairments" is included in special education and covers a wide range of disabilities, genetic abnormalities, and many other medical problems.

It may be that your child does not need a special education class but just some daily help in special ways which is called accommodation. Accommodation also means making accessible areas used by a student with special needs, such as bathrooms, classrooms, or the cafeteria.

In general, when special education services are needed they are provided on the regular school campus. However, in some states, there are still classes, designated as "orthopedically handicapped," where children with physical disabilities are taught and receive therapy. These are outdated, but still very much in existence in many states. The argument is that if physical and occupational therapists are on site, children can receive the special help they need without transporting them to a special therapy unit and back to their regular schools. The reality is that children in these special schools often do not get the education or socialization they need when the emphasis is primarily on their disability. I have had many children like this as patients, and find that most fall far behind when they go on into regular school programs.

> Be sure that your child is included in everything at school, or he or she can become very isolated and lonely.

If a child has to be hospitalized for a considerable period of time, it is possible to have instruction provided by the school district. However, children with neuromuscular disorders seldom need this, because even after major procedures, such as surgery on the spine, the kids are out of the hospital quickly and back at school. It would be a rare situation where a child needs tutoring out of the classroom, unless he or she were hospitalized on a long-term basis in a nursing care facility or rehabilitation center. This could happen if a family elected to use a mechanical means of life support and yet did not feel capable of caring for the young person at home. Today however, there are children with ventilators who attend school with their personal aides.

Adaptive Physical Education

All children need some kind of daily exercise, and for kids with muscle weakness, exercise can make the difference in their ability to continue walking for a much longer time if their disorder is progressive.

Many schools make no arrangements for a special needs kid unless it is written into the child's Individual Educational Plan (IEP). Even if it is, exercise plans may not be made without some real pushing by the parents.

Children who are unable to keep up with their classmates in physical activities should have a program that is adapted to their needs. This is called "adaptive physical education," and there are specific individuals who are trained as adaptive physical education teachers. They work with children and young people who cannot take part in regular physical education (P.E.) programs

> You may have to fight your school to get any kind of sports activities for your child. They can adapt things for his needs, and he'll be much happier.
>
> ◆
>
> You may find that constipation is one of the worst problems that your child has. It took us a long time to find out that it was related to our child's muscle weakness and her limited diet.

by planning games or other activities in which the child can participate. This helps maintain muscle strength and also prevents a child from sitting on the sidelines.

It always saddens me to see a child watching basketball or some other sport, no arrangements having been made for him or her to participate. There are many activities that can be readily adapted for kids, as has been demonstrated by wheelchair sports organizations and worldwide teams for tennis, basketball, and soccer. Any school can have a tether ball lowered to meet the needs of a child using a wheelchair, and other activities, such as shuffleboard, can also be adapted. Blowing Ping-Pong balls or balloons across a line can improve lung function, as can other similar activities. No child should ever have to sit by the side of a playground, but, instead, adaptive P.E. needs to be written into the child's Individual Educational Plan, and the child should receive this daily or at least three times a week.

Most schools prefer to keep children with disabilities out of physical education programs because of the fear that kids will fall and be injured. I understand this concern, but every sport carries a risk for the players, and I've never heard of a high school that eliminated its football team just because a player might be injured!

> You may find that your director of special education is always "missing in action."

I recently heard quite an unbelievable story from one of my teenage patients who has the severe form of autosomal recessive muscular dystrophy. She was getting no exercise at school and, when I inquired if there were other kids getting adaptive P.E., she said, "Yes, but all they do is walk around and pick up the trash."

When I asked our special-education attorney consultant how we could get adaptive P.E. worked into the teenager's school program, it seemed that it wasn't as simple as I had thought. Because this student is a bright A student, she needs no accommodations or other special help in school. So, the first step was to draft a letter for the girl's mother to send to the Department of Special Education to have the student assessed for adaptive P.E. Since the administrator was probably going to say that she didn't qualify under special education criteria, the next step, according to the attorney, would be to contact the 504 coordinator. The attorney explained to me that under Section 504 of the Rehabilitation Act, individuals with disabilities in programs funded by the federal government "should not be excluded from participation in, be denied the benefits of, or be subjected to discrimination under any program or activity receiving federal financial assistance." Thus, if a program is supported by or receives money from the government, it is required to allow individuals with disabilities to participate. In 1990, this law was amended to cover education so that accommodations are now required for disabled students who need adaptive P.E., special equipment such as tape recorders or word processors, or accommodations that may be necessary for students who require extra time to take tests or who are unable to write.

Each school district *must* have a 504 coordinator, and you should be able to find out who this is and how the law pertains to your child by calling your school district's department of education. Interestingly enough, I called one school district recently, and the director of special education refused to tell me who the 504 coordinator was. I simply turned it over to a special education attorney, and she took care of it. The mother in this particular case, who had been fighting for three years to get some help, said, "How interesting that a little piece of paper from an attorney can make such a difference."

If a district is out of compliance or not providing what your child needs, call the Office of Civil Rights. You should be provided with information and a complaint form. A complaint filed with the federal Office of Civil Rights will result in an investigation and this office has real clout. Also they are mandated to investigate any compliance complaints.

> Be aware that administrators may try to keep you, the parents, and your child's teachers in the dark about available services so the district won't have to pay for them.

A due process hearing can also be requested, I'm told, under Section 504 for determination of necessary accommodations or services. Unfortunately, however, the guidelines are not as clearly defined as those under the IDEA.

One important thing for parents to know is that Section 504 continues coverage for kids on into the college years and adult life, whereas the IDEA law does not.

Unfortunately, even though the Section 504 and the IDEA have specific requirements, no federal money was provided to enforce and pay for the services mandated by

> Be sure that your child's school uncouples the educational needs of your child from any financial considerations.

Section 504. Also, the funds provided under IDEA are more and more inadequate to provide necessary programs for disabled children, so many times kids are not identified who need help.

Special Education Qualifications

Each state has different guidelines as to how quickly a child must be tested or assessed to see if he or she qualifies for special education. These guidelines should be clearly stated in the brochure that you obtain from your local school or county special education office. If you feel, after you review these guidelines, that your child needs special education services, a school district has a limited number of days to work out an assessment plan once you have requested it. Tests may be done by a psychologist, a physical, occupational, or speech therapist, a special education teacher, or an adaptive P.E. teacher, depending on your child's special needs. In California, for example, a school district has fifteen days to develop an assessment plan after parents fill out an application for special education. Then, once a parent or parents sign and approve this testing plan, the district must hold an IEP, or Individual Educational Program, meeting within fifty days. It is required that a child must have completed all the tests that he or she needs by that time.

If you decide that your child does need special education help, I suggest that you put on your desk or wall calendar both the date you have applied and the date the assessments must be completed. It is extremely important to keep on top of this, so if you haven't heard from the school district by the dates you've marked, then I would call your district's special education office. It is wise to have handy the name of one person there with whom you can keep in touch. Having a good relationship with the secretary or secretaries in the special education office is important, because they can be extremely helpful in seeing that your application is filled out correctly and that it gets to the right individual or individuals. Mail can be sent to the wrong address or even get lost, so keep checking.

> Go right to the top of the school system. Get to know the director of special education, the president of the school board, the principal, and the resource specialist.

If your child has reading or learning problems, and you can afford an outside assessment, I would urge you to do so. For this, you will need an educational psychologist with special training and experience in testing children with learning problems or those with physical disabilities or mental delay. An outside assessment should take several hours; sometimes it is done over a period of two or three days, whereas school personnel do not have the luxury of this kind of time and may do a much more limited assessment. Since most children don't settle down in short periods of time, this testing can be unsatisfactory. One mother said that the school psychologist did her child's assessment over the phone, basing it on the answers she gave to questions! If your child is deemed by the special education department to be ineligible for help, you can ask that the assessment be repeated the following year. This may also be necessary if there has been a change in the status of your child's disorder, such as increasing muscle weakness. The purpose of testing is to see if a child's disability has a significant impact on his or her ability to learn.

A child who has significant muscle weakness, contractures, or difficulty walking because of a neuromuscular disorder, should qualify for special help under the category of "orthopedic disability." Some children, unfortunately, have more than one physical disability or even one or more genetic abnormalities. There may be an associated significant hearing loss, as was the case with one of my patients who had limb girdle muscular dystrophy, or a learning disability, as is the case with a young patient of mine who has Emery-Dreifuss muscular dystrophy. One of my little patients with Duchenne dystrophy also has Down syndrome, and another teen-ager with Charcot-Marie-Tooth disease is autistic. Thus, these children require several different kinds of special help.

If a boy has early Duchenne dystrophy with no learning disability or developmental delay, he may not need special education help until the muscle weakness becomes progressive; then some accommodations will be needed. A child with Duchenne dystrophy who is quite

> Tell your child's teacher as much as you can about his or her muscle problem. Otherwise, no matter what happens, the teacher and other school people will think that the muscle disease is the cause of *any* problem.

learning-disabled or even mentally delayed may need help right from the beginning. I had one patient with Duchenne dystrophy who was quite bright, while his younger sibling who also had Duchenne dystrophy, was severely delayed cognitively and required a very different program.

The process of assessment differs with the individual who is testing, but by law a child must be tested in his primary language for the test results to be valid. A test such as the Stanford-Binet is inadequate for children with marked muscle weakness, since it requires good hand function and motor ability. If you have any questions about a school assessment, I urge you to have outside testing done. This testing can be worth its weight in gold.

Once the tests have been completed, an Individual Educational Program (IEP) should be developed by you, school personnel, and any outside consultants you wish to bring to the IEP meeting. By law, an IEP meeting cannot be held unless one parent is present.

Individual Educational Program (IEP)

> The IEP is an individual educational plan, but most schools don't tailor their programs to the individual.

It is extremely important that you know what is required in an IEP if your child is going to need special help. Under Federal Law 94-142, which is now IDEA, a procedure called an Individual Educational Program, or IEP, was established whereby a child with special needs must have specific assessments. Then, a program tailored to these needs must be developed. Assessments may include occupational or physical therapy, speech, adaptive P.E., and educational tests. Sometimes these tests are done by experienced professionals, but if there is a shortage of personnel or money, a school's test results may lack substance.

> Try to always include your child's next year's teacher at the spring IEP meeting.

The IEP is developed by a team that may include a psychologist, a speech therapist, a special education teacher, a resource specialist (who sometimes has special training in testing children for learning disabilities), an adaptive P.E. teacher, a physical therapist, an occupational therapist, and an administrator or representative from the special education department.

Components of the IEP

Once the assessments have been completed, a specific time and date are established for an IEP team meeting. This meeting should be at your convenience as well as that of the professionals or support people you want to bring with you. It can be difficult to arrange a time convenient for everyone, since some of the school personnel may come from other sites. However, it is required that a minimum of four school personnel be present including your child's regular teacher and a district representative other than the child's special education teacher—and one or both of the child's parents. Often, many other professionals are included, such as a speech therapist, a psychologist, occupational and physical therapists, as well as an adaptive P.E. teacher. *Remember, though, that the IEP team must include you, the parent!*

> The school people may try to intimidate you at your child's IEP meeting. Take along a friend or an advocate and also tape-record the meeting; it makes a real difference. It seems that IEP meetings and fair hearings are just an employment program for special-education people, so quickly learn the laws and what you can expect for your child.

The IEP meeting should include the following:

1. Each professional should give the result of the assessments that were done. (Do not hesitate to ask questions and request explanations of any terms or words you do not understand.)

2. A list of short-term objectives and long-term goals must be established for the year.

> Join a parent advocacy group if there's one in your area. They often have seminars and discussions about how to get the most out of IEPs and other school problems.

3. Related services, such as a one-to-one aide, specialized tutoring, transportation, counseling, physical therapy, occupational therapy, or adaptive P.E., need to be discussed.

4. The dates that services will start and how often they are to be given should be specified. (For example, if speech therapy is to

be given once a week on an individual basis, or several times a week in a group, this should be noted, and also the length of time that the therapy is to last—i.e., thirty to sixty minutes.)

5. If a child is to be in a regular school class for any time during the day, this should also be clearly stated.

Goals and services that could be specific for kids with neuromuscular disease are the following (these should be individualized, and they are dependent on a child's (1) age, (2) intellectual ability, and (3) motor ability):

If, for example, a five-year-old boy with Duchenne dystrophy is severely mentally delayed, the goals would be more limited—learning colors, naming objects, and naming the parts of his body, for instance. The development of self-help skills might be more appropriate for this child, which would require the services of an occupational therapist, and would thus be educationally required.

If a child has progressive mental deterioration, as is seen with some of the severe mitochondrial disorders, goals will need to be adjusted as the condition changes. When this occurs, it can be difficult for both parents and school personnel to keep up.

If a child can't write because of muscle weakness or contractures, special arrangements may be needed for untimed tests, a specially adapted computer keyboard, a typewriter, and/or a calculator. Also, the services of an occupational therapist or physical therapist are important, in this case, to help a child perform school tasks. An aide might be needed to give the special help required. Once again, as a child grows, the child's condition may develop increased muscle strength, as can occur with some of the congenital myopathies, or goals can be changed if contractures improve with good stretching.

Monitoring the IEP

If an IEP has been developed previously, there should be an ongoing discussion about what goals and objectives the child has achieved.

You can request a new IEP at any time, if you put this stipulation in writing. So if you are not satisfied with an IEP—for example, if a professional or partner whose input you wanted was unavailable at the time the IEP was written—your child is not locked into it.

Once the IEP is signed and put into effect, parents should constantly monitor services to see that they are being provided at the level that was originally agreed upon. Many schools have a frequent turnover of personnel, and even though services may have been specified in an IEP, they frequently are not given, so, as a parent, you need to watch closely.

> You'll find that a school will move more quickly if you tell them they are not in compliance with the IEP.

One way to check what your child is doing is to have a notebook go back and forth from his or her regular teacher to you. A record can be kept about what services your child is receiving and how things are going. I would also suggest frequent visits to the classroom to be sure that all is well. Be sure to first request permission to visit a class, both from the principal and from your child's teacher, so that no problems develop. Remember that establishing a good working relationship with the staff in your child's school is extremely important.

Most school personnel want to give your child the best possible educational program, but, as in real life, there are the control-folks, the manipulative ones, and those who are just plain inefficient and uninterested.

Using Outside Consultants

By law, parents can have done any outside testing or assessments that they wish, and the results of these tests must be reviewed at the IEP meeting. (Some school personnel may be unhappy about having this occur and may say that it is not legally possible. Do stand your ground because outside testing of your child is your right.) You are also permitted to have any outside specialists come to your child's IEP meeting. I have attended many such meetings and found the climate to be friendly in some cases, while it was quite chilly in others. My presence sometimes made some of the school personnel most uncomfortable. One mother noted that she was treated far differently when she went with her husband to an IEP meeting and feels that it is important that you take your partner, if at all possible. She said that "it shows the school that you are a united team, especially if you want something done for your child."

To get the most out of your child's individual educational program meeting, I suggest the following guidelines:

1. Doing your homework about what IEPs should cover.
2. Role-playing what you want to say with a friend or your partner.
3. Buying and using a small handheld tape recorder.*
4. Bringing a file of your child's assessments to the IEP.
5. Dressing in a businesslike way when you attend the IEP.
6. Being pleasant but matter-of-fact.
7. Having both parents attend, if possible. If just one parent can go, take another child's parent who understands the process.

*You must inform the school 24 hours in advance that you plan to tape the IEP.

Remember that the IEP is a procedure established by law. You don't want to be lulled into thinking that it is just a friendly school get-together where you might feel uncomfortable about clearly stating your child's needs.

If you are not satisfied with the proceedings or content of the IEP meeting, don't be intimidated. Remember, you as a parent, are an important member of the IEP team, and the law is on your side. *You do have power*, which can be exercised by:

1. Not signing the IEP if you disagree with anything in it, or requesting to observe the proposed placement for your child before signing and agreeing to the IEP.
2. Tape-recording the IEP meeting, so your advocate or partner can listen to it again.
3. Asking for a new IEP.
4. Asking for a procedure called a due process hearing if the IEP is unsatisfactory.
5. Enlisting the help of a lawyer who specializes in special education problems.

Some things to watch out for from school personnel at IEP meetings:

1. Telling you that your child must be in the class they suggest.
2. Refusing to read or review reports from outside assessments.

3. Setting the IEP for a time or place that is inconvenient for you or anyone else whom you wish to have attend.
4. Delaying in setting a date for the IEP.
5. Making you feel you are a demanding, difficult parent or parents. (One parent noted that "this is a situation that parents must deal with a lot, depending on the child. Sometimes parents just give up the fight because they get worn down.")
6. Not allowing enough time for the IEP, so that reports and discussions are rushed.

Disputes Between Families and Schools

If you have a dispute with your child's school regarding either the education or needed services, then a regular procedure has been set up to help resolve the disagreement. If you do not agree with the IEP, you can file a request asking for an administrative due process hearing. When you file for a due process hearing, a list of attorneys or advocates must be provided so that you can choose to have representation. One parent noted that "sometimes just threatening to have a hearing can get results."

The maximum number of days allowed between the day you file your request and the hearing of the dispute is variable from state to state. For example, in California, the hearing officer must make a decision about the dispute within fifty days of receiving the request for a hearing. The state contracts with a private group that provides an impartial hearing officer, who issues a decision after hearing the facts. The decision can be appealed to either a state or federal court if you disagree.

If you encounter major problems, there are special education and children's attorneys who will take cases to court. However, the success record with this approach is variable, and you have to factor in the cost of your time and money. If you win your case, the school district is required to reimburse you for attorneys' fees and costs.

Mediation

Parents who have filed for a due process hearing are now given the opportunity to first meet with a mediator. In California, once a due process hearing is requested, parents are automatically assigned a mediator. However, mediation can be waived by either you or the school district. Many disputes are settled during mediation, saving both you and the district emotional stress, time, money, and energy. Remember, though, that a mediated agreement is binding.

Moving

If you have to move, examine your child's school records to be sure nothing with which you don't agree is going to be sent on.

If you are moving to a new school district and have been satisfied with your child's IEP and overall school program, there are some things you should know:

1. The IEP should go with you to the new school district.
2. Placement in the new school can be as it was under the old IEP for thirty days, and then a new IEP should be written.
3. If you are not pleased with the new IEP, don't sign it and write your concerns on the forms. Also, remember that it can always be changed within a few months.

One parent told me that they moved their daughter from one school to another within the same district, and the staff and the principal at the new school were wonderful about following all the goals and requirements of the IEP.

Conclusion

Because an education is so important for your child, it should be a top priority after you establish the medical care you need. The most important thing to remember in trying to get the best possible education for your child is that *you do have power*. If you focus your energies on just the two or three problems you want resolved and stay in close communication with key special education people, this will help a lot. Remember that it's important to establish a good rapport with the personnel at your child's school. One parent told me that their adaptive P.E. teacher acted as a go-between between the school individuals and herself, and she felt that this help has been "invaluable" in achieving goals for her daughter.

I would certainly urge you to avoid using an attorney, if possible. No one wants to be a thorny, difficult parent, and schools don't want to take on time-consuming and expensive legal battles. As one parent of a child with a congenital muscle disease noted, "sometimes just mentioning that you are willing to consult an attorney will help resolve problems that may have perhaps been long-standing."

So don't give up, but just keep in mind the long-term goal that kids with a good education have a better chance at succeeding than do those in classrooms with teachers who have limited expectations and allow them to get by with minimal effort. You will find some wonderful, dedicated teachers and school personnel along the way, so if you can enlist their help and keep focused on your goals, the educational battle will hopefully be a successful one. Good luck!

THIRTEEN

◆ ◆ ◆

How to Be a Strong Advocate for Your Child

P arents of children with neuromuscular diseases tell me that one of their hardest, almost daily tasks is battling to get the treatment and services that their children need.

You probably will become very "bureaucratically challenged" in your efforts to get adequate education, equipment, and help for your child.

◆

When you get tired of all the bureaucratic runarounds, take a mental vacation from time to time. Go inward for a while to retreat. Then, once your energies are renewed, you can pick up the battle again.

First and foremost, they have to fight through the medical maze to find a doctor knowledgeable about children's neuromuscular disorders and be sure that the diagnosis is correct.

Second, they have to constantly battle to get and keep adequate medical coverage.

Third, they have to push hard to find agencies, such as state children's services, regional centers, and the Muscular Dystrophy Association, to help pay for equipment, respite care, home health aides, physical therapy, occupational therapy, and many other things.

Last, they have to watch, and

often fight, their child's school to be sure that the best possible education, therapy, and adequate facilities are provided.

I'm sure each day seems like a long uphill climb to many of you.
Then, just when the top of the mountain is reached, a peaceful valley
doesn't lie ahead, but, instead, another even steeper hill is there to
climb. And on and on it goes, often
to the point of exhaustion.

So how can you and your partner, family members, and friends
find ways to be the best possible advocates for your child? There are
some important basics:

> Spend a little extra money
> on yourself, even if you think
> you can't afford it.
> (A mother)

1. Make sure you take care of yourself by eating a good diet, getting
   some exercise, and sprinkling some moments of relaxation and
   fun in whenever you can.
2. Do as much research as possible about a particular problem by
   talking to:
   a. other parents
   b. social workers
   c. physicians
   d. educators
   e. agency personnel
3. Join a parent support group.
4. Use national information resource centers (see Appendix D)
   and newsletters to keep up to date, and use the Internet when
   possible.
5. Form an advocacy group if
   one is not available in your
   area.
6. Become active in your child's
   school PTA.
7. Research affordable legal
   help that is available if all
   else fails.
8. Become active in the local
   Muscular Dystrophy Associ-
   ation chapter or other nonprofit agency that provides information and support for your child.

> Try to find an association of
> other parents who are deal-
> ing with the same problem,
> because you need lots of
> support if you're going to
> be a strong advocate for
> your child.

Record Keeping

1. Telephone logs in which you record the date, time, and content of conversations about specific problems can be invaluable, because it is easy to forget information that later may be necessary to resolve school or other problems. These logs can be kept in notebooks of different colors to separate areas of concern.

2. Keep a correspondence notebook in chronological order.

3. Keep a small notebook to record (a) medical visits and tests; (b) dates of IEPs; (c) names, addresses, and telephone numbers of important individuals.

4. A tape recorder can be used to record information about medical, educational, or community resources or other information. It can also be taken to IEP meetings.

Letter Writing

1. Get to know your local, state, and national elected officials, since they can be invaluable in helping you solve a problem. Don't be shy about calling or writing them; elected officials are there to serve you.

2. Letters to the editor in newspapers or magazines such as *Exceptional Parent* can help connect you with parents who have a similar problem. An article in your local newspaper can also help you find parents with similar interests.

3. Both thank-you letters and letters of criticism will be needed. Hopefully, the first will outweigh the second. A single thank-you note can accomplish a great deal. The old saying that you catch more flies with honey than you do with vinegar is very true. When people know that they are appreciated, they often work that much harder to help you.

4. If you are trying to have an insurance claim processed or secure funding for some needed equipment or special therapy through a state or local government program, you will probably need to write letters over several weeks or months. Keeping copies of these letters, in chronological order, and establishing what is called a "paper trail" is all important. Letters should be as short as possible and to the point. Also, remember to either type or write them clearly, on clean white paper; the more professional they look, the more attention you will get. If you are getting no replies after repeated tries, you may need to send a carbon

copy to a lawyer who specializes in advocacy for children with special needs. It never fails to amaze me how doors begin to open when an attorney's name is mentioned. Yes, lawyers are generally expensive, but some special ones do work on sliding fee scales or for nonprofit organizations, so that they are affordable. They can be a very helpful part of your support system and also save you stress and much-needed time.

The Nuts and Bolts of Developing and Keeping a Good Support System

To be a strong advocate for your child, you need to make frequent phone calls to other parents, social workers, physicians, and other professionals who will document any special needs your child has. There are some important ways to ensure that your support system will be there for you:

> Don't ever feel vulnerable and passive, but become a warrior for your child. After a few years of dealing with bureaucratic nonaction and frustration, you will soon get fed up with all the wasted times and delays of service, but you can win if you put your energies in just a few places.

1. Appointments: If you get to your child's appointments on time without canceling frequently, you will be remembered by the staff, since punctuality seems to be getting less and less common. Also, if you pay your bills on time and bring the needed insurance and other billing information, you will also make points.

2. Needed information: When you call agencies, insurance companies, and doctor's offices, have needed information ready. A great deal of delay results when insurance forms and numbers are lost or misplaced, and when your information is outdated.

3. Your medical team: Your pediatrician or family doctor, as well as other specialists, will hopefully be part of your support system as you try to be the best possible advocate for your child. Remember, though, that the letters and phone calls that they make on your child's behalf take time and cost money. Few physicians charge for these letters and calls, and I know they often wonder if parents really appreciate the amount of time, energy, and money involved in being their advocate. So an occasional thank-you note or verbally expressing your appreciation

is all important. Many physicians say that parents who demand the most are often the least appreciative, whereas those who expect very little can't seem to say "thank you" enough.

Your doctor's staff also needs your thanks, because they are the ones who see that the letters get dictated or written and sent out, the forms are completed, and the insurance claims are submitted. Getting to know the staff's names is also important, so that you develop both good communication and accountability.

4. Schools: Getting to know the staff at your child's school can make a real difference. You can still be a strong advocate for your child even if you are friendly with the personnel. People tend to avoid prickly individuals, so try to be as pleasant as possible even though you may be angry about a placement or lack of services. If you can both develop and keep open the lines of communication with school personnel, or find one individual on the staff with whom you can communicate, this can make a real difference in achieving the desired goals for your child.

5. Community Agencies: By being knowledgeable about local or national nonprofit groups who can help your child, you can determine whether or not they are living up to their stated mandates. Remember that, as parents, you do have power, so speak up if you feel a local agency is not following its designated guidelines. But remember, it is better to work *within* the system than to take on the organization by yourself. By talking to other parents and knowledgeable community individuals, you can get some history and perspective on the organization and develop a strategy plan. No good general takes his troops into battle without knowing the strength of the enemy, their weaknesses, and the minefields he may encounter during the battle.

> As parents, the greater awareness you have of your power, the more doors you can open.

Special Help

Attorneys

Today there are lawyers who specialize in many of the problems that disabled individuals and their parents encounter. Unfortunately, good attorneys who work for nonprofit agencies often become overburdened so quickly that they cannot take on new cases. Some lawyers will take cases they feel they have a good chance of winning for no up-front money. They may bill, however, for secretarial services and litigation costs, which is called taking a case on contingency. If you find an attorney willing to do this, be sure that you have a written agreement that you understand. If you lose your case, you should not be charged anything, unless you have agreed to pay filing fees and secretarial costs. Under some of the laws protecting disabled children in school, there are provisions for district payment of fees and costs of the parents' attorney when the parent is the prevailing, or winning, party. You should ask your attorney about this provision on any issue related to your child's schooling.

The best way to find a lawyer to be your champion is to network with other parents. Many parent support groups have a telephone hot line with a contact person who can answer this kind of question. Information is also available on the Internet.

If you plan to hire an attorney on behalf of your child, there are some basic facts to know ahead of time:

1. Establish the lawyer's expertise.
2. Define what his or her services will be.
3. Understand the fees and charges for the services.
   Specific questions to ask an attorney when you meet for the first time are the following:
   a. What are your charges, and how do you charge?
   b. Do you require a retainer, and if so, how much?
   c. How do you bill, and what is your charge per hour?
   d. Do you charge for telephone consultations?
   e. How do you bill for typing, photocopying, and other routine office jobs?
   f. How often do you bill?
   g. How will the services be itemized?
   h. Will you continue to be my attorney or will you, at some point, assign me to a junior member of the firm? (This is a real problem in many lawsuits, and it should be firmly established that the lawyer you choose will continue to represent you.)
   i. Will you be available for phone calls?

If you meet an attorney and do not have a good feeling about him or her, keep looking. It is very important to have a comfortable working relationship, a feeling of trust, and mutual respect. If a lawyer does not make you feel confident or make you feel that you have a chance to win your case, then he or she is not one you want as your champion.

Advocates

Not only are there attorneys who specialize in issues for people with disabilities, but there are also people who have had special training in this area, and some who have become experts by advocating for their own child. Advocates can be found through community nonprofit agencies or by word of mouth. Also, the federal government has personnel and divisions where complaints can be lodged, but far too often these get overloaded.

In view of the increasing power of insurance companies and HMOs, parents and advocates need to know that there are regulations which govern these organizations under state and federal corporation laws. Also, each state has an insurance commission where complaints can be lodged. Remember that HMOs and insurance companies are FOR PROFIT companies and should be accountable to those they serve.

Becoming embroiled in a legal battle with a school, HMO, or insurance company is not something I would recommend unless you have lots of time, energy, financial resources, and a tremendously strong support system. Unless the problem involves just your child, it is best to combine forces with other parents. Parents do have power, and the more they can take on battles together, the greater their chances of winning.

If you decide to become engaged in a legal battle, take plenty of time to outline your battle plan. Finding an advocate or attorney to help is wiser than trying to go into battle alone. Schools, HMOs, and insurance companies employ many powerful, high-priced attorneys to fight their battles, so do have your eyes wide open before you step into the legal arena. Otherwise, you may end up with many battle scars, having accomplished little.

> If you don't run your own life and your child's, someone else will, so you need to be a very strong advocate.

You will probably find some strong support when you work as your child's advocate, but unfortunately, you will also encounter people who thrive on power and control and don't like to be challenged. These are the individuals you will have to outmaneuver, and if you can do it skillfully without losing a great amount of sleep, you will be on your way to success. You may never achieve all you wish for your child, but by developing a game plan, and knowing that there will be both wins and losses, you will be far ahead.

> Every time you think you've achieved some success, something else will happen. Things will never be stable, but keep trying.

Don't just wallow in despair, but *get up, get moving, and get organized.* You may develop such skills in advocacy that you decide to do this for others for pay, as does one of my patient's parent, or as an attorney, as does another single-parent mother.

Achieving even small successes will help build your confidence, and the more you accomplish as an advocate, the more doors will open for you and your child. You will develop strengths you probably didn't know you had, and feel real pride in your accomplishments. As fathers and mothers, you will also benefit by developing more and more confidence in your ability to overcome obstacles. Good luck on this difficult journey.

FOURTEEN

◆ ◆ ◆

What Lies Ahead?

I t's hard, as parents and grandparents, not to continually look ahead and worry about the future. Almost daily, I urge mothers and fathers to try to live just in that twenty-four hours and not beyond. With the tremendous amount of medical research that is going on worldwide, today's unanswered questions may be tomorrow's discoveries. Although the underlying causes of most childhood neuromuscular diseases are not yet known, more and more is being learned almost daily. For example, we now know that in Duchenne muscular dystrophy, an important protein called dystrophin is missing or abnormal.

The most promising line of research for developing cures appears to be genetic engineering. With this technique, viruses, or miniviruses, are introduced into cells after specific genetic changes have been programmed. The hope is that missing factors can be manufactured so that normal muscle function and strength can be restored.

> It's hard to think that your child may outlive you and not be able to take care of himself or herself. So make plans for the future.
>
>
>
> You may find that the Americans with Disabilities Act helps put big sums in consultants' pockets but doesn't really benefit your child very much. You do need to learn as much as you can about the law and how it can help.

Already, with careful control of infection, ongoing exercise and physical therapy, and appropriate orthopedic surgery, children with muscle weakness are living longer, healthier, and more productive lives. Technological advances are also helping children and adults with neuromuscular disease to be more independent. Electric wheelchairs, computers, and other equipment, as well as the increased accessibility made possible by the Americans With Disabilities Act, have resulted in many more opportunities for those with neuromuscular disorders.

Your Role as Parents

One of the most important things you can do for your son or daughter is to see that he or she is as active as possible *each day.* If your child dislikes sports or outdoor activities, getting a child moving can be a problem. One of the best ways I know to accomplish this is by *turning off the TV* and getting a child outdoors, playing games, or in-

> Some days you'll wish that your child could be normal, even for a day. (A mother)

volved in other activities. If you let kids know that this is what is expected, it will be easier to get them outside and moving. Many children, particularly those with muscle weakness, prefer to be "couch potatoes" because it's the easy way out.

If your child has muscle weakness and can't keep up with friends, some modifications to equipment or games may be necessary. For example, a tether ball, a croquet mallet, and a badminton set can all be adapted to a child's needs, and a bicycle can have training wheels put on it. Your child's physical therapist, an adaptive P.E. teacher, or other parents can probably all suggest some fun activities.

> It's much more productive to channel your energies into coping with the problems of the muscle disease than to grieve over them.

Just as you expect kids to brush their teeth and dress and feed themselves if they can, you can also expect as much activity from them as possible. You may have to make rules about how many minutes a day of exercise is necessary. A chart with gold stars can be used, or a bank into which a certain number of pennies go when exercise is performed, or taken out when it is not. Some families do this with M & Ms or other treats, which usually motivates kids; but be careful because too many treats can cause weight problems.

The best way to ensure that your child get the exercise he or she needs is simply to make it part of the daily routine, as commonplace as brushing teeth. If you are matter-of-fact about it and allot the time, there is no reason why your child can't get some daily exercise. This could be on a stationary bicycle in the house or by the use of weights and pulleys. Exercising with your child can also work. Most of us adults don't get enough exercise, and also kids love to do things like this with their parents.

> Be careful about doing too much for your child. You can rob her of a chance to do things for herself, and then you'll cheat her of a sense of self-worth and feeling as independent as possible.

When a child is constantly waited on by others, big troubles lie ahead. Kids who are expected to do things for themselves and are rewarded by their parents' approval will be much more motivated.

You will become—and will need to become—the expert for your child. Also it's wise to become as knowledgeable as possible about your child's disorder, because you will probably need to educate teachers, therapists, counselors, and even some physicians about your child's muscle disorder. You have not only the daily contact but also the love and concern that will guide and sustain your child through the problems associated with his or her neuromuscular disorder.

You will discover strengths that you didn't know you had and soon find that you are acting as consultants to other parents who have children with muscle weakness. Each day you may feel as if you've gone two steps forward and one step back, but if you keep climbing, you will be very surprised at the view from the top of the mountain when you reach the end of your journey.

> Accept the reality of your child's muscle weakness but not the limitations. Don't give up!

Yes, there may be other mountains to climb, but if you don't give up, you will eventually come to a place that will bring you unexpected feelings of accomplishment, as well as moments of pride.

FIFTEEN

◆ ◆ ◆

Questions and Answers

Q: My doctor said that my child needs an MRI, EMG, and nerve conduction times before a definite diagnosis of a neuromuscular disease can be made. His only problem seems to be muscle weakness, so why are all these things necessary? The doctor hasn't suggested a muscle biopsy.

A: Unless your child is having convulsions or seizures, or there are some unusual findings on his neurological examination, I would suggest that a muscle biopsy and genetic tests be done before anything else.

Q: My child has spinal atrophy and gets frequent colds and lung infections. The pediatrician doesn't take his own calls, but they are answered by a nurse. She prescribes just Tylenol and a decongestant. I know that he needs an antibiotic right away to prevent pneumonia again. What should I do?

A: I would go to the emergency room and insist on antibiotics, or call another doctor. Also, I would write a note to your present doctor telling him about the problem or make an appointment to discuss it with him. He may be able to put your son's name on a special list so that you get the attention you need when you call and speak to a nurse. You may need to change doctors or health plans to get the care you want.

Q: I have a friend whose child has the same neuromuscular problem as my child. She receives a daily dose of antibiotics during the winter months and is never ill, like my child. Yet our doctors won't let us do this. What can we do?

A: Ask your pediatric neuromuscular consultant to talk to your pediatrician or send a letter. Also, you could refer your doctor to the discussion of maintenance antibiotics in this book (Chapter Four).

Q: My daughter is having hip surgery next week, but the orthopedist hasn't said anything about physical therapy either while she's in the hospital or afterward. I have asked him, but he says we'll wait and see. What should we do?

A: I would call and talk to him about your concerns, and ask your pediatric neuromuscular consultant to talk to the orthopedist also. Your school physical therapist might be able to find out from the hospital physical therapist if the orthopedist has a physical therapist involved in the postop care of his children with neuromuscular diseases. A little networking can pay big dividends.

Q: The school wants to put my child in a special day class with children who have little ability to learn. When we had him tested by an outside educational psychologist, she said that he needed a speech-based, small class. What should we do?

A: I would send a letter to the department of special education requesting a new IEP. Then I would find out exactly how many days they have in your particular district to answer you. Another parent, an advocate, or a special education lawyer may be needed to get the proper classroom for your child.

Q: Our son has severe Duchenne muscular dystrophy and is very weak. He is now in the hospital, and the doctors say that they are planning to do a tracheotomy so he can breathe better. They didn't really discuss the pros and cons of this with either us or our son. Shouldn't this have happened? And do we have to have a tracheotomy done?

A: A tracheotomy should be the choice of both your son and you. Many young men with Duchenne dystrophy elect not to have a tracheotomy but want to try other means of ventilation, such as a mask or nighttime oxygen. I would suggest that you request a consultation from another pulmonary physician if the first one has not given you any choices.

Q: Our child has been weak since birth, and the doctors say that he has congenital hypotonia. They say that it's not possible to make another diagnosis, and yet in our reading we found out about things like congenital myopathies and spinal atrophy. How can we push the doctor to get a more exact diagnosis?

A: I would suggest that you find out if your physician has had training in a children's neuromuscular unit and, if not, I would find another doctor who has. Congenital hypotonia simply means that a child is weak, and a muscle biopsy needs to be done to determine the exact cause.

Q: Our son has mild muscle weakness, and we have been told that he needs a muscle biopsy. However, it's to be done in the operating room under a general anesthetic, and we understand that this is very risky. Another parent's child had a problem with high fever when a biopsy was done under a general anesthetic. What should we do?

A: I would discuss this with your physician and say that you understand that a biopsy can be done on a come-and-go basis under a local anesthetic, and that you simply do not want a general anesthetic. It should never be necessary unless another procedure has to be done for which the general anesthetic is needed. If necessary, you may need to find another physician who will do it under a local anesthetic.

Q: My teenage daughter has been diagnosed as having Charcot-Marie-Tooth disease. We are having real problems buying her shoes, and she is also having difficulty keeping her balance. Do you have some suggestions?

A: Often as Charcot-Marie-Tooth disease progresses, it's important for young people to either have stabilization or surgery on their ankles or to wear special shoe inserts or short-leg braces. Both surgery and braces may be necessary, and these can make a real difference in balance as well as the ability to walk.

Q: Our teenager in a wheelchair is exhibiting signs of real anger and frustration. We try to get him out with both disabled and nondisabled kids, but he is beginning to withdraw more and more, and we are worried. What should we do?

A: It sounds as though it's time for some counseling. I would ask your family physician or pediatrician if he or she has some referrals, and also ask your neuromuscular consultant. Usually, individual therapy with a psychologist or psychiatrist is needed, but sometimes group therapy with several disabled young people is successful.

Q: My eight-year-old son has Duchenne muscular dystrophy. His five-year-old sister has started wetting her bed and acting very upset. Do you have any suggestions?

A: I would ask how much one-to-one time you've been able to spend recently with your daughter. She may be feeling left out, since you probably have had to spend extra time with your son.

Q: My son gets a lot of muscle cramps. Does this mean he has a muscle disorder?

A: Some children have muscle cramps after very active playing and don't have an underlying problem. Others improve with more protein and more calcium in their diets. A good diet can make a difference. However, muscle cramps are also quite common in some of the neuromuscular disorders. If there is any muscle weakness at all, then I would suggest a specialist be seen.

Q: I have a teenage son who has a congenital myopathy. He is very thin and narrow and hates his body. Will working out in the gym help him build up his muscles?

A: When boys with congenital myopathies work out, they don't so much improve their muscle bulk as increase the muscle tone. I would be sure that the trainer in the gym is aware of his muscle problem and doesn't try to get him to do things he should not be doing. Moderate exercise is certainly good for anyone with a muscle disease.

Q: My son falls frequently, and I am wondering if he should wear a helmet.

A: In general, the neurosurgeons that I've spoken to suggest that a helmet is not necessary. However, if your son is very active and falls on hard surfaces such as concrete, I suggest that he wear a helmet during times of increased activity or where he is most at risk.

Q: My son has Charcot-Marie-Tooth disease and one foot is smaller than the other. He also has very high arches, and we have trouble buying him shoes. Do you have any suggestions?

A: I am told that the Nordstrom stores will sell shoes in different sizes. Also, your orthopedist may be able to refer you to a store that makes shoes specially. These usually are quite expensive, however.

Q: My son has muscular dystrophy and is now a wheelchair user. For the last two to three months he has been having some soiling in his shorts. I know he's shy about asking people to take him to the bathroom. Do you have any suggestions?

A: When it's not easy to get to the bathroom, individuals often try to keep from having a bowel movement and thus develop rather severe constipation. It may be that your son is soiling around a large mass of stool. A rectal examination should be done by a physician to see if this is the case. If there is not a problem with constipation, it's important to try to get your son to have a bowel movement either after breakfast or in the evening, and to be on a regular bowel movement schedule. Sometimes you can get regular bowel movements started by inserting a suppository for two or three nights. This way, your son can have a bowel movement at home and be spared the embarrassment of soiling during the daytime.

Q: My two-year-old daughter has spinal atrophy type II. The pediatrician has refused to give her any immunizations, saying that could make her condition worse. Is that true?

A: There is no contraindication to giving immunizations to a child with spinal atrophy or any other neuromuscular disease. If your pediatrician has any question about this, he should refer to the American Academy of Pediatrics' *Red Book* on immunizations or talk to a pediatric infectious disease expert. A physician in your local health department might also be able to help, but I would use this as the last resort.

Q: The school nurse suggests that my son, who has muscular dystrophy and is in a wheelchair, wear a urine collection device attached to a leg bag. I wonder if this is a good idea.

A: There really is no reason for a youth with muscular dystrophy to need a urine collection device and a leg bag. These devices can leak, and they can also have an odor. It's better that he carry a urinal and feel comfortable about asking to be taken to the bathroom. Urinary incontinence is not a symptom of muscular dystrophy.

Q: My son is in a wheelchair because of mitochondrial myopathy and is afraid to stay home alone even for a few minutes. I don't leave him very often, but once in a while I just have to.

A: I would make two suggestions: The first is that you buy a special-alert gadget that either ties in with a business such as a security company or makes a loud piercing noise so that neighbors can be alerted to come running if they hear it.

My other suggestion is that you have a family emergency drill so that your son, as well as everyone else, knows what to do in case of a fire or other problem.

Q: My son has withdrawn from all activities he used to do with his friends. He seems unhappy and depressed. What do you suggest?

A: It sounds as though your son is beginning to realize the full impact of his neuromuscular weakness. If he needs attendant care, it may help to have a male attendant who can take him out and do things with him. Even going out with one person is better than not getting out at all. I strongly advise against having either a woman attendant or a female member of the family give him care. It sounds as though he needs a buddy. Also, I strongly suggest counseling on an individual basis. A hobby might be helpful, too. Does he communicate with anybody on the Internet? There are lots of on-line resources now for individuals with disabilities.

Q: We have a problem in trying to hire and keep attendants. Do you have any suggestions?

A: I would advertise in both college and state employment offices. Also, calling churches to see if they have any suggestions may be help-ful. Sometimes even a strong, healthy, retired man is willing to act as an attendant. Perhaps you could call some senior centers.

Q: My daughter has a progressive neuromuscular disorder and is find-ing it difficult to sleep at night. I have to get up frequently to turn her. Do you have any suggestions?

A: First, I would ask what kind of a mattress you are using? For some individuals a foam rubber mattress, eggcrate mattress, or even a water bed can make sleeping more comfortable. Also, an over-the-counter Be-nadryl capsule given at bedtime will often help an individual relax at night. These are not addictive and should not cause any side effects. If you need something stronger, your doctor may be able to prescribe Val-ium or a similar drug.

Q: My daughter is in a wheelchair and frequently gets very upset. Her stomach hurts considerably at these times, and the doctor doesn't want to do any testing. Could she have an ulcer?

A: Yes, she certainly could. In my experience, patients with chronic dis-abilities often express their unhappiness or anger by developing either ulcers or other kinds of stomach disorders. Zantac, which your doctor will need to prescribe, often works well, as do antacids such as Tums or Mylanta. However, please discuss this with your doctor before doing anything on your own. An X ray of the feeding tube, or esophagus, and stomach may be needed to see if there is any trouble there.

Q: My son is in a wheelchair and complains frequently of back pain. Is this common?
A: Yes, unfortunately spasm of the back muscles is quite common in people who sit in wheelchairs a great deal. Often a seat can be made more comfortable with special personalized seating. Talk to your doctor and your equipment company about a special insert. But first have your doctor check and see if there is some spasm of the back muscles.

Q: My son has begun to complain of rapid beating of his heart, and he gets very anxious. Is this common?
A: Yes. If there is progressive muscle weakness, it's very easy to become anxious about even little things. Sometimes a few counseling sessions can help; if not, medication may be needed to relieve the anxiety. I would not wait too long before getting some help.

Q: My son, who has Duchenne muscular dystrophy, is sixteen and has begun complaining of morning headaches and shortness of breath. He does better if he sleeps on two or more pillows. What should we do?
A: I would discuss this with your physician and request a referral to a pulmonary doctor. It sounds very much as though your son is experiencing an oxygen lack. Most likely, a heart doctor should also be consulted.

SIXTEEN

◆ ◆ ◆

Surviving the Loss of a Child

The loss of a child is probably the most painful, most devastating experience that any parent can have. Even if you anticipate that the end is near for your child and have tried to prepare yourself, there is just no way to truly do this. When a child dies, a void of immense proportions is left.

> You have to just go one day at a time, because the future without your child may be so frightening that you think you can't go on without her or him.

Immediately after the loss of your child, you will probably be too numb and too busy to grieve, but grieve you must. Many parents keep their pain so tightly locked away that it doesn't come out until years later. Then it surfaces as marital difficulties, or headaches, fears, ulcers, and even back pain.

Allowing yourself to grieve every day for even a few minutes or hours is important. Letting the tears flow will help relieve some of the pain and hopefully, in time, at least a small feeling of peace will come.

Acceptance of a child's death never comes, one parent told me, but in time there is a gradual adjustment to the loss. Screaming to or at a supreme being who allowed such a thing to happen is okay. Parents have told me that they lost their belief in a just and fair god when their son or daughter died. Priests, ministers, and rabbis may try to give parents answers to the question of why an innocent child should suffer and die, but most parents find little consolation from these explanations. If the individual has never known such a loss or had children, it's even harder to accept their statements.

I believe that each parent has to work out his or her own answers to the question of "why." For some, no answer ever comes, but that in itself can be a reply. I've seen parents remain angry and bitter all of their lives instead of turning their rage into a productive force. Think of the foundations, scholarships, agencies, and buildings that have had their birth in the loss of a child: Stanford University and the Kevin Collins and Polly Klaas Foundations all came about because the parents turned their anger and grief into action.

> I don't know how you make it if you lose your trust in God. My faith has made it possible to go on.

Not only must you, as a parent, allow yourself to grieve if you have lost a much-loved child, but you also have to find ways simply to get through the days ahead. Initially, you can probably make it through just an hour at a time, but gradually you will be able to get through a day at a time.

Quiet time alone is important, although at first it may be difficult to turn off the phone, the TV, or the radio because of the intense emotional pain. I can promise you, though, that if you hold in your pain it will only increase. So sitting in a quiet park, a beautiful church, or walking on a silent seashore will help you confront the pain, let you shed some tears, and give you the courage and strength to go on for just a little longer.

Learning to handle your anguish is a little like learning to walk again after an accident or stroke. You take one tentative step and then another, and slowly, by exercising muscles that you didn't know were there, you begin to be able to go longer and longer distances.

Being particularly kind to yourself during this sad, difficult time is important. A few extra minutes spent in the tub or shower, a new CD or tape, and other special treats for yourself make the hours and days pass more quickly.

Family, Friends, and Neighbors

The grief of another person is extremely difficult for most individuals to see or share, and you may feel slighted by family members or friends who can't seem to understand what you are going through. If someone close to you seems to go on with their life and not be grieving, that may just be their way of coping. Perhaps they feel that you couldn't handle their grief in addition to your own. Or, they may feel that allowing their grief to surface could cause a loss of self-control, which would just be an additional problem for you.

Insensitive remarks may be said because of an individual's own anger about what has happened to your child. It is sometimes hard to put these disturbing words into perspective. Perhaps other people do understand your pain and grief but just don't know how to tell you. So you may have to help keep the lines of communication open and realize that other people, too, may be feeling a terrible loss. If you can reach out to them and help them with their grief it may also help you handle your own.

Exercise

Even a brisk ten-minute walk or some exercise at home, such as throwing a few basketballs, can help you let go of some of your pain. Group sports may be too difficult at first, but later you may welcome the company of others and the feeling of normality you get from these activities, if even just for a while.

Sharing Grief With Your Partner

Many fathers feel that they have to be the strong one in a relationship and that it shows weakness to express any grief. If you are a father who feels this way, please think about what your wife or partner will feel if you wall off your grief. She may feel such a sense of guilt over either being the genetic carrier of a particular disorder, or from not doing enough while your child was alive, that she becomes numb and is simply unable to express what she is feeling. Your silence could be misinterpreted as a lack of caring, or an inability to feel the loss as deeply as your partner. If you and your partner can shed tears together and share at least some of your grief, increased closeness will result. But by closing out your mate emotionally, not only will you have lost your child, but you could distance or lose your partner as well. I've seen this happen far too often, even though in every case I've tried hard to get the couple to talk to each other about their grief or find a counselor to help them do so. One mother who lost her son to Duchenne muscular dystrophy said that she and her husband have never talked about their boy's death. Instead, her husband has gone weekly to put flowers on the youth's grave while she has retreated into a world of her own. A great deal of communication has been lost, and these partners have essentially forgotten how to share at a feeling level.

Counselors and Therapists

Individual or group therapy can make a tremendous difference in helping you to go on with your life after the loss of a child. In some cities there are support groups composed of parents who have lost a child or children. For some fathers and mothers, this kind of a group offers a place where grief can be shared. Other parents say that these groups are real downers because a few members seem forever stuck in their grieving, leaving the impression that life will always be dark and gloomy. If you want to find out about a support group for parents who have lost children in your own community, call your local hospital and speak to one of the social workers, who should be able to give you a number to call. Your physician, other parents, a parenting hot line, and a community agency where you have sought help are oher places you might try.

If the idea of a group of grieving parents is more than you can handle, find someone who you know has survived a painful loss and still has a positive outlook on life. A social worker or a physician might be able to help you locate one.

Individual therapy can be costly, but even a few sessions could make a real difference in your ability to go on. A good therapist or counselor should be able to help you work through the stages of grieving so that some inner healing can occur. But it must be someone who has had real pain in his or her own life and has worked through it. A wise counselor once said to me during a time of great pain: "It's important to find someone to help who has walked your path and gone beyond your pain."

Many counseling centers have sliding fee scales, and even private therapists may let you work out a payment schedule. It is extremely important to have someone with whom you can share your grief and deepest feelings, and there is always a way to get therapy if you need it.

Siblings

When a much-loved child is lost, parents often forget that the child's brothers and sisters will also be suffering. In addition, a sibling may have feelings of guilt that the death was caused by something that the brother or sister thought, said, or did. So siblings, too, need someone with whom they can talk and share their grief. Otherwise, important lines of communication may be cut off and irrevocable emotional damage may result. If children are deprived of the love and support they need at this critical time, it can have ramifications on their adult relationships, and even on any children they might have.

Soon after a child's death special one-to-one time with each brother or sister needs to be planned. It's important to talk about what has happened and answer as many questions as possible in a straightforward manner. Sometimes just sharing some silent time together or sitting quietly with your arms around each other can help a great deal.

Grief Without End

Some parents become so stuck in their grief that they never move beyond it, and their lives get put on hold. They essentially stop living in the real world, and every day becomes a replay of previous days. Either they do a great deal of crying during the day, or they talk incessantly about the son or daughter they have lost. Nothing is ever moved in the child's room, and it often becomes a shrine. One mother, who lost a much-loved seven-year-old daughter unexpectedly after surgery, sits alone in her house with the curtains drawn despite all efforts to help her, sinking further and further into depression. She has refused medication as well as counseling, despite the fact that she has a bright, healthy, ten-year-old still at home. I am not sure what the outcome is going to be for this mother, but I hope that eventually she will accept some therapy and turn her grief into a positive force.

> If your child has had a full life, you should be proud of yourself and grateful. Some parents just sit back and become immobile, waiting for a kid to be gone.

Rejoining the World

One mother said she felt out of place in the nondisabled world after her son died. Disability had been such a big part of her life for so many years that she missed seeing those with whom she had had daily contact: parents, teachers, physical and occupational therapists, and many others. For this woman, volunteering to assist parents of disabled children find resources and raising money for a center for disabled children helped fill the void.

Another mother became a hospital social worker and began holding grief groups for families. She has wonderful insight into what these families are feeling, because she said it took her many years to adjust to her son's death and that the first year is still a total blur to her.

A father with a great deal of mechanical ability handled his grief by helping other parents devise ramps, bathroom lifts, and other needed aids. So, instead of getting stuck in their grief, these parents worked through it and found ways to help others. By doing this, they helped themselves.

There is no set time that it takes to adjust to the loss of a child. For some it is a few years, and for others, many years. We each handle grief and pain in different ways, but therapy or counseling can hasten healing.

After the loss of a child, your life will never be the same again, but not all the changes will be gray or negative. Instead, you will hopefully notice that small things become more important, as does any happiness or joy. You will probably also feel everything more deeply, as the poet Kahlil Gibran says: "The deeper that sorrow carves into your being, the more joy you can contain."

> Time does bring some healing, but you'll always ask yourself: "Why us?" "Why him?" "Why her?"

The loss of a child is like a dam breaking, allowing water to flood the countryside. As the water recedes, terrible destruction will be present, but ultimately new trees, green grass, and beautiful flowers will grow and even more secure buildings will be erected. I hope that any of you who lose a child will someday find a new place of growth and beauty in your life.

APPENDIX A

◆ ◆ ◆

The ABCs of Genetics

This section may not be important to you right now, but I want to make it available in case you need to refer to it at some time in the future.

E ach of us has unique and special characteristics, such as the color of our eyes or a special ability. Many of these traits are determined by genes, which are very complex pieces of chemical material located on larger, very well-defined units called chromosomes. Most individuals have 46 chromosomes in 23 pairs, of which half come from our fathers and half from our mothers. The sex chromosomes are the exceptions in that a mother has two X's, which are the female chromosomes, and a father has an X and a Y, or a male and female, chromosome. Otherwise, the chromosomes are matched pairs.

At the present time, about 100,000 different genes are believed to be present, though only a small number have been identified. *Each gene carries a code for a protein, which then carries out a specific function. Any change in a gene is called a mutation.* For example, we now know that a protein,which has been named dystrophin, is present in normal muscle cells. This protein is missing in the muscle of boys with Duchenne dystrophy. Thus, the gene that is responsible for the production of dystrophin has been altered or mutated in these boys. Though researchers have not yet determined exactly how the lack of dystrophin accounts for many of the problems that occur in Duchenne dystrophy, they most likely will in the not-too-distant future with all the international research. In chapters 2, 3, and 4, each childhood neuromuscular disease is discussed and what is known about the specific genetic change is given. Understanding some basic genetics should help you have a better understanding of the genetic cause of your child's disorder, if it is known.

Classification of Chromosomes

Of the 23 pairs of human chromosomes, 22 pairs are called *autosomes*, which means that they are identical in males and females. The chromosomes can each be identified under the microscope, and they are known by their number from chromosome 1 (the largest) to chromosome 22 (the smallest). The *sex chromosomes* are the 23rd pair, the ones that determine whether we are male or female. We say that females are XX and males are XY. This means that a female has a matching pair of X chromosomes, and a male has one X chromosome exactly like the female ones (which he inherits from his mother) and a Y chromosome (which he inherits from his father). A picture of the 22 chromosome pairs as seen under the microscope, arranged in a specific pattern, is called a *karyotype*.

Each chromosome has a short arm (referred to as "p") and a long arm (referred to as "q"). Genes are arranged along the chromosomes, with each gene having a specific position, or *locus*. For example, the location of the defective gene in Duchenne dystrophy is at Xp21 on the short arm of the X chromosome.

Sometimes one or more chromosomes are missing, or present in too many copies. For example, most children with Down syndrome have an extra chromosome 21 in all of their cells. Sometimes pieces of chromosomes can break off and move to a different location, which is a called a *translocation*. An example would be that Duchenne muscular dystrophy can occur in females if a translocation occurs.

Genes

Genes are made up of DNA strands located along the chromosomes. Each gene is composed of a particular sequence of subunits called *nucleotides*, which carry one of four different "bases," known as A, T, G, and C. These subunits of any gene are in a specific order (sequence). If this sequence is disturbed, the gene may not function correctly, and an abnormality or disorder can result.

A special kind of alteration in genes has been recently discovered in which some hereditary disorders are known to be caused by small *repeats*, which are like "stutters" within a gene. For example, in myotonic dystrophy, there are *triplet repeats* just three bases long that may occur several or many times in a row. With this particular pattern the resulting disease becomes more severe, because in each subsequent generation the affected members tend to have more repeats.

APPENDIX B

◆ ◆ ◆

Tables

Table 1. Myopathies

Disorder	Age of Onset	Inheritance	Sex	Diagnosis	Course	Prognosis
Duchenne muscular dystrophy	2 to 5 years	X-linked recessive	Male	Elevated CPK Genetic studies Muscle biopsy Absent dystrophin*	Slowly progressive muscle weakness heart and lung involvement	Poor, with death in teens or twenties
Becker muscular dystrophy	Usually in childhood	X-linked recessive	Male	Elevated CPK Genetic studies Muscle biopsy Clinical picture	Slowly progressive in general	Good, and usually without cardiac involvement
Limb Girdle dystrophies Calpain 3	8 to 15 years	Autosomal recessive and dominant	Male/ female	Elevated CPK Genetic studies Muscle biopsy	Variable	Variable
Sarcoglycanopathies Severe childhood autosomal recessive muscular dystrophy (SCARMD) alpha (α)	3 to 12 years	Autosomal recessive	Male/ female	Clinical picture Muscle biopsy Absent or decreased 50kDAG	Rapidly progressive loss of ambulation can occur about age 12	Progressive but may have good heart and lung function
gamma (γ)	2 to 10 years	Autosomal recessive	Male/ female	Muscle biopsy Decreased 35DAG	Variable	Guarded

Disorder	Age of Onset	Inheritance	Sex	Diagnosis	Course	Prognosis
Emery-Dreifuss muscular dystrophy	5 years and up	X-linked Autosomal recessive	Male	Elevated CPK Muscle and skin biopsies Molecular studies	Slowly progressive, with onset of heart problems usually in teens	Good with heart pacemaker insertions in teens or twenties
Congenital muscular dystrophy Merosin-deficient Merosin-positive	At birth	Autosomal recessive	Male/ female	Elevated CPK Muscle and skin biopsies Merosin studies	Nonwalkers, severe problems / May do well	Sudden death can occur / Depends on involvement
Facioscapulohumeral	Childhood to adolescence	Dominant	Male/ female	Genetic studies Muscle biopsy Clinical picture	Slowly progressive	Good, in general
Congenital myopathies	Usually at birth*	Variable	Male/ female	Muscle biopsy Genetic studies Clinical picture	Improvement, then plateau*	Variable, depending on respiratory function
Dermatomyositis/Polymyositis	At any age	None	Male/ female	Elevated CPK Muscle biopsy Laboratory studies Clinical picture	Dependent on treatment	Good, with early treatment*

*Exceptions occur.

Table 2. Neuropathies

Disorder	Age of Onset	Inheritance	Sex	Diagnosis	Course	Prognosis
SPINAL MUSCULAR ATROPHY						
Werdnig-Hoffmann (Type I)	Birth	Autosomal recessive	Male/female	History and physical exam Muscle biopsy CPK Molecular tests	Rapid onset of weakness	Poor, with death usually by age 2
Intermediate (Type II)	After 6 months	Autosomal recessive	Male/female	History and physical exam Muscle biopsy CPK Molecular tests	Reaches a plateau	Depends on lung status
Kugelberg-Welander (Type III)	Childhood	Autosomal recessive	Male/female	History and physical exam Muscle biopsy CPK Molecular tests	Gradual onset of weakness	Good, with walking into twenties and beyond*

HEREDITARY MOTOR AND SENSORY NEUROPATHIES (HMSN) or CHARCOT-MARIE-TOOTH DISEASE

	Onset	Inheritance	Sex	Diagnosis	Course	Prognosis
HMSN I	Childhood	Autosomal dominant	Male/ female	History and physical exam Biopsy EMG/NC Molecular tests	Slowly progressive	Good, but dependent on rapidity of progression
HMSN II	Childhood or later	Autosomal dominant	Male/ female	History and physical exam Biopsy EMG/NC Molecular tests	Slowly progressive	Good, but dependent on rapidity of progression May use walker as adults
HMSN III	First 3 years	Autosomal recessive	Male/ female	History and physical exam Biopsy EMG/NC	Slowly progressive	May use wheelchair as adult
Friedreich's ataxia	First 10 years	Autosomal recessive	Male/ female	History and physical exam Biopsy EMG/NC EKG Molecular tests within families	Variable	Guarded, may lose ability to walk in childhood

*Exceptions occur.

Table 3. Metabolic Myopathies

Disorder	Age of Onset	Inheritance	Sex	Diagnosis	Course	Prognosis
GLYCOGENOSES						
Type II (Pompe's) Acid maltase deficiency	Infancy Variable	Autosomal recessive	Male/female	Clinical picture Biopsy EMG	Rapidly progressive	Fatal within a few months May live into the forties
Type III (Cori's/Forbes) Debranching enzyme deficiency	Infancy or childhood	Autosomal recessive	Male/female	Muscle biospy EM pictures Blood tests	Improvement, but may have liver problems	May have normal adult life
Type V (McArdle's) Myophosphorylase deficiency	Childhood to teens	Autosomal recessive	Male/female	EKG Blood tests Muscle biopsy	Need to regulate exercise	Good
Type VII (Tarui's) Phosphofructokinase deficiency	Childhood or later	Autosomal recessive	Male/female	Muscle biopsy	Need to regulate exercise	Good
Type VIII Phosphorylase b kinase deficiency	Childhood	Autosomal recessive X-linked	Male/female Male	Muscle biopsy	Variable	Good
Type IX Phosphoglycerate kinase deficiency	Variable, childhood and up	X-linked	Male	Muscle biopsy	Variable	Dependent on liver and muscle involvement
Type X Phosphoglycerate mutase deficiency	Variable	Autosomal recessive	Male/female	Biopsy Blood tests	May be mild, with exercise regulation	Dependent on blood and kidney involvement and treatment

Disorder	Age of onset	Inheritance	Sex	Tests	Course	Prognosis
Type XI Lactate dehydrogenase deficiency	Variable	Autosomal recessive	Male/female	CPK Biopsy Blood tests	May be mild, with exercise regulation	Good, with exercise regulation and treatment of myoglobinuria
LIPID DISORDERS						
Carnitine deficiency	Infancy and on	Autosomal recessive	Male/female	Biopsy Blood tests	Mild weakness Slowly progressive	Variable, dependent on heart involvement
Carnitine palmitoyl transferase deficiency	Childhood	Autosomal recessive	Male/female	Muscle biopsy	Normal between attacks	Good, with diet
MITOCHONDRIAL DISORDERS						
Kearns-Sayre (KSS) syndrome	Childhood	Sporadic deletions in genes	Male/female	EKG Biopsy EM Molecular tests	Rapidly progressive	Poor, with death in thirties or forties
MELAS	Before 40 years	From mother	Male/female	Biopsy EM Molecular tests	Progressive	Poor, with death at variable ages
MERRF	Childhood or later	From mother	Male/female	Biopsy EM Molecular tests	Progressive, with mental decline	Poor, with death in teens, thirties, or forties
Cytochrome Oxidase (COX) deficiency (Complex IV)	Infancy or later	Not known	Male/female	Muscle biopsy	Depends on which type	May be fatal within one year or can recover completely

Table 4. Ion Channel Disorders

Disorder	Age of Onset	Inheritance	Sex	Diagnosis	Course	Prognosis
PERIODIC PARALYSIS						
Hyperkalemic	Infancy to childhood	Dominant	Male/female	Blood potassium Molecular tests	Bout of weakness	Depends on treatment
Hypokalemic	10 to 20 years	Dominant	Male/female	Blood potassium Molecular tests	Bouts of weakness	Good
MYOTONIC SYNDROMES						
Myotonia congenita	Birth	Dominant Autosomal recessive	Male/female	Clinical picture History Genetic tests Molecular tests	Good, but may need prescription drugs	Good
Paramyotonia congenita (Eulenburg's disease)	Any age	Dominant	Male/female	Clinical picture Molecular tests	Good	Normal life expectancy
Chondrodystrophic myotonia (Schwartz-Jampel syndrome)	Birth	Usually autosomal recessive	Male/female	Clinical picture	No progression	Good
Myotonic dystrophy (Steinert's disease)	Birth or later	Dominant Autosomal recessive	Male/female	History Physical exam Biopsy, EMG Molecular tests	Progressive weakness with other symptoms	Guarded, with heart, eye, and GI problems

Chores Chart for Children

Ages 3–5 years

Dust
Set table
Empty wastebaskets
Put away toys

Ages 5–7 years

Make beds
Sweep steps and floor
Fold clothes
Sort clothes
Water plants
Care for pets
Wash and dry salad greens
    and vegetables
Polish silver

Ages 7–10 years

Clean bedroom
Help make lunches
Empty dishwasher
Wash and dry dishes
Load washing machine
Clean bathroom
Make dessert, salad, or cookies
Vacuum
Iron simple things
Take out garbage

Ages 10+ years

Load dishwasher
Help fix dinner
Iron
Mop floors
Change beds
Yard work
Wash windows
Clean bathroom

APPENDIX D

◆ ◆ ◆

Resource Directories

AGENCIES THAT CAN GIVE YOU INFORMATION

Arthrogryposis

AMC Support Group of the
Netherlands:
Wanja Van den Elsen
Kamillestraat 15
5741 VN   Beck En Donk
The Netherlands

Alabama-Based Support Group
for AMC:
Debbie and Robert Adams
700 Redwood Dr.
Maylene, AL 35114
205-664-3196

The Arthrogryposis Association
of Ireland:
Christine Healy
19 Lower Beachwood Ave.

Ranelagh, Dublin 6
Ireland

The Arthrogryposis Group
(TAG):
Diana Piercy
1, The Oaks
Common Mead Lane
Gillingham, Dorset SP8 4SW
England
07476-7655

The Arthrogryposis Group of
New Zealand (TAG-NZ):
Marianne Devengoes
40 Eversam Rd.
Mr. Maunganni
New Zealand

Arthrogryposis UTAH Support
Group:

Sue Bryson
2241 So. 500 West
Bountiful, UT 84010
801-292-8323

The Australian Arthrogryposis
Group (TAAG):
Jacqueline Bland
Lot Willards Lane
Oakhampton Heights
N.S.W. 2320
Australia

Canadian Arthrogryposis
Support Team (C.A.S.T.):
Joyce Jepperson
365 Fiddlers Green Rd. So.
Ancaster, Ontario LPG 1X2
Canada
416-648-2007

Georgia Chapter—National
Foundation for AMC
2347 Melinda Dr.
Atlanta, GA 30345
404-325-8982

G.I.S.A. (AMC Support Group
of Italy):
Robert Mezzaroma
Viale Dell 'Esperanto, 71
00144 Rome
Italy

Initiative Arthrogryposis:
Karl Heinz and Cornelia Umber
Hauptstrasse 130
W-7880 Bad Sackingen
Germany

National Support Groups for
Arthrogryposis
c/o Mary Ann and Jim Schmidt
P.O. Box 5192
Sonora, CA 95370
209-928-3688

Southern Arizona Support Group
for AMC:
Georgia Mclaughlin
232 James Dr.
Sierra Vista, AZ 85635
602-458-2306

Ataxia

National Ataxia Foundation
750 Twelve Oaks Center
15500 Wayzata Blvd.
Wayzata, MN 55391
612-473-7666

Carnitine Deficiency

Assistance for Babies & Children
with Carnitine Deficiency
(ABCD)
720 Enterprise Dr.
Oak Brook, IL 60521
800-554-ABCD

Charcot-Marie-Tooth Disease

Charcot-Marie-Tooth Association
601 Upland Ave.
Upland, PA 19015
800-606-2682

Deafness

Deaf Counseling Advocacy and
Referral Agency (DCARA)
1539 Webster St.
Oakland, CA 94610
510-251-6400

Dentistry

National Foundation of Dentistry for the Handicapped
1800 Glenarm Pl. Suite 500
Boulder, CO 80202
303-298-9650

Epilepsy

Epilepsy Foundation of
America
4351 Garden City Dr.
Landover, MD 20785
301-459-3700

Guillain-Barré Syndrome

Guillain-Barré Foundation
International
P.O. Box 262
Wynnewood, PA 19096
610-667-0131

Hydrocephalus

Hydrocephalus Association
870 Market St.—#955
San Francisco, CA 94102
415-776-4713

Learning Disabilities

Foundation for Children with
Learning Disabilities
381 Park Ave. So. Suite 1420
New York, NY 10016
212-545-7510

Mitochondrial Disorders

Cox Foundation for Mitochondrial Diseases
P.O. Box 156
Hartman, AZ 72840-0156
501-497-1563

Education and Support Exchange
for Mitochondrial Disorders
P.O. Box 1151
Monroeville, PA 15146-1151

Mitochondrial Disorder Foundation of America
5100-B Clayton Rd. Suite 187
Concord, CA 94521
510-798-8798

Myotubular Myopathy X-Linked
Myotubular Myopathy Research
Group
2413 Quaker Dr.
Texas City, TX 77590
409-945-8569

Muscular Dystrophy

Muscular Dystrophy Association
of America
3300 E. Sunrise Dr.

Tucson, AZ 85718
602-529-2000

Myasthenia Gravis

Myasthenia Gravis Foundation
22 So. Riverside Plaza
Suite 1540
Chicago, IL 60606
800-541-5454
312-258-0522

Prader-Willi Syndrome

Prader-Willi Syndrome
Association
2510 So. Brentwood Blvd.
Suite 220
St. Louis, MO 63144
800-926-4797

Special Agencies

The Association for Persons with
Severe Handicaps (TASH)
11201 Greenwood Ave. No.
Seattle, WA 98133
206-361-8870

Girl Scouts of the USA
420 5th Ave.

New York, NY 10018
212-940-7500

Home Care for Medically Fragile
Children
Sick Kids (Need) Involved People
410-647-0164

National Library for the Blind
and Physically Handicapped
1291 Taylor St. N.W.
Washington, D.C. 20542
202-707-5100

The National Rehabilitation
Information Center
Silver Spring, MD
301-588-9284

Special Olympics Inter-
national, Inc.
1325 "G" St. N.W. Suite 500
Washington, D.C. 20005
202-628-3630

Spinal Atrophy

Families of Spinal Muscular
Atrophy
P.O. Box 1465
Highland Park, IL 60035
708-432-5551

STATE-BY-STATE RESOURCE DIRECTORY

Alabama

Government Agencies

General Disabilities
Children's Rehabilitation
Services
2129 E. South Blvd.
P.O. Box 11586
Montgomery, AL 36111
205-288-0220

Special Needs Programs
Division of Vocational
Educational Services
Department of Education
5239 Gordon Persons Bldg.
P.O. Box 302101
Montgomery, AL 36130
205-242-9111

Developmental Disabilities
Developmental Disabilities
Planning Council
Department of Mental Health
and Mental Retardation
200 Interstates Park Dr.
P.O. Box 3710
Montgomery, AL 36109
205-271-9207

Private Agencies

General Disabilities
Alabama Easter Seal Society
2125 E. South Blvd.
Montgomery, AL 36111
205-288-8382

Cerebral Palsy
UCP Association of Alabama
2430 11th Ave. No.
Birmingham, AL 35234
205-251-0165

Mental Retardation
Arc of Alabama
215 21st Street Ave. So.
Birmingham, AL 35205
205-856-2877

Alaska

Government Agencies

General Disabilities
Exceptional Children and Youth
Department of Education
810 W. 10th St., Suite 200
Juneau, AK 99801
907-465-2970

Office of Vocational
Rehabilitation
Department of Education
810 W. 10th St., Suite 200
Juneau, AK 99801
907-465-2814

Special Needs, Career, and
Vocational Education
810 W. 10th St., Suite 200
Juneau, AK 99801
907-465-2970

Health Care Program for
Children with Special Needs
1231 Gambell St., Suite 30
Anchorage, AK 99501
907-272-1534

Developmental Disabilities
Governor's Council of Disabilities
and Special Education
P.O. Box 240249
Anchorage, AK 99524
907-563-5355

Private Agencies

General Disabilities
Easter Seal Society of Alaska
2525 Blueberry Rd., Suite 106
Anchorage, AK 99503
907-277-7325

American Samoa

Government Agencies

General Disabilities
Division of Special Education
State Department of Education
Pago Pago, American
Samoa 96799
011-684-633-5237

Maternal & Child Health &
Crippled Children's Program
LBJ Tropical Medical Center
Division of Public Health
Pago Pago, American
Samoa 96799
011-684-633-4606

Arizona

Government Agencies

General Disabilities
Division of Special Education
State Department of Education
1535 W. Jefferson
Phoenix, AZ 85007
602-542-3183

Children's Rehabilitation Services
Department of Health Services
1740 W. Adams
Phoenix, AZ 85007
602-542-1860

State Library for Blind and
Physically Handicapped
1030 No. 32nd St.
Phoenix, AZ 85008
602-255-5578
800-255-5578 (in Arkansas)

Developmental Disabilities
Governor's Council on Developmental Disabilities
1717 W. Jefferson
Phoenix, AZ 85007
602-542-4049

Private Agencies

Cerebral Palsy
UCP Association of Central
Arizona
321 W. Hatcher, Suite 102
Phoenix, AZ 85021
602-943-5472

Arkansas

Government Agencies

General Disabilities
Special Education
Department of Education
Arch Ford Education Bldg.,
Room 105-C
Little Rock, AR 72201
501-682-4221

Children's Medical Services
Department of Human Services
P.O. Box 1437—Slot 526
Little Rock, AR 72203
501-682-2277
800-482-5850 (in Arkansas)

Developmental Disabilities
Governor's Developmental
Disabilities Planning Council
Freeway Medical Center
5800 W. 10th, Suite 805
Little Rock, AR 72204
501-661-2589

Private Agencies

General Disabilities
Arkansas Easter Seal Society
3920 Woodland Heights
Little Rock, AR 72212
501-227-3600

Cerebral Palsy
UCP of Central Arkansas
10400 W. 36th St.
Little Rock, AR 72204
501-224-6067

Mental Retardation
Arc of Arkansas
2000 So. Main St.
Little Rock, AR 72206
501-375-7770

California

Government Agencies

General Disabilities
Special Education Division
Department of Education
515 "L" St., Suite 270
Sacramento, CA 95814
916-445-4568

Developmental Disabilities
California State Council on Developmental Disabilities
2000 "O" St., Suite 100
Sacramento, CA 95814
916-322-8481

Children's Medical Services
(CCS)
714 "P" St., Room 350
Sacramento, CA 95814
916-654-0499

Private Agencies

Cerebral Palsy
UCP of California
480 San Antonio Rd.
Mountainview, CA 94040
650-917-6900

Mental Retardation
Arc of California

111120 "I" St., 2nd floor
Sacramento, CA 95814
916-522-6619

Colorado

Government Agencies

General Disabilities
Special Education Services Unit
Colorado Department of
Education
201 E. Colfax Ave., Suite 300
Denver, CO 80203
303-866-6694

Health Care Program For
Children with Special Needs
Colorado Department of Health
4300 Cherry Creek Dr. So.
Denver, CO 80222
303-692-2370

Developmental Disabilities
Developmental Disabilities
Planning Council
777 Grant St., Suite 304
Denver, CO 80203
303-692-2370

Private Agencies

General Disabilities
Colorado Easter Seal Society
5755 W. Alameda Ave.
Lakewood, CO 80226
303-233-1666

Cerebral Palsy
UCP of Denver

2727 Columbine St.
Denver, CO 80205
303-355-7337

Mental Retardation
Arc of Colorado
4155 E. Jewell, Suite 916
Denver, CO 80222
303-756-7234

Connecticut

Government Agencies

General Disabilities
Early Childhood Unit
Department of Education
25 Industrial Park Rd.
Middletown, CT 06457
203-638-4204

Children with Special Health
Care Needs
Department of Health
999 Asylum Ave.
Hartford, CT 06106
203-566-3994

Developmental Disabilities
Connecticut Council on Developmental Disabilities
90 Pitkin St.
East Hartford, CT 06108
203-725-3829

Visual Impairments
Board of Education and Services
for the Blind
170 Ridge Rd.
Wethersfield, CT 06109

203-566-5800
800-842-4510 (in Connecticut)

Private Agencies

Cerebral Palsy
UCP of Connecticut
80 Whitney St.
Hartford, CT 06105
203-236-6201

Epilepsy
Epilepsy Association of
Connecticut
2102 Main St.
Bridgeport, CT 06606
203-334-0854

Mental Retardation
Arc of Connecticut
1030 New Britain Ave.
West Hartford, CT 06110
203-953-8335

Delaware

Government Agencies

General Disabilities
Children with Special Health
Needs Program
State Department of Public
Health
P.O. Box 637
Dover, DE 19903
302-739-4735

Developmental Disabilities
Developmental Disabilities
Planning Council
Townsend Bldg.—Lower Level

P.O. Box 1401
Dover, DE 19903
302-739-3333

Mental Retardation
Woodside Center
State Department of Mental
Retardation
R.D. 1, Box 750-D
Dover, DE 19901
302-739-4494

Private Agencies

General Disabilities
Easter Seal Society of Del-Mar
61 Corporate Circle
New Castle, DE 19720
302-324-4444

Cerebral Palsy
UCP of Delaware, Inc.
700-A River Rd.
Wilmington, DE 19809
302-764-2400

Mental Retardation
Arc of Delaware
240 No. James St., Suite B-2
Newport, DE 19804
302-996-9400

District of Columbia

Government Agencies

General Disabilities
Special Education Branch
District of Columbia Public
Schools

Logan School
215 "G" St. N.E.
Washington, D.C. 20002
202-724-4801

Health Services for Children with
Special Needs
State Department of Human
Services
19th and Massachusetts Ave. S.E.
Washington, D.C. 20003
202-675-5214

Developmental Disabilities
State Developmental Disabilities
Planning Council
Department of Human Services
St. Elizabeth Campus
2700 Martin Luther King Ave. S.E.
Bldg. 801 East—Room 1301
Washington, D.C. 20032
202-279-6085

Private Agencies

General Disabilities
Easter Seal Society for Disabled
Children And Adults
2800 13th St. N.W.
Washington, D.C. 20009
202-232-2342

Cerebral Palsy
United Cerebral Palsy
3135 8th St. N.E.
Washington, D.C. 20017
202-269-1500

Muscular Dystrophy
Muscular Dystrophy Association

6564 Loisdale Ct., Suite 305
Springfield, VA 22150
703-922-2880

Florida

Government Agencies

General Disabilities
Bureau of Education for Exceptional Students
Department of Education
Florida Education Center
325 W. Gaines St., Suite 614
Tallahassee, FL 32399
904-488-1570

Children's Medical Services
Program
Department of Health and
Rehabilitation Services
1317 Winewood Blvd.
Bldg. B.—Room 128
Tallahassee, FL 32399
904-487-2690

Developmental Disabilities
Developmental Services Program
Department of Health and
Rehabilitation Service
1317 Winewood Blvd.
Bldg. B.—Room 215
Tallahassee, FL 32399
904-488-4257

Developmental Disabilities
Council
820 E. Park Ave., Room I-100
Tallahassee, FL 32301
904-488-4180

Visual Impairments
Department of Education
Division of Blind Services
2540 Executive Center
Circle West
203 Douglas Blvd.
Tallahassee, FL 32399
904-488-1330

Private Agencies

General Disabilities
Florida Easter Seal Society
1010 Executive Center Dr.,
Suite 231
Orlando, FL 32803
407-896-7881

Cerebral Palsy
UCP of Florida
2003 Apalachee Pkwy.,
Suite 175
Tallahassee, FL 32301
904-878-2141

Mental Retardation
Arc of Florida
411 E. College Ave.
Tallahassee, FL 32301
904-921-0460

Georgia

Government Agencies

General Disabilities
Center for Exceptional Children
State Department of Education
1970 Twin Towers East
205 Butler St.

Atlanta, GA 30334
404-656-2425

Children's Medical Services
Department of Human Resources
2600 Skyland Dr. N.E.
Atlanta, GA 30319
404-679-4700

Developmental Disabilities
The Governor's Council on
Developmental Disabilities
2 Peachtree St. N.W.,
Suite 3-210
Atlanta, GA 30303
404-657-2126

Emotional Disturbance
Child and Adolescent Mental
Health Services
Division of Mental Health
Department of Human Resources
2 Peachtree St. N.W.,
3rd Floor West
Atlanta, GA 30303
404-657-2165

Mental Retardation
Division of Mental Health,
Mental Retardation, and
Substance Abuse
2 Peachtree St. N.W., Suite 315
Atlanta, GA 30303
404-657-2113

Private Agencies

General Disabilities
Georgia Easter Seal Society
3035 No. Druid Hills Rd.

Atlanta, GA 30329
404-633-9609

Cerebral Palsy
UCP of Greater Atlanta
Georgia, Inc.
1776 Peachtree St. N.W.,
Suite 522 South
Atlanta, GA 30309
404-892-3667

Down Syndrome
National Down Syndrome
Congress
1605 Chantilly Dr., Suite 250
Atlanta, GA 30324
800-232-6372

Hawaii

Government Agencies

General Disabilities
Special Needs Branch
State Department of Education
3430 Leahi Ave.
Honolulu, HI 96815
808-733-4990

Children with Special Health
Needs Branch
State of Hawaii Department
of Health
741 Sunset Ave.
Honolulu, HI 96816
808-733-9055

Developmental Disabilities
State Planning Council of

Developmental Disabilities
Department of Health
919 Ela Moana Blvd.,
Room 113
Honolulu, HI 96814
808-586-8100

Emotional Disturbance
Child and Adolescent Mental
Health Division
Department of Health
3627 Kilauea Ave., Room 101
Honolulu, HI 96816
808-733-9333

Private Agencies

Cerebral Palsy
UCP Association of Hawaii
245 No. Kukui St., Suite A
Honolulu, HI 96817
808-563-6789

Mental Retardation
The Arc of Hawaii
3989 Diamond Head Rd.
Honolulu, HI 96816
808-737-7995

Idaho

Government Agencies

General Disabilities
State Department of Education
Special Education Section
P.O. Box 83720
Boise, ID 83720
208-334-3940

Children's Special Health
Program
Department of Health and
Welfare
P.O. Box 83720, 4th Floor
Boise, ID 83720
208-334-5962

Bureau of Child Health
Department of Health and
Welfare
P.O. Box 83720, 4th Floor
Boise, ID 83720
208-334-5967

Developmental Disabilities
Idaho State Council of Developmental Disabilities
280 No. 8th St., Suite 208
Boise, ID 83720
208-334-2179

Emotional Disturbance
Bureau of Community Mental
Health
Division of Family and Community Services
P.O. Box 83720
Boise, ID 83720
208-334-5528

Mental Retardation
Bureau of Developmental
Disabilities
Division of Family and Community Services
450 W. State—7th Floor
Boise, ID 83720
208-334-5512

Visual Impairments
Commission for the Blind and
Visually Impaired
341 W. Washington
Boise, ID 83720
208-334-3220

Private Agencies

General Disabilities
Easter Seal Society
1350 Vista Ave.
Boise, ID 83705
208-384-1910

Cerebral Palsy
UCP Association of Idaho
5530 Emerald
Boise, ID 83706
208-377-8070

Epilepsy
Epilepsy League of Idaho
310 W. Idaho St.
Boise, ID 83702
208-344-4340

Illinois

Government Agencies

General Disabilities
Department of Specialized Education Services
State Department of Education
100 No. 1st St.
Springfield, IL 62777
217-782-6601

Division of Specialized Care for
Children
2815 W. Washington Ave.,
Suite 300
Springfield, IL 62794
217-793-2350

Hearing and Visual Impairments
Philip Rock Center and School
818 Du Page Blvd.
Glen Ellyn, IL 60137
708-790-2474

Illinois Instruction Material
Center
Services for the Visually Impaired
Springfield School District
No. 186
3031 Stanton
Springfield, IL 62703
217-525-3300

Private Agencies

General Disabilities
Family Resource Center on
Disabilities
20 E. Jackson—Room 900
Chicago, IL 60604
312-939-3513

National Easter Seal Society
230 W. Monroe St., Suite 1800
Chicago, IL 60606
312-726-6200

Down Syndrome
National Association for Down
Syndrome (NADS)
P.O. Box 4542

Oakbrook, IL 60522
708-325-9112

Indiana

Government Agencies

General Disabilities
Department of Special
Education
Department of Education
State House—Room 229
Indianapolis, IN 46204
317-232-0570

Children's Special Health Care
Services
Indiana State Department of
Health
1330 W. Michigan
P.O. Box 1964
Indianapolis, IN 46206
317-383-6273

Developmental Disabilities
Developmental Disabilities
Advisory Council
Department of Mental Health
429 No. Pennsylvania St.
Indianapolis, IN 46204
317-232-7885

Private Agencies

General Disabilities
Indiana Easter Seal Society
4740 Kingsway Dr.
Indianapolis, IN 46205
317-466-1000

IN*SOURCE (Indiana Resource Center for Families with Special Needs)
833 Northside Blvd., Bldg. 1 Rear
South Bend, IN 46617
219-234-7101

Cerebral Palsy
UCP Association of Indiana
615 No. Alabama St., Room 322
Indianapolis, IN 46204
317-632-3561

Mental Retardation
Arc of Indiana
22 E. Washington St., Suite 210
Indianapolis, IN 46204
317-632-4387
800-382-9100 (in Indiana)

Iowa

Government Agencies

General Disabilities
Child Health Specialty Clinic
University of Iowa
247 Hospital School
Iowa City, IA 52242
319-356-1469

Bureau of Special Education
Department of Education
Grimes State Office Bldg.
Des Moines, IA 50319
515-281-3176

Developmental Disabilities
Governor's Planning Council for
Developmental Disabilities

Hoover State Office Bldg.,
1st Floor
Des Moines, IA 50319
515-281-7632

Hearing Impairments
Deaf Services Commission
of Iowa
Department of Human Rights
Lucas State Office Bldg.
Des Moines, IA 50309
515-281-3164

Visual Impairments
Department for the Blind
524 Fourth St.
Des Moines, IA 50309
515-281-7999

Private Agencies

General Disabilities
Easter Seal Society of Iowa
P.O. Box 4002
Des Moines, IA 50333
515-289-1933

March of Dimes
4845 Merle Hay Rd., Suite C
Des Moines, IA 50322
515-252-1458

Epilepsy
Epilepsy Association
3326 Indianola Rd.
Des Moines, IA 50315
515-241-8294

Mental Retardation
Arc of Iowa

715 E. Locust
Des Moines, IA 50309
515-283-2358

Kansas

Government Agencies

General Disabilities
Special Education Outcomes
Kansas State Board of
Education
120 E. 10th Ave.
Topeka, KS 66612
913-296-7454

Services for Children with
Special Health Care Needs
State Department of Health and
Environment
900 S.W. Jackson, Room 1005-N
Topeka, KS 66612
913-296-1313

Developmental Disabilities
Kansas Planning Council for
Developmental Disabilities
Docking State Office Bldg.
915 Harrison, Room 141
Topeka, KS 66612
913-296-2608

Mental Retardation
Division of Mental Health and
Retardation Services
Docking State Office Bldg.,
5th Floor
Topeka, KS 66612
913-296-3471

Private Agencies

General Disabilities
Easter Seal Society of Kansas
3636 No. Oliver
Wichita, KS 67220
316-744-9291

Cerebral Palsy
UCP Association of Kansas, Inc.
P.O. Box 8217
Wichita, KS 67208
316-688-1888

Mental Retardation
TARC (Topeka Association for
Retarded Citizens)
2701 Randolph
Topeka, KS 66611
913-232-0597

Kentucky

Government Agencies

General Disabilities
Office of Education for Excep-
tional Children
State Department of Education
Capital Plaza Tower,
 8th Floor
Frankfort, KY 40601
502-564-4970

Department of Health Services
Cabinet for Human Resources
275 E. Main St.
Frankfort, KY 40621
502-564-3970

Commission for Children with
Special Health Care Needs
982 Eastern Pkwy.
Louisville, KY 40217
502-595-3264

Developmental Disabilities
Department of Mental
Health/Mental Retardation
 Services
Cabinet for Human Resources
275 E. Main St.
Frankfort, KY 40621
502-564-7842

Emotional Disturbance
Department of Mental
Health/Mental Retardation
 Services
Division of Mental Health
275 E. Main St.
Frankfort, KY 40621
502-564-4448

Visual Impairments
Department for the Blind
Work Force Development
Cabinet
427 Versailles Rd.
Frankfort, KY 40601
502-573-4754

Hearing Impairments
Commission on Deaf and Hard
of Hearing
134 Brighton Park Blvd.
Frankfort, KY 40601
502-573-2604

Private Agencies

General Disabilities
Kentucky Easter Seal Society
233 E. Broadway
Louisville, KY 40202
502-584-9781

Louisiana

Government Agencies

General Disabilities
Special Educational Services
P.O. Box 94064
Baton Rouge, LA 70804
504-342-3631

Children's Special Health
Services
Department of Health and
Hospitals
Office of Public Health
P.O. Box 60630, Room 607
New Orleans, LA 70160
504-568-5055

Developmental Disabilities
Louisiana State Planning Council
on Developmental Disabilities
P.O. Box 3455
Baton Rouge, LA 70821
504-342-6804

Emotional Disturbance
Office of Mental Health
Department of Health and
Human Resources
4615 Government St., Bldg. B

Baton Rouge, LA 70806
504-925-1806

Mental Retardation
Office for Citizens with Developmental Disabilities
Department of Health and Human Resources
4615 Government St., Bldg. B
Baton Rouge, LA 70806
504-925-1910

Private Agencies

General Disabilities
Easter Seal Society
P.O. Box 8425
Metairie, LA 70011
504-885-0480

Cerebral Palsy
UCP Association of Louisiana
1500 Edwards Ave., Suite M
Harahan, LA 70123
504-733-6851

Mental Retardation
Arc of Baton Rouge
8326 Kelwood
Baton Rouge, LA 70806
504-927-0855

Maine

Government Agencies

General Disabilities
Division of Special Education Services
State Department of Education

State House, Station No. 23
Augusta, ME 04333
207-287-5950

Bureau of Children with Special Needs
Department of Mental Health and Mental Retardation
State House, Station No. 40
Augusta, ME 04333
207-287-4250

Developmental Disabilities
Maine Developmental Disabilities Council
The Nash Bldg., Station No. 139
Augusta, ME 04333
207-287-4213

Mental Retardation
Division of Mental Retardation
Department of Mental Health and Mental Retardation
State Office Bldg.—Room 411
Station No. 40
Augusta, ME 04333
207-287-4200

Private Agencies

General Disabilities
Pine Tree Society of Handicapped Children and Adults
84 Front St.
P.O. Box 518
Bath, ME 04530
207-443-3341

Eastern Hancock County Educational Cooperative
P.O. Box 37

Ellsworth, ME 04605
207-667-5388

Cerebral Palsy
UCP of Northeastern Maine
103 Texas Ave.
Bangor, ME 04401
207-941-2885

Parent Organization
Special Needs Parent Information
Network (SPIN)
P.O. Box 2067
Augusta, ME 04338
207-582-2504

Maryland

Government Agencies

General Disabilities
Division of Special Education
State Department of Education
200 W. Baltimore St.
Baltimore, MD 21201
410-767-0238

Prevention and Early Intervention for Young Children
Governor's Office of Children,
Youth, and Families
1 Market Center
300 W. Lexington St.—Suite 304,
Box 15
Baltimore, MD 21201
410-333-8110

Developmental Disabilities
Developmental Disabilities
Council

300 W. Lexington St., Box 10
Baltimore, MD 21201
410-333-3688

Children's Medical Services
Department of Mental Health
201 W. Preston St., 4th Floor
Baltimore, MD 21201
410-225-5580

Mental Retardation
Developmental Disabilities
Administration
Department of Health and Mental
Hygiene
201 W. Preston St.
Baltimore, MD 21201
410-225-5600

Private Agencies

General Disabilities
Central Maryland Chapter of the
National Easter Seal Society
3700 Fourth St.
Baltimore, MD 21225
410-298-0991

Cerebral Palsy
UCP of Maryland
1616 Forest Dr.
Annapolis, MD 21403
410-269-6364

Mental Retardation
Arc of Maryland
6810 Deerpath Rd., Suite 310
Baltimore, MD 21227
410-379-0400

Massachusetts

Government Agencies

General Disabilities
Program Quality Assurance
Services
State Department of Education
350 Main St.
Malden, MA 02148
617-388-3300, x497

Massachusetts Office on
Disability
1 Ashburton Pl., Room 1303
Boston, MA 02108
617-727-7440

Division for Children with
Special Health Needs
Bureau of Family and Community Health
150 Tremont St.
Boston, MA 02111
617-727-3372

Developmental Disabilities
Massachusetts Developmental
Disabilities Council
600 Washington St., Room 670
Boston, MA 02111
617-727-6374

Emotional Disturbance
Department of Mental Health
25 Staniford St.
Boston, MA 02114
617-727-5603

Mental Retardation
State Mental Retardation
Program
Department of Mental Health
160 No. Washington St.
Boston, MA 02114
617-727-5608

Private Agencies

General Disabilities
Massachusetts Easter Seal Society
484 Main St., 6th Floor
Worcester, MA 01608
508-757-2756
800-922-8290 (in Massachusetts)

Federation for Children with
Special Needs
95 Berkeley St., Suite 104
Boston, MA 02116
617-482-2915

Information Center for Individuals with Disabilities
Fort Point Pl.—1st Floor
27–43 Wormwood St.
Boston, MA 02210
617-727-5540
617-345-9743 (TDD)
800-462-5015 (in Massachusetts)

Cerebral Palsy
UCP Association of Metro Boston
71 Arsenal St.
Watertown, MA 02172
617-926-5480

Learning Disabilities
Learning Disabilities Association

of Massachusetts
1275 Main St.
West Newton, MA 02154
617-891-5009

Mental Retardation
Arc of Massachusetts
217 South St.
Waltham, MA 02154
617-891-6270

Eunice Kennedy Shriver Center
for Mental Retardation
200 Trapelo Rd.
Waltham, MA 02254
617-642-0001

Visual Impairments
Vision Foundation, Inc.
818 Mt. Auburn St.
Watertown, MA 02172
617-926-4232
800-852-3029 (in Massachusetts)

Michigan

Government Agencies

General Disabilities
Office of Special Education
Services
Department of Education
P.O. Box 30008
Lansing, MI 48909
517-373-0923

Children's Special Health Care
Services
Department of Public Health

3423 No. Martin Luther King
Blvd.
P.O. Box 30195
Lansing, MI 48909
517-335-8961

Developmental Disabilities
Developmental Disabilities
Council
Department of Mental Health
Lewis Cass Bldg.
320 So. Walnut St.
Lansing, MI 48913
517-334-6123

Emotional Disturbance
Department of Mental Health
Lewis Cass Bldg.
320 So. Walnut St.
Lansing, MI 48913
517-373-3500

Mental Retardation
Department of Mental Health
Lewis Cass Bldg.
320 So. Walnut St.
Lansing, MI 48913
517-373-3500

Visual Impairments
Michigan Commission for
the Blind
Department of Labor
201 No. Washington St.
P.O. Box 30015
Lansing, MI 30015
517-373-2062

Private Agencies

General Disabilities
Easter Seal Society of
Michigan
4065 Saladin Dr. S.E.
Grand Rapids, MI 49546
616-942-2081

Cerebral Palsy
UCP Association of Metropolitan
Detroit, Inc.
23077 Greenfield Rd., Suite 205
Southfield, MI 48075
810-557-5070

Mental Retardation
The Arc of Michigan
333 So. Washington St., Suite 200
Lansing, MI 48933
517-487-5426
800-292-7851 (in Michigan)

Minnesota

Government Agencies

General Disabilities
Special Education Section
Minnesota Department of
Education
Capital Square Bldg.,
500 Cedar St.
St. Paul, MN 55101
612-296-6104

Minnesota Children with Special
Health Needs
Division of Family Services

Department of Health
717 Delaware St. S.E.,
P.O. Box 9441
Minneapolis, MN 55440
612-623-5150

Minnesota State Council on
Disability
121 E. 7th Pl., Suite 107
St. Paul, MN 55101
612-296-6785
800-945-8913 (in Minnesota)

Developmental Disabilities
Minnesota Governor's Planning
Council on Developmental
Disabilities
Centennial Office Bldg.—3rd
Floor
658 Cedar St.
St. Paul, MN 55155
612-296-4018

Mental Retardation
Division of Developmental
Disabilities
Department of Human
Services
444 Lafayette Rd.
St. Paul, MN 55155
612-296-2160

Visual Impairments
Services for the Blind and Visu-
ally Handicapped
Department of Economic
Security
2200 University Ave. W.
St. Paul, MN 55114
612-642-0500

Hearing Impairments
Regional Service Center for
Deaf and Hard of Hearing
444 Lafayette Rd.
St. Paul, MN 55155
612-297-1316

Private Agencies

Cerebral Palsy
UCP Association of Minnesota
Grigg's Midway Bldg.,
Room S-286
1821 University Ave.
St. Paul., MN 55104
612-646-7588

Mental Retardation
Arc Minnesota
3225 Lyndale Ave. So.
Minneapolis, MN 55408
612-827-5641
800-582-5256 (in Minnesota)

Parent Organization
Parent Advocate Coalition for
Education Rights (PACER)
PACER Center, Inc.
4826 Chicago Ave. So.
Minneapolis, MN 55417
612-827-2966

Mississippi

Government Agencies

General Disabilities
Bureau of Special Services
Department of Education

P.O. Box 771
Jackson, MS 39205
601-359-3490

Children's Medical Program
P.O. Box 1700
Jackson, MS 39215
601-987-3965

Developmental Disabilities
Developmental Disabilities
Council
239 No. Lamar St.—Room 1101
Jackson, MS 39201
601-359-1288

Emotional Disturbance
Department of Mental Health
1101 Robert E. Lee Bldg.
239 No. Lamar St.
Jackson, MS 39201
601-359-1288

Mental Retardation
Bureau of Mental Retardation
Department of Mental Health
1101 Robert E. Lee Bldg.
239 No. Lamar St.
Jackson, MS 39201
601-359-1288

Missouri

Government Agencies

General Disabilities
Division of Special Education
Department of Elementary and
Secondary Education

P.O. Box 480
Jefferson City, MO 65102
314-751-2965

Bureau of Special Health Care
Needs
Department of Health
P.O. Box 570
Jefferson City, MO 65102
314-751-6246

Developmental Disabilities
Division of Mental Retarda-
tion/Development Disabilities
P.O. Box 687
Jefferson City, MO 65102
314-751-4054

Emotional Disturbance
Department of Mental Health
P.O. Box 687
Jefferson City, MO 65102
314-751-3070

Visual Impairments
Rehabilitation Services for the
Blind
Division of Family Services
619 E. Capitol Ave.
Jefferson City, MO 65101
314-751-4249

Private Agencies

**Speech and Hearing
Impairments**
Missouri Speech-Language-
Hearing Association
Central Missouri State University

Department of Speech Pathology
and Audiology
Warrensburg, MO 65093
816-543-4993

Montana

Government Agencies

General Disabilities
Special Education Unit
Office of Public Instruction
State Capital
Helena, MT 59620
406-444-5661

Children with Special Health
Needs
Bureau of Maternal and Child
Health
1400 Broadway—Room 314
Helena, MT 59620
406-444-4740

Mental Retardation
Developmental Disabilities
Division of Social and Rehabilita-
tive Services
P.O. Box 4210
Helena, MT 59604
406-444-2995

Private Agencies

Mental Retardation
Association for Retarded Citizens
c/o Beverly Owens
602 18th Street West

Billings, MT 59801
406-656-9549

Nebraska

Government Agencies

General Disabilities
State Education Office
State Department of Education
301 Centennial Mall South
P.O. Box 94987
Lincoln, NB 68509
402-471-2471

Medically Handicapped
Children's Program
Department of Social Services
301 Centennial Mall South
Lincoln, NB 68509
402-471-3121

Hotline for Disability
Services/Nebraska Child Find
Nebraska Department of
Education
301 Centennial Mall South,
6th Floor
Lincoln, NB 68509
402-471-3656

Developmental Disabilities
Developmental Disabilities
Department of Health
301 Centennial Mall South
P.O. Box 95007
Lincoln, NB 68509
402-471-2330

Emotional Disturbance
State Mental Health Agency
Lincoln Regional Center
P.O. Box 94949
Lincoln, NB 68509
402-471-4444

Mental Retardation
Developmental Disabilities
Division
P.O. Box 94728
Lincoln, NB 68509
402-471-2851, x5110

Nevada

Government Agencies

General Disabilities
Special Education Branch
Nevada Department of Education
400 W. King St.
Capitol Complex
Carson City, NV 89710
702-687-3140

Children's Special Health Care
Needs
Department of Human Resources
Kinkead Bldg.
505 E. King St.—Room 205
Carson City, NV 89710
702-687-4885

Developmental Disabilities
Developmental Disabilities
Council
711 So. Stewart

Carson City, NV 89710
702-687-4452

Mental Retardation
Division of Mental
Hygiene/Mental Retardation
Department of Human
Resources
Kinkead Bldg.
505 E. King St.—Room 603
Carson City, NV 89710
702-687-5162

Private Agencies

General Disabilities
Easter Seal Society of Nevada
5785 W. Tropicana Ave., Suite 2
Las Vegas, NV 89103
702-873-4000

Parent Advocacy Group
Nevada Association for the
Handicapped
620 W. Oakey
Las Vegas, NV 89102
702-870-7050

Cerebral Palsy
UCP of Southern Nevada
1500 E. Tropicana Ave.,
Suite 230
Las Vegas, NV 89119

Mental Retardation
Churchill Association for
Retarded Citizens
P.O. Box 1641
Fallon, NV 89407
702-423-4760

New Hampshire

Government Agencies

General Disabilities
State Department of Education
101 Pleasant St.
Concord, NH 03301
603-271-3741

Bureau of Special Medical
Services
Office of Family and Community
Health
Division of Public Health
Services
6 Hazen Dr.
Concord, NH 03301
603-271-4499
800-852-3345 (in New Hampshire)

Developmental Disabilities
New Hampshire Developmental
Disabilities Council
10 Ferry St., Unit 315
Concord, NH 03301
603-271-3236

Emotional Disturbance
Adolescent Services
New Hampshire State Hospital
105 Pleasant St.
Concord, NH 03301
603-271-5300

Mental Retardation
Mental Health and Developmental Services
State Office Park South
105 Pleasant St.

Concord, NH 03301
603-271-5000

Private Agencies

General Disabilities
Easter Seal Society
555 Auburn St.
Manchester, NH 03103
603-623-8863

Parent Information Center
(PIC)
P.O. Box 1422
Concord, NH 03302
603-224-7005

Mental Retardation
Arc New Hampshire
10 Ferry St., Unit 4
Concord, NH 03301
603-228-9092

New Jersey

Government Agencies

General Disabilities
Special Child Health Services
Department of Health
CN 364
Trenton, NJ 08625
609-292-5676

Division of Special Education
Department of Education
225 W. State St., CN 500
Trenton, NJ 08625
609-292-0147

Developmental Disabilities
Developmental Disabilities
Council
32 W. State St., CN 700
Trenton, NJ 08625
609-292-3745

Emotional Disturbance
Division Mental Health
Services
Department of Human Services
CN 727
Trenton, NJ 08625
609-777-0700

Mental Retardation
Division Developmental
Disabilities
Department of Human Services
50 E. State St., CN 726
Trenton, NJ 08625
609-292-3742

Visual Impairments
Commission for the Blind
Department of Human
Services
153 Halsey St.
P.O. Box 47017
Newark, NJ 07101
201-648-3333
800-962-1233 (in New Jersey)

Private Agencies

Cerebral Palsy
UCP Association of New Jersey
354 So. Broad St.
Trenton, NJ 08608
609-392-4004

Epilepsy
Epilepsy Foundation of New
Jersey
58 E. State St., Suite 212
Trenton, NJ 08608
609-392-4900

Mental Retardation
Association for Retarded
Citizens
225 No. Center Dr.
North Brunswick, NJ 08901
908-821-1199

New Mexico

Government Agencies

General Disabilities
Division of Special Education
State Department of Education
300 Don Gaspar Ave.
Santa Fe, NM 87503
505-827-6541

Children's Medical Services
State Department of Health
P.O. Box 968
Santa Fe, NM 87503
505-827-3703

Developmental Disabilities
Developmental Disabilities
Division
State Department of Health
1190 St. Francis Dr.
Santa Fe, NM 87502
505-827-2574

Emotional Disturbance
Division of Mental Health
State Department of Health
1190 St. Francis Dr.
Santa Fe, NM 87502
505-827-2651

Mental Retardation
Developmental Disabilities
Division
State Department of Health
1190 St. Francis Dr.
Santa Fe, NM 87502
505-827-2574

Private Agencies

General Disabilities
Easter Seal Society of New
Mexico
2819 Richmond Dr. N.E.
Albuquerque, NM 87107
505-888-3811

Mental Retardation
Association for Retarded Citizens
of Albuquerque (ARCA)
1515 Fourth St. N.W.
Albuquerque, NM 87102
505-247-0321

New York

Government Agencies

General Disabilities
Office for Special Education
Services

New York State Department of
Education
One Commerce Plaza—Room
1624
Albany, NY 12234
518-474-5548

Physically Handicapped
Children's Services
Bureau of Child and Adolescent
Health
Corning Tower Bldg.—Room 208
Empire State Plaza
Albany, NY 12237
518-474-2001

Developmental Disabilities
New York State Developmental
Disabilities Planning Council
155 Washington Ave., 2nd Floor
Albany, NY 12210
518-432-8233

Emotional Disturbance
Office of Mental Health
44 Holland Ave.
Albany, NY 12229
518-474-4403

Mental Retardation
Office of Mental Retardation and
Developmental Disabilities
44 Holland Ave.
Albany, NY 12229
518-473-1997

Visual Impairments
Commission for the Blind and
Visually Handicapped

State Department of Social
Services
40 No. Pearl St.
Albany, NY 12243
518-473-1801
800-342-3715, x46812 (in New
York)

Private Agencies

General Disabilities
New York Easter Seal Society
845 Central Ave.
Albany, NY 12206
518-438-8785

Cerebral Palsy
UCP Association of New York
State
330 W. 34th St.
New York, NY 10001
212-947-5770

Mental Retardation
New York State Association for
Retarded Children, Inc.
(NYSARC)
393 Delaware Ave.
Delmar, NY 12054
518-439-8311

North Carolina

Government Agencies

General Disabilities
Division of Exceptional Children
Department of Public Instruction

Education Bldg.
301 No. Wilmington
Raleigh, NC 27601
919-715-1563

Children's Special Health
Services
Department of Environment,
Health, and Natural Resources
P.O. Box 27687
Raleigh, NC 27611
919-733-7437

Developmental Disabilities
North Carolina Council on
Developmental Disabilities
Department of Human
Resources
1508 Western Blvd.
Raleigh, NC 27606
919-733-6566

Emotional Disturbance
Division of Mental Health,
Developmental Disabilities, and
Substances Abuse Services
Department of Human
Resources
325 No. Salisbury St.
Raleigh, NC 27603
919-733-7011

Mental Retardation
Developmental Disabilities
Services
Division of Mental Health,
Developmental Disabilities, and
Substances Abuse Services
Department of Human Resources

325 No. Salisbury St.
Raleigh, NC 27603
919-733-3654

Visual Impairments
Division of Services for the Blind
Department of Human Resources
309 Ashe Ave.
Raleigh, NC 27606
919-733-9822

Private Agencies

General Disabilities
Easter Seal Society of North
Carolina
2315 Myron Dr.
Raleigh, NC 27607
919-783-8898

Cerebral Palsy
UCP of North Carolina
P.O. Box 27707
Raleigh, NC 27611
919-832-3787

Mental Retardation
The Arc of North Carolina
P.O. Box 20545
Raleigh, NC 27619
919-782-4632

North Dakota

Government Agencies

General Disabilities
Special Education Division

Department of Public
Instruction
State Capitol
600 E. Boulevard Ave.
Bismarck, ND 58505
701-328-2277

Children's Special Health
Services
Department of Human Services
State Capitol
600 E. Boulevard Ave.
Bismarck, ND 58505
701-328-2436

Developmental Disabilities
Developmental Disabilities
Division
Department of Human Services
State Capitol Bldg.
Bismarck, ND 58505
701-328-2768

Emotional Disturbance
Division of Mental Health
State Department of Human
Services
600 East Blvd.
Bismarck, ND 58505
701-328-2766

Private Agencies

General Disabilities
Easter Seal Society of North
Dakota, Inc.
211 Collins
Mandan, ND 58554
701-663-6828

Mental Retardation
Arc of North Dakota
418 E. Broadway
Bismarck, ND 58501
701-223-5349

Ohio

Government Agencies

General Disabilities
Division of Special Education
State Department of Education
933 High St.
Worthington, OH 43085
614-466-2650

Bureau for Children with Medical
Handicaps
Division of Maternal and Child
Health
P.O. Box 1603
Columbus, OH 43266
614-466-1700

Governor's Office of Advocacy
for Disabled Persons
30 E. Broad St., Suite 1201
Columbus, OH 43266
614-466-9956

Developmental Disabilities
Office of Developmental Disabili-
ties Council
Department of Mental
Health/Developmental
Disabilities
8 E. Long St., 6th Floor

Columbus, OH 43215
614-466-5205

Emotional Disturbance
Department of Mental Health
30 E. Broad St., 8th Floor
Columbus, OH 43266
614-466-2337

Mental Retardation
Ohio Department of Mental
Retardation and Developmental
Disabilities
Rhodes Tower—12th Floor
30 E. Broad St.
Columbus, OH 43266
614-466-5214

Private Agencies

General Disabilities
Ohio Easter Seal Society
565 Children's Dr. West
Columbus, OH 43205
800-860-5523

Cerebral Palsy
UCP of Ohio
2141 Overlook Rd.
Cleveland, OH 44106
216-791-8363

Mental Retardation
The Arc of Ohio
1335 Dublin Rd., Suite 205-C
Columbus, OH 43215
614-487-4720

**Speech and Hearing
Impairments**
Ohio Speech and Hearing
Association
9331 Union Rd. So.
Miamisburg, OH 45342
513-866-4972

Oklahoma

Government Agencies

General Disabilities
Special Education Services
State Department of Education
2500 No. Lincoln Blvd.
Oklahoma City, OK 73105
405-521-3351

Special Health Care Needs Unit
Oklahoma Health Care Authority
Lincoln Plaza—Suite 124
4545 No. Lincoln Blvd.
Oklahoma City, OK 73105
405-530-3400

Oklahoma Office for Handicapped Concerns
4300 No. Lincoln Blvd., Suite 200
Oklahoma City, OK 73105
405-521-3756

Developmental Disabilities
Developmental Disabilities
Services
P.O. Box 25352—Room 510
Oklahoma City, OK 73125
405-521-3571

Emotional Disturbance
Department of Mental Health
and Substance Abuse
Services
P.O. Box 53277
Capitol Station
Oklahoma City, OK 73152
405-522-3908

Mental Retardation
Developmental Disabilities
Services
P.O. Box 25352—Room 510
Oklahoma City, OK 73125
405-521-3571

Private Agencies

General Disabilities
Easter Seal Society, Inc.
2100 N.W. 63rd St.
Oklahoma City, OK 73116
405-848-7603

Cerebral Palsy
UCP of Oklahoma
1917 So. Harvard
Oklahoma City, OK 73128
405-681-9611

**Speech and Hearing
Impairments**
Oklahoma Speech-Language-
Hearing Association
P.O. Box 53217
Oklahoma City, OK 73152
405-769-7329

Oregon

Government Agencies

General Disabilities
Special Education Office
Department of Education
c/o Public Service Bldg.
255 Capitol St. N.E.
Salem, OR 97310
503-378-3598

Child Development and Rehabilitation Center
P.O. Box 574
Portland, OR 97207
503-494-8095

Developmental Disabilities
Oregon Developmental Disabilities Council
540 24th Place N.E.
Salem, OR 97301
503-945-9941

Emotional Disturbance
Mental Health Division
2575 Bittern St. N.E.
Salem, OR 97310
503-378-2671

Mental Retardation
Mental Health and Develop-
mental Disabilities Services
Division
Department of Human Resources
2575 Bittern St. N.E.
Salem, OR 97310
503-378-2429

Visual Impairments
Oregon Commission for the
Blind
535 S.E. 12th St.
Portland, OR 97214
503-731-3221

Private Agencies

Cerebral Palsy
UCP of Oregon
7830 S.E. Foster Rd.
Portland, OR 97206
503-777-4166

Mental Retardation
The Arc of Oregon
1745 State St. N.E.
Salem, OR 97301
503-581-2726

**Speech and Hearing
Impairments**
Hearing and Speech Institute
3515 S.W. Veterans Hospital Rd.
Portland, OR 97201
503-228-6479

Pennsylvania

Government Agencies

General Disabilities
Bureau of Special Education
State Department of Education
333 Market St.
Harrisburg, PA 17126
717-783-6913

Division of Children's Special
Health Care Needs
Bureau of Maternal and Child
Preventative Health
State Department of Health
P.O. Box 90—Room 714
Harrisburg, PA 17118
800-852-4453

Developmental Disabilities
Developmental Disabilities
Planning Council
569 Forum Bldg.
Harrisburg, PA 17120
717-787-6057

Mental Retardation
State Mental Retardation
Program
P.O. Box 2675—Room 512
Harrisburg, PA 17105
717-787-3700

Emotional Disturbance
State Mental Health Agency
P.O. Box 2675—Room 501
Harrisburg, PA 17105
717-787-6443

Private Agencies

Cerebral Palsy
UCP of Pennsylvania
925 Linda La.
Camp Hill, PA 17011
717-737-3477

Mental Retardation
The Arc of Pennsylvania
2001 No. Front St.

Bldg. 2—Suite 221
Harrisburg, PA 17102
717-234-2621

Visual Impairments
Blindness and Visual Services
Department of Public Welfare
P.O. Box 2675
Harrisburg, PA 17105
717-787-6176

Puerto Rico

Government Agencies

General Disabilities
Crippled Children's Services
125 Diego Ave.
Puerto Nuevo, PR 00921
809-781-2728

Developmental Disabilities
Developmental Disabilities
Council
P.O. Box 9543
San Juan, PR 00908
809-722-0590

Rhode Island

Government Agencies

General Disabilities
Office of Special Needs
Department of Education
Roger Williams Bldg.—
Room 209
22 Hayes St.

Providence, RI 02908
401-277-3505

Child Development Center
Rhode Island Hospital
593 Eddy St.
Providence, RI 02903
401-444-5685

Developmental Disabilities
Developmental Disabilities
Council
600 New London Ave.
Cranston, RI 02920
401-464-3191

Emotional Disturbance
Division of Children's Mental
Health and Education
Department of Children, Youth,
and Families
610 Mt. Pleasant Ave.
Providence, RI 02908
401-457-4514

Private Agencies

General Disabilities
Easter Seal Society of Rhode
Island
667 Waterman Ave.
East Providence, RI 02914
401-438-9500

Cerebral Palsy
UCP of Rhode Island
500 Prospect St.
Pawtucket, RI 02860
401-728-7800

Mental Retardation
The Arc of Rhode Island
3445 Post Rd.
Warwick, RI 02887
401-739-2700

Visual Impairments
Services for the Blind and Visu-
ally Impaired
Social and Rehabilitative
Services
275 Westminister St.
Providence, RI 02903
401-277-2300

South Carolina

Government Agencies

General Disabilities
Programs for Exceptional
Children
Department of Education
1429 Senate St.
Columbia, SC 29201
803-734-8806

Children's Rehabilitative Services
Division of Children's Health
Department of Health and
Environment Control
2600 Bull St.
Columbia, SC 29201
803-737-4050

Developmental Disabilities
Developmental Disabilities
Council

1205 Pendleton St.—Room 372
Columbia, SC 29201
803-734-0465

Emotional Disturbance
Department of Mental Health
P.O. Box 485
Columbia, SC 29202
803-734-7766

Mental Retardation
Department of Disabilities and
Special Needs
3440 Harden St. Extension
P.O. Box 4706
Columbia, SC 29240
803-734-7520

Visual Impairments
Commission for the Blind
1430 Confederate Ave.
Columbia, SC 29201
803-734-7520

Private Agencies

General Disabilities
Easter Seal Society of South
Carolina
3020 Farrow Rd.
Columbia, SC 29203
803-256-0735

Mental Retardation
The Association for Retarded
Citizens of South Carolina
7412 Fairfield Rd.
Columbia, SC 29202
803-894-5591

South Dakota

Government Agencies

General Disabilities
Office for Special Education
Department of Education and
Cultural Affairs
700 Governors Dr.
Pierre, SD 57501
605-773-3678

Children's Special Health
Services
Department of Health
445 E. Capital
Pierre, SD 57501
605-773-3737

Developmental Disabilities
Division of Developmental
Disabilities
Department of Human Services
Hillsview Plaza
c/o 500 E. Capital
Pierre, SD 57501
605-773-3438

Private Agencies

General Disabilities
Easter Seal Society of South
Dakota
1351 No. Harrison
Pierre, SD 57501
605-224-5879

Cerebral Palsy
Community Disabilities Services

3600 So. Duluth
Sioux Falls, SD 57105
605-334-4220

Mental Retardation
Arc of South Dakota
P.O. Box 220
Pierre, SD 57501
605-224-8211

Tennessee

Government Agencies

General Disabilities
Division of Special Education
Gateway Plaza—8th Floor
710 James Robertson Pkwy.
Nashville, TN 37243
615-741-2851

Children's Special Services
Department of Health
Tennessee Tower—11th Floor
312 Eighth Ave. North
Nashville, TN 37247
615-741-8530

Developmental Disabilities
Developmental Disabilities
Council
Gateway Plaza—10th Floor
710 James Robertson Pkwy.
Nashville, TN 37243
615-532-6615

Emotional Disturbance
Department of Mental Health and

Mental Retardation
710 James Robertson Pkwy.
Nashville, TN 37243
615-532-6500

Mental Retardation
Department of Mental Health
and Mental Retardation
710 James Robertson Pkwy.
Nashville, TN 37243
615-532-6530

Visual Impairments
Services for the Blind
88 Hermitage Ave.
Nashville, TN 37210
615-741-1685

Private Agencies

General Disabilities
Easter Seal Society of Tennessee
1701 W. End Ave., Suite 300
Nashville, TN 37203
615-215-0070

Cerebral Palsy
UCP of Tennessee
2670 Union Ave. Extended,
Suite 522
Memphis, TN 38112
901-323-0190

Mental Retardation
Arc of Tennessee
1805 Hayes St., Suite 100
Nashville, TN 37203
615-327-0294

Texas

Government Agencies

General Disabilities
Texas Education Agency
Division of Special Education
1701 No. Congress Ave.
Austin, TX 78701
512-463-9362

Children's Health Division
Texas Department of Health
1100 W. 49th St.
Austin, TX 78756
512-458-7355

Developmental Disabilities
Texas Planning Council for
Developmental Disabilities
4900 No. Lamar
Austin, TX 78751
512-483-4080

Emotional Disturbance
Department of Mental Health
and Retardation
909 W. 45th St.
Austin, TX 78751
512-454-3761

Mental Retardation
Department of Mental
Health/Developmental
Disabilities
909 W. 45th St.
Austin, TX 78751
512-454-3761

Private Agencies

General Disabilities
Easter Seal Society
1331 River Bend, Suite 200
Dallas, TX 75247
214-358-5261

Mental Retardation
The Arc of Texas
1600 W. 38th St., Suite 200
Austin, TX 78731
512-454-6694

Cerebral Palsy
UCP of Texas
9027 Northgate Blvd.
Austin, TX 78758
512-834-1827

Visual Impairments
Texas Commission for the
Blind
4800 No. Lamar
Austin, TX 78756
512-459-2500

Utah

Government Agencies

General Disabilities
Special Education and Students
at Risk
Utah State Office of Education
250 E. 500 South
Salt Lake City, UT 84111
801-538-7702

Children with Special Health
Care Needs
Community and Family Health
Services
Utah Department of Health
44 No. Medical Dr.
Salt Lake City, UT 84114
801-584-8284

Developmental Disabilities
Governor's Council for People
with Disabilities
555 East 300 South, Suite 201
Salt Lake City, UT 84102
801-533-4128

Emotional Disturbance
Division of Mental Health
Department of Human
Services
120 No. 200 West, 4th Floor
Salt Lake City, UT 84103
801-538-4720

Mental Retardation
Division of Services for People
with Disabilities
Department of Human
Services
120 No. 200 West
Salt Lake City, UT 84103
801-538-4200

Visual Impairments
State Services for the Blind and
Visually Impaired
309 East 100 South
Salt Lake City, UT 84111
801-533-9393

Private Agencies

General Disabilities
UCP of Utah
1831 E. Fort Union Blvd.
Salt Lake City, UT 84121
801-944-8965

Parent Organization
Utah Parent Center
2290 East 4500 South, Suite 110
Salt Lake City, UT 84117
801-272-1051

**Speech and Hearing
Impairments**
Utah Speech-Language-
Hearing Association
P.O. Box 171363
Holiday, UT 84117
801-596-7553

Vermont

Government Agencies

General Disabilities
Special Education Unit
Department of Education
120 State St.
Montpelier, VT 05620
802-828-3141

Children with Special Health
Needs
Department of Health
108 Cherry St.
Burlington, VT 05401
802-863-7338

Developmental Disabilities
Vermont Developmental Disabilities Council
103 So. Main St.
Waterbury, VT 05671
802-241-2612

Emotional Disturbance
Department of Mental Health
103 So. Main St.
Waterbury, VT 05671
802-241-2610

Mental Retardation
Community Mental Retardation
Programs
Department of Mental Health
103 So. Main St.
Waterbury, VT 05671
802-241-2614

Visual Impairments
Division for the Blind and
Visually Impaired
Department of Aging
103 So. Main St.
Waterbury, VT 05671
802-241-2210

Private Agencies

General Disabilities
Central Vermont A.R.C.
73 Main St., Room 17
Montpelier, VT 05601
802-223-6149

Cerebral Palsy
Association for Cerebral Palsy
73 Main St., Room 402
Montpelier, VT 05601

Mental Retardation
Champlain A.R.C.
Champlain Mill
Box 37
Winooski, VT 05404
802-655-4014

Virginia

Government Agencies

General Disabilities
Special Education and Student
Services
Virginia Department of
Education
101 No. 14th St.
Richmond, VA 23219
804-225-2402

Children's Specialty Services
Virginia Department of Health
1500 E. Main St., Suite 135
Richmond, VA 23219

State Mental Health Agency
Virginia Department of Mental
Health and Mental Retardation
109 Governor St.
Richmond, VA 23214
804-786-3921

Developmental Disabilities
Developmental Disabilities
Program
Virginia Department of Mental
Health and Mental Retardation
109 Governor St.
Richmond, VA 23214
804-786-5313

Mental Retardation
Mental Retardation Program
Virginia Department of Mental
Health and Mental Retardation
109 Governor St.
Richmond, VA 23214
804-786-1746

Visual Impairments
Virginia Department for the
Visually Handicapped
397 Azalea Ave.
Richmond, VA 23227
804-371-3140

Private Agencies

General Disabilities
Easter Seal Society of
Virginia, Inc.
4841 Williamson Rd.
Roanoke, VA 24012
703-362-1656

Mental Retardation
The Arc of Virginia
6 No. Sixth St., Suite 403
Richmond, VA 23219
804-649-8481

(U.S.) Virgin Islands

Government Agencies

General Disabilities
Division of Special Education
Department of Education
44-46 Kongens Gade

St. Thomas, USVI 00802
809-774-4399

Services for Children with
Special Health Care Needs
Division of Maternal and Child
Health
Department of Health
3500 Estate Richmond
Christiansted
St. Croix, USVI 00820
809-773-1311

Developmental Disabilities
Division of Developmental
Disabilities and Rehabilitation
Services
Department of Human Services
3011 Golden Rock
Christiansted
St. Croix, USVI 00820
809-773-2323

Mental Retardation
Mental Health, Alcoholism, and
Drug Dependency Services
Department of Health
Barbel Plaza South
St. Thomas, USVI 00802
809-774-4888

Washington

Government Agencies

General Disabilities
Special Education Programs
Office of Public Instruction
P.O. Box 47200

Olympia, WA 98504
360-753-6733

Children with Special Health
Care Needs
P.O. Box 47880
Olympia, WA 98504
360-753-0908

Maternal and Child Health
P.O. Box 47880
Airdustrial Way—Bldg. 7
Olympia, WA 98504
360-586-9015

Developmental Disabilities
Developmental Disabilities
Planning Council
906 Columbia St. S.W.
P.O. Box 48314
Olympia, WA 98504
360-753-3908

Emotional Disturbance
Division of Mental Health
Department of Social and Health
Services
P.O. Box 45320
Olympia, WA 98504
360-753-5414

Mental Retardation
Division of Developmental
Disabilities
Department of Social and Health
Services
P.O. Box 45310
Olympia, WA 98504
360-753-3900

Private Agencies

General Disabilities
Easter Seal Society of
Washington
521 Second Ave. West
Seattle, WA 98119
206-281-5700

Cerebral Palsy
UCP Association
4409 Interlake Ave. North
Seattle, WA 98103
206-632-2867

Mental Retardation
The Arc of Washington State
1703 State Ave. N.E.
Olympia, WA 98506
360-357-5596

West Virginia

Government Agencies

General Disabilities
Office of Special Education
Capitol Complex
Bldg. 6—Room B-304
Charleston, WV 25305
304-558-2696

Handicapped Children's
Services
Office of Maternal and Child
Health
Bureau of Public Health
1116 Quarrier St.
Charleston, WV 25301
304-558-3071

Mental Retardation
Mental Health and Community
Rehabilitation Services
Division of Behavioral Health
Bureau of Public Health
Capital Complex
Bldg. 6—Room B-717
Charleston, WV 25305
304-558-0067

Developmental Disabilities
Developmental Disabilities
Planning Council
110 Stockton St.
Charleston, WV 25312
304-558-0416

Wisconsin

Government Agencies

General Disabilities
Division for Learning Support:
Equity and Advocacy
P.O. Box 7841
Madison, WI 53707
608-266-1649

Program for Children with
Special Health Care Needs
Department of Health and Social
Services
1414 E. Washington Ave.,
Room 167
Madison, WI 53703
608-266-2886

Developmental Disabilities
Wisconsin Council of

Developmental Disabilities
P.O. Box 7851
Madison, WI 53707
608-266-7826

Mental Health
Adolescent and Diagnostic
Treatment Unit (A.D.T.U.)
Mendota Mental Health Institute
301 Troy Dr.
Madison, WI 53704
608-243-3000

Mental Retardation
Bureau of Developmental
Disabilities Services
Division of Community Services
P.O. Box 7851
Madison, WI 53707
608-266-0805

Private Agencies

General Disabilities
Easter Seal Society of Wisconsin
101 Nob Hill Rd.
Madison, WI 53713
608-277-8288

Cerebral Palsy
UCP of Wisconsin
1502 Greenway Cross
Madison, WI 53713
608-273-4434

Mental Retardation
Arc of Wisconsin
121 So. Hancock St.

Madison, WI 53703
608-251-9272

Wyoming

Government Agencies

General Disabilities
Special Education Division
State Department of
Education
Hathaway Office Bldg.
Cheyenne, WY 82002
307-777-7414

Children's Health Services
Hathaway Office Bldg.—
Room 462
Cheyenne, WY 82002
307-777-7941

Developmental Disabilities
Governor's Planning Council
on Developmental
Disabilities
Herschler Bldg.—4th Floor
122 W. 25th St.
Cheyenne, WY 82002
307-777-7230

Emotional Disturbance
Division of Behavioral Health
Department of Health
Hathaway Office Bldg.—
4th Floor
Cheyenne, WY 82002
307-777-7094

NATIONAL MUSCULAR DYSTROPHY ASSOCIATIONS

Argentina

Assoc Distrofia Muscular (ADM)
Av. Cordoba 5428 (1414)
BUENOS AIRES
tel: +54 1 9817522

Republic of Armenia

Charity Assoc of Neurohereditary
Diseases
Tigran Mets Ave. 40–70
YEREVAN 375005
tel: +7 885 538387
fax: +7 885 564983

Australia

The Muscular Dystrophy Association of South Australia
GPO Box 414
ADELAIDE SA 5001
tel: +61 8 212 82345266
fax: +61 8 212 82345866

Austria

Osterreichische Gesellschaft für
Muskelkranke
Währinger Gurtel 18-20
Postbach 23
A-1097 WIEN
tel: +43 1 40400 3112
fax: +43 1 40400 3141

Belgium

Vlaamse Vereniging Neuromusculaire Aandoeningen (NEMA)

Hutsepotstraat 50
B-9052 ZWUNAARDE / GENT
tel: +32 9 2226446
fax: +32 9 2226446

Assoc belge contre les Maladies
Neuro-Musculaires
Rue du Blanc Bois 2
B-1360 PERWEZ
tel: +32 81 655885
fax: +32 81 655885

Brazil

Assoc Brasileira de Distrofia
Muscular
Rua Eugenheiro Teixeira Soares
715
955 055 Butanta
SAO PAULO S.P.
tel: +55 11 8148562
fax: +55 11 8154272

Bulgaria

Bulgarian Neuromuscular
Diseases Assoc
96, Pliska Street Entrance 2,
App. 4
BG-7004 ROUSSE
tel: +359 82 452055
fax: +359 82 237045

Canada

Muscular Dystrophy Association
of Canada
2345 Yonge Street, Suite 900

TORONTO, ONTARIO
M4P 2E5
tel: +1 416 4880030
fax: +1 416 4887523

Muscular Dystrophy Association
of Canada
1425 René-Levesque Ouest
Bureau 506
MONTRÉAL, QUÉBEC
H3G 1T7
tel: 1-800-567-2236 or
514-393-3522
fax: 1-514-393-8113

305 St. Valier, C.P.27
CHICOUTIMI, QUÉBEC
G7H 5H6
tel: 1-800-520-2236 or
418-693-8223
fax: 1-418-393-1318

Society of Muscular Dystrophy
Information International
P.O. Box 479
BRIDGEWATER, NOVA SCOTIA
B4V 2X6
tel: +1 902 6853961
fax: +1 902 6853962
e-mail: smdi@Atcon.com

China

Chinese MDA
Div Neuromuscular Disorders,
Research
Chinese Pla Gen Hospital
28 Fuxin Road
BEIJING 100853

tel: +86 1 6887329
fax: +86 1 8217073

Colombia

Fund Omega
Carrara 30 No. 89-79 (la Castel-
lana)
BOGOTA
tel: +57 1 2365004

Croatia

Union of Muscular Dystrophy
Societies of Croatia
Nova Ves 44
10000 ZAGREB
tel: +38 41 271849

Cyprus

The Cyprus Institute of Neurology & Genetics
P.O. Box 3462
NICOSIA
tel: +357 2 358600
fax: +357 2 358237/238

Czech Republic

Asociace Muskularnich
Dystrofiku
Petyrkova 1953/24
1490 PRAHA 4-CHODOV
tel: +42 2 7933777

Denmark

Muskelsvindfonden
Kongsvang Allé 23
DK 8000 AARHUS

tel: +45 89482222
fax: +45 89482212

Dominican Republic

Instituto de Neurociencias y
Especialidades
Club Rotario 67
En Sanche Ozama
SANTO DOMINGO
tel: +1 809 5496659

Ecuador

Fundacion Ecuatoriana por la
Distrofia Muscular
Colon Avenue and La Rabida
Colon Building, 3rd Floor,
Of. 301
QUITO
tel: +593 2 565401
fax: +593 2 565401

Estonia

Eesti Lihasehaigete Selts
Vilde 121A—57
TALIN EE0026
tel: +372 014 598992

Finland

Lihastautiliitto R.Y. De Muskel
Handikappades
Forbund R.F.
Lantinen Pitkakatu 35
20100 TURKU
tel: +358 2 2500233
fax: +358 2 2335503

France

Association Française contre les
Myopathies
13 Place de Rungis
75013 PARIS
tel: +33 1 44162700
fax: +33 1 45803736

Germany

Deutsche Gesellschaft für
Muskelkranke e. V.
Im Moos 4
79112 FREIBURG
tel: +49 7665 94470
fax: +49 7665 94472

Guam

Guam Lytica & Bodig Assoc
P.O. Box 1458
AGANA 96910
tel: +671 4723581
fax: +671 4723583

Guatemala

Assoc Gutemalteca de Rehabilita-
cion de Lisiados
6a. Avenida 'A' 36-01, zona 11
GUATEMALA CITY
tel: +76 7295
fax: +76 2365

Holland (*see* The Netherlands)

Honduras

Instituto Hondureno de Rehabil-
itacion

Apartado Postal #1056
TEGUCIGALPAV, Municipio del
Distrito Central
tel: +504 32 8761

Hungary

National Federation of the Assoc
of Persons with Disabilities
P.O. Box 141
H-1300 BUDAPEST

India

Indian Muscular Dystrophy
Association
21-136 Batchupet
MACHILIPATNAM 521 001
tel: +91 8672 2817

Ireland

Muscular Dystrophy Ireland
Carmichael House
North Brunswick Street
DUBLIN 7
tel: +353 1 8721501
fax: +353 1 8724482
e-mail: mdi@iol.ie

Israel

Muscle Disease Association of
Israel
Alyn Hospital
Olswanger Street / P.O. Box 9117
KIRYAT YUVEL, JERUSALEM
tel: +972 26 494222
fax: +972 26 437338

Israel Society of Neuromuscular
Diseases
c/o Hadassah Medical
Organisation
P.O. Box 24035
91240 JERUSALEM
tel: +972 25 844751
fax: +972 25 823515

Italy

Unione Italiana Lotta alla
Distrofia Muscolare
Via P.P. Vergerio 17
35126 PADOVA
tel: +39 49 8021002
fax: +39 49 757033

Japan

Muscular Dystrophy Association
of Japan
National Recuperation–Education
Center
2-2-8 Nishi-Waseda
Shinjuku-Ku, TOKYO 162
tel: +81 3 52732930
fax: +81 3 32087030

Jordan

Al-Hussein Society for the
Rehabilitation
of the Physically Handicapped
P.O. Box 5102
AMMAN

Korea

Muscular Dystrophy Association
of Korea

Suite 402, Seochang B/D
Banpo-Dong, Seocho-Gu
SEOUL, KOREA #137-040
tel: +82 2 599-9201
fax: +82 2 532-3336

Lithuania

Lithuanian Neuromuscular
Association
Eiven in—2
KAUNAS 3007
tel: +370 7 228753
fax: +370 7 798585

Malaysia

Muscular Dystrophy Association
of Malaysia
13 Jalan 12/10
47200 Petaling Jaya
SELANGOR DURAL EHSAN
tel: +60 3 7581294
fax: +60 3 7582377

Malta

Muscular Dystrophy Group
Malta
1 Block 1, Govt. H/E
Sliema Road
GZIRA
tel: +356 572696

Mexico

Sociedad Mexicana de la Distrofia
Muscular A.C.
Peten No. 185
Col. Narvarte

Delegacion Benito Juarez
MEXICO, 03110 D.F.
tel: +52 5 239003

Association Leonesa para la
Distrofia Muscular-AC
Arquitectos #112
C.P. 37160
Colonia Panorama
Leon, Gto.
37170 MEXICO
tel: (47) 17-61-67

Moldova

Myopathy Association
16 Livezilor Street
279452 Villa Taul
d-ct DONDUSENI
tel: +373 8 0422 25161349

Morocco

Association Marocaine contre les
Myopathies
B.P. 6568
Rabat Institut
RABAT
tel: +212 7 750539

The Netherlands

Vereniging Spierziekten
NEDERLAND
Lt. Gen. van Heutszlaan 6
NL-3743 JN Baarn
tel: +31 35 5480480
fax: +31 35 5480499
e-mail: vsn@vsn.nl

New Zealand

Muscular Dystrophy Association
of New Zealand
P.O. Box 23-047
PAPATOETOE, AUCKLAND
tel: +64 9 2787216 / 2783734

Norway

Foreningen for Muskelsyke
Postboks 116, Kjelsas
0411 OSLO 4
tel: +47 2 235050
fax: +47 2 235700

Pakistan

Association of Physically
Disabled Persons
House 2, Street 40, F.7/1
ISLAMABAD
tel: +92 (051) 823925

Association of Physically Handicapped Adults (APHA)
5-E 14/6 Nazimabad-5
KARACHI 74600
tel: +92 21-621647

MA Ayesha Memorial Centre
(For Care & Control of Neuro-
muscular Disorders)
SPNA-22, Block 7/8, Near
Commercial Area
K.M.C.H.S.
KARACHI
tel: +92 21-447686

Papua New Guinea

C/-Dauli Teachers College
P.O. Box 16

TARI, Shp
tel: +675 508080
fax: +675 508079

Philippines

The ALS Association Philippines
Support Group
78 Misi kap Extension
Central District
Diliman
QUEZON CITY 1100
Metro Manila
tel: +63 2 922 8274
fax: +63 2 922 9199

Poland

Polish Neuromuscular
Association
c/o Department of Neurology
Bancha 1a, bid D
02-097 WARSZAWA
tel: +48 22 6597505
fax: +48 22 6688512

Portugal

PMG /DNM—Hospital de Santa
Maria
Centro Estudos Egas Moniz
Av. Prof. Egas Moniz
1699 LISBOA
tel: +351 1 7976882
fax: +351 1 7957474

Associacion Portuguesa de Dun-
cas Neuromusculares
Servico de Neurologica
Hospital de Santa Maria
7600 LISBOA

tel: +351 1 7978821
fax: +351 1 7977782

Romania

Asociatia Distroficilor Muscular
din Romania
Str. Bailor nr. 197
VILCELE JUD. COVASNA
Cod 4017
tel: +40 67 315665
fax: +40 67 315665

Neuromuscular Diseases
Association of Romania
Institute of Neurology
C.P. 61-42
RO 75622 BUCHAREST
tel: +40 10 756273

Russia

Russian Muscular Dystrophy
Association
Rublevskoe shosse, d.44-1
Apt. 162
121609 MOSCOW
tel: +7 095 4129158
fax: +7 095 9246655

Myafond Charity Myasthenic
Foundation
Chasovaya Street 20
1253 15 MOSCOW
tel: +7 095 1512651
fax: +7 095 1512651

Serbia

Sovez Distroficara Jugoslavije
Maksima Gorkog 28a

11000 BEOGRAD
tel: +381 11 439854
fax: +381 11 439854

Slovakia

Muscular Dystrophy Organisation of Slovakia
Sportova 5
83104 BRATISLAVA
tel: +42 7 215830
fax: +42 7 215830

Slovenia

Drustvo Misicno Obolelih
Slovenije
Linhartova 1/111
61000 LJUBLJANA
tel: +386 61 312047
fax: +386 61 326695

South Africa

Muscular Dystrophy Research
Foundation of South Africa
P.O. Box 1535
PINEGOWRIE 2123
tel: +27 11 7897634
fax: +27 11 7897635

Spain

Association Espanola de Enfer-
medades Musculares
Appartado de Correos 14.170
08080 BARCELONA
tel: +34 3 4516544
fax: +34 3 4516904

Coordinadora de Minusvalidos
Fisicos de Madrid

Eugenio Salazar 2—la
28002 MADRID
tel: +34 1 4137441

Sweden

The Swedish Association of
Neurologically Disabled (NHR)
Box 3284
103 65 STOCKHOLM
tel: +46 8 6777010
fax: +46 8 241315

Swedish Association for Disabled
Children and their Families
(RBU)
Box 6607
113 84 STOCKHOLM
tel: +46 8 7362600
fax: +46 8 301410

Switzerland

Association Suisse Romande
contre la Myopathie
c/o Hospital regional d'Aubonne
1170 AUBONNE
tel: +41 21 8087411
fax: +41 21 8088111

Scheizerische Gesellschaft für
Muskelkrankheiten (SGMK)
Forchstrasse 136
8032 ZÜRICH
tel: +41 1 4221634
fax: +41 1 4225941

Taiwan

Muscular Dystrophy Association
of Taiwan

No. 100, Shih-Chuan 1st Road
Department of Neurology
Kaohsiung Medical College
KAOHSIUNG 807
tel: +886 7 3121101 ext. 6771
fax: +866 7 3234237

Tunisia

Association des Myoathes de
Tunisie
Rue Azzouz Rebaï Impasse 6
Nozha 4, Appt 1
MANAR 2—2092
tel: +216 1 883513
fax: +216 1 884979

Turkey

Association of Muscle Disorders
Hatboyu Cad. no. 12
YESILKOY, ISTANBUL
tel: +90 212 5730975
fax: +90 212 6630168

Uganda

The Biruduma Students MDA
P.O. Box 596
MBARARA

United Kingdom

Muscular Dystrophy Group of
Great Britain & Northern
Ireland
7–11 Prescott Place
LONDON SW4 6BS
tel: +44 171 7208055
fax: +44 171 4980670

Uruguay

Centro de Ayuda Social a Los
Enfermos Neuromusculares
Dulcinesa 3030
MONTEVIDEO
tel: +598 2 816823
fax: +598 2 810045

USA

Muscular Dystrophy
Association
3300 East Sunrise Drive
TUCSON, AZ 85718
tel: +1 520 5292000
fax: +1 520 5295300
e-mail: mda@mdausa.org

Venezuela

Foudacion de la Distrofia
Muscular
Conjunto Res. Jardin Bello Campo
Apto. B-1D Ave. Libertado.
Chacaco
CARACAS 1060
tel: +58 2 2621565
fax: +58 2 26307084

Zimbabwe

Muscular Dystrophy Association
of Zimbabwe
Stand 14063 Torchwood Road
THRONGROVE, BULAWAYO
tel: +263 9 79954

Glossary

Adaptive P.E. Specifically adapted exercise programs for children with disabilities who cannot take part in regular physical education.

Adhalin The missing protein in severe childhood autosomal recessive muscular dystrophy; of importance in the diagnosis of the disorder.

ADL Activities of daily living.

AFO Ankle-foot-orthoses, or short-leg brace.

Amniocentesis The process of taking fluid from a pregnant woman's abdomen with a needle.

> You'll find difficulty with the vocabulary, because each professional often uses different terms. Learn as much as you can.

Anesthesiologist A medical doctor who has had several additional years of training in sedating patients for surgery and monitoring them during the surgical procedures.

Assistive technology A term used for mechanical ways to help individuals to communicate.

Atelectasis Area of collapse in a lung.

Atrophic fibers Small fibers seen in a muscle biopsy.

Atrophy Loss of muscle bulk owing to disease in the muscle or the nervous system.

Autosomal dominant A hereditary disorder that is present in a parent and passed on to a child.

Bilateral Involvement of both sides of the body or both legs, as in "bilateral braces."

Cardiac Related to the heart.

Congenital A condition present at birth; may have an unknown cause.

Chromosomes The small bodies that contain our genetic information or characteristics.

Contracture Tightness of muscles that limits the full range of motion.

CPK Creatine phosphokinase, an enzyme found in muscle and other tissues of the body.

Development The process by which a child gains specific skills such as sitting, walking, or talking.

Distal The muscles away from the center of the body.

DNA Deoxyribonucleic acid, the principal matter of all living cells. It is found primarily in the nucleus, or center portion, of the cell, and it is the principal material found in chromosomes.

Due process hearing A legal proceeding that has been established for special-education students so that parents can disagree with school findings under Public Law 94-142, now called IDEA.

Dystrophin The protein usually lacking in Duchenne dystrophy.

Dystrophinopathies Disorders due to abnormalities of the dystrophin gene, as Duchenne dystrophy.

EKG A tracing of the electrical activity of the heart.

EMG A procedure that records the electrical activity of muscles.

Evaluation An overall comprehensive review, either by a physician or school personnel, to determine a child's specific medical or educational needs.

Extension The straightening of a limb or a body part.

Fine motor skills Pertaining to the use of the hands in performing tasks.

Flexion Forward bending.

Genes Present on chromosomes, each gene determines a specific body characteristic. Each cell has many thousands of genes.

Germ cells Special cells that produce sperm in the males and the egg cells in females.

Gowers' sign First described by Sir William Gowers, a diagnostic sign of muscle weakness where a child has to push up with his hands on his legs to get up from a sitting position on the floor.

Histochemical stains Special laboratory procedures that are performed to more clearly define specific structures or the lack of them in a muscle biopsy.

Hypertrophy Enlargement of muscles.

Hypotonia An absence of muscle tone that may be due to muscle weakness, nerve damage, or changes in the body chemistry.

IEP An individualized educational program (or plan) for special education students.

Immunoglobulins Special proteins found in all parts of the body that help fight disease.

Internist A physician who has additional training in medical problems of adults.

KAFO Knee-ankle-foot orthoses, or long-leg braces.

Karyotype The specific chromosomal pattern found in individual species.

Kyphosis A humplike prominence of the upper back.

Least restrictive environment The school setting in which a child with special needs has the most freedom.

Mainstream Enrollment in regular school classes by students who have qualified for special education.

Mask ventilation Air given by pressure through a mask to help the patient breathe.

Medicaid A combined federal and state program that pays for medical care for individuals who also receive SSI, or supplementary security income.

Medicare A federal program that pays for medical care for individuals who receive Social Security.

Merosin A protein missing in one of the pure forms of congenital muscular dystrophy—i.e., merosin-negative CMD.

Metabolic Pertaining to the chemical processes that occur in our bodies.

MRI A detailed picture, which does not use radiation, of a specific area in the body.

Muscle tone The tension of muscles which can be described as low tone or increased tone.

Myoglobinuria The loss of the protein myoglobin in the urine, which can cause severe kidney damage.

Myopathic Denoting disease in the muscles.

Myotonia Increased tone or stiffness of the muscles.

Nemaline rods Threadlike particles (*nemaline* = "thread" in Greek) seen in the muscle biopsy of patients with nemaline disease and some other muscle disorders.

Neurologist A medical doctor who has training in either pediatric or adult disorders of the brain and nervous system.

Neuropathic Denoting disease or abnormalities in the nervous system.

Occupational therapy or therapist (O.T.) An individual with training in the muscle function of the body, particularly the upper extremities. Problems such as dressing, eating, and adaptation of equipment for activities of daily living are addressed.

Orthopedic surgeon A physician with several years of postgraduate training in disorders of bones and joints who can perform surgical procedures. There are subspecialists who see just children.

Orthotics Braces or shoe inserts that are prescribed to help support extremities or the back.

Orthotist An individual with special training in making and fitting braces of all kinds.

Pathologist A medical doctor with additional training in studying tissues both visually and under the microscope.

Pediatrician A medical doctor who has had additional training in the care of children and young people.

Pediatric cardiologist A physician who is a pediatrician with additional training in heart problems in children and young people.

Pediatric geneticist A professional who may not be a physician but has had special training in genetic disorders of babies and children.

Pediatric ophthalmologist A surgically trained eye doctor who has had additional training in eye diseases of infants and children.

Physiatrist A medical doctor with special training in helping individuals overcome loss of physical abilities. They do not perform surgery.

Physical disabilities Problems due to hereditary disorders, trauma, or defects that affect the body so that normal motor function is not possible.

Physical therapist (P.T.) A professional who has been trained to evaluate and treat individuals who have dysfunction of the muscles due to brain injuries, accidents, or genetic disorders such as muscular dystrophy.

Physical therapy The evaluation and treatment of individuals with muscle problems, as well as help with ordering needed equipment.

Postop Following surgery.

Ptosis Weakness of the eye muscles, making it difficult to open the eyes completely.

Public Law 94-142 The Education of All Handicapped Children Act (EAHCA), now called IDEA. It states that children with special needs should be placed in the least restrictive environment.

Pulmonary Pertaining to the lungs and respiratory system.

Pulmonary function tests Tests done to determine the adequacy of lung function.

Ragged red fibers Small particles seen in muscle biopsies in mitochondrial myopathies.

Range of motion (ROM) Pertains to the degree that a body part is able to rotate.

Related services Any services that a child with special needs has, including physical therapy, occupational therapy, adaptive P.E., and transportation.

Respiratory infections Viral or bacterial infections of the nose, throat, sinuses, or lungs.

Respite care Care in or out of the home by someone other than the immediate family.

Rheumatologist A medical doctor who has had specific training in disorders that affect the joints and muscles, such as arthritis or dermatomyositis.

RNA Ribonucleic acid, the blueprint copied from DNA used in the cells to make protein.

Scoliosis Curvature of the spine.

Sed rate (sedimentation rate) A blood test that indicates signs of infection or a disease in the body.

Sex-linked recessive (X-linked) A genetic disorder that is passed through the mother to one or more of her male children. Each boy has a 50 percent chance of being affected.

SGOT and SGPT Enzymes in the body that can be elevated in the blood in some muscle diseases as well as diseases of the liver.

Social worker An individual with special training in counseling and finding resources. They have either an M.S.W. (medical social worker) or L.C.S.W. (licensed clinical social worker) degree.

Special education Established to meet the educational needs of pupils with disabilities.

Tenotomy An incision made through a tendon to lengthen it if there is a contracture.

Treatment plan A plan by which a hospital, physician, or other professionals map out a course of treatment for an individual patient.

Triplet repeat disorders Refers to the presence of substances repeated three times in sequence in the DNA and includes myotonic dystrophy and spinocerebellar degeneration.

Ventilator A mechanical method to support breathing.

Vertebrae The bones in the back or spine.

Suggested Readings

Subject Category in Order of Appearance in Book

Coping

Harold S. Kushner, *When Bad Things Happen to Good People* (New York: Avon, 1989).

Robin Simons, *After The Tears* (New York: Harcourt Brace Jovanvich, 1996).

Books for Kids

Laura Dwight, *We Can Do It!* (New York: Checkerboard Press, 1997).

Medical Maze

Health Insurance

Robert Enteen, *Health Insurance—How to Get It, or Improve What You've Got* (Santa Barbara, California: Special Needs Project, 1996). (1-800-333-6867)

Hospitalization

Carole Livingston and Claire Ciliotta, *Why Am I Going to the Hospital?* (New York: Carol Publishing Group, 1981).

Fred Rogers, *Going to the Hospital* (New York: G. P. Putnam's Sons, 1988).

Special Needs

Adaptive Clothing

Laurel Designs, 5 Laurel Ave., #6, Belvedere, CA 94920 (1-415-435-1891).

Dental Care

American Dental Association, *Dental Care for Special People* (Chicago: American Dental Association, 1991). (211 E. Chicago Ave., Chicago, Illinois 60611)

Perlman, C. Friedman, and D. Tesini, *Prevention and Treatment Considerations for the Dental Patient with Special Needs* (Chicago: American Academy of Pediatric Dentistry). (211 E. Chicago Ave., Chicago, Illinois 60611)

Parenting

Mothers and Fathers

Jane Bluestein, *Parents, Teens, and Boundaries: How to Draw the Line* (Deerfield Beach, FL: Health Communications, 1993).

Bobbi Conner, *The Parent's Journal Guide to Raising Great Kids* (New York: Bantam Books, 1997).

Martin Greenberg, *The Birth of a Father* (New York: Avon, 1986).

Donald J. Meyer, *Uncommon Fathers: Reflections on Raising a Child with a Disability* (Bethesda, MD: Woodbine House, 1995).

Linda G. Pillsbury, *Survival Tips for Working Moms* (Seattle, WA: Parenting Press, Inc., 1994).

Elizabeth Crary, *365 Wacky Wonderful Ways to Get Your Children to Do What You Want* (Seattle, WA: Parenting Press, Inc., 1995).

James May, *Fathers of Children with Special Needs* (Bethesda, MD: Association for the Care of Childrens' Health, 1997). (Available through The Special Needs Project, Santa Barbara, California, 1-800-683-2341)

Discipline

Thomas Gordon, *Parent Effectiveness Training* (New York: Penguin Books, 1994).

Thomas W. Phelan, *1, 2, 3 Magic Effective Discipline for Children 2-12* (Glen Ellyn, IL, 1996). (Book and video available in Spanish and English through The Special Needs Project, Santa Barbara, California, 1-800-683-2341)

Melvin Silberman and Susan Wheelan, *How to Discipline Without Feeling Guilty* (New York: Hawthorne Books, 1980).

Grandparents

Rosemary and Peter Dolton, *The Encyclopedia of Grandparenting* (San Leandro, CA: Bristol Publishing Enterprises, Inc., 1990).

Eda Leshan, *Grandparenting in a Changing World* (New York: New Market Press, 1997).

Single Parents

Caryl W. Krueger, *Single With Children* (Nashville, TN: Abbington Press, 1993).

Siblings

Debra J. Lobato, *Brothers, Sisters, and Special Needs* (Baltimore, MD: Paul Brooks Publishing Co., 1990). (Available through The Special Needs Project, Santa Barbara, California, 1-800-683-2341)

Play

Art

Judy Press, *The Little Hands Art Book* (Charlotte, VT: Williamson Publishing, 1994).

Cathy Savage-Hubbard, *Paint Adventures* (Cincinnati, OH: F. & W. Publications, 1993).

Rawley Silver, *Developing Cognitive and Creative Skills Through Art* (Sarasota, FL: Ablin Press, 1989).

General Activities

Steve and Ruth Bennett, *365 TV-Free Activities You Can Do With Your Child* (Holbrook, MA: Adams Media, 1996).

Joan M. Bergstrom, *School's Out! It's Summer* (Berkeley, CA: Ten Speed Press, 1992).

Joan M. Bergstrom, *School's Out!* (Berkeley, CA: Ten Speed Press, 1990).

Joan Eckstein and Joyce Gleit, *Fun With Making Things* (New York: Avon, 1991).

Leslie Hamilton, *Child's Play* (New York: Crown Publishing Group, 1989).

Priscilla Herschberger, *Make Costumes* (Cincinnati, OH: F. & W. Publications, 1992).

June Johnson, *Eight Hundred and Thirty-Eight Ways to Amuse A Child* (New York: Random House, 1988).

Adrienne Katz, *What to Do With Kids on a Rainy Day or in a Car, on a Train, or When They Are Sick . . .* (New York: St. Martin's Press, 1989).

Roy McConkey and Dorothy Jeffree, *Making Toys for Handicapped Children* (Englewood Cliffs, NJ: Prentice Hall, 1983).

Eating Healthy

Penny Warner, *Healthy Snacks for Kids* (San Leandro, CA: Bristol Publishing Enterprises, 1996).

Travel

Wendy Roth and Michael Tompane, *Easy Access to National Parks* (San Francisco, CA: Sierra Club Books, 1992).

Special Education

Paul Nordoff, *Music Therapy in Special Education* (Evansville, IL: MMB Music, 1983).

Kenneth Shore, *Special Education Handbook: A Comprehensive Guide for Parents and Educators* (New York: Warner Books, 1986).

Lisa Wahl and Paul Hendrix, *Computer Resources for People with Disabilities* (Alameda, CA: Hunter House, 1996).

Learning Disabilities

Rhoda Cummings and Gary Fisher, *The School Survival Guide for Kids with Learning Disabilities—Ways to Make Learning Easier and More Fun* (Minneapolis, MN: Free Spirit, 1991). (Available through The Special Needs Project, Santa Barbara, CA, 1-800-683-2341)

ADHD

Colleen Alexander-Roberts, *Practical Advice for Parents from Parents* (Dallas, TX: Taylor Publishing, 1994). (Available through The Special Needs Project, Santa Barbara, California, 1-800-683-2341)

Death and Dying

Elisabeth Kübler-Ross, *On Death and Dying* (New York: Simon & Schuster, 1997).

Index

Accessibility
  in community, 113, 173
  in Europe, 114
  at home, 112–113
Accessible Technology Centers, 108–
    109
Accommodation, 150
Acid maltase deficiency, 63–64, 198
Activities of daily living (ADLs), 85
Adaptive physical education, 151–
    154
Adaptive utensils, 142
ADLs, 85
Advocacy, 174
  advocates and, 170–171
  attorneys and, 168–170
  means of, 164–167
  support system and, 167–168
Advocates, 170–171
After school recreation programs, 122
Airplane travel, 113–114
Allowance, 145
Alpha sarcoglycanopathy, 34–35
Americans with Disabilities Act, 173
Amniocentesis, 28

Anesthesia, 87
  arthrogryposis and, 50
  Central Core disease and, 41
  questions and answers about, 177
Anger, 5, 6
  of child with a muscle disorder,
    131, 146
  of family, 129–130
  at HMO, 91
Antibiotics, 175–176
Antigen testing, 17
Antinuclear test, 17
Anxiety, of child, 136–137
  questions and answers about, 181
Art therapy, 128, 134
Arthrogryposis
  description and treatment of,
    50–51
  joint problems and, 82
Artificial insemination, 53, 56
Assessments, special education, 154–
    156
Atelectasis, 102
Attorneys
  advocacy and, 167